A
Gift
to
The
Colorado College
by

The National
Association of
Biology Teachers

CHARLES
LEAMING
TUTT
LIBRARY

*A good book is the precious
life blood of a master spirit,
embalmed and treasured up
on purpose to a life be-
yond life.* —*John Milton*

THE PHYSIOLOGY OF
AGGRESSION AND DEFEAT

THE PHYSIOLOGY OF AGGRESSION AND DEFEAT

Proceedings of a symposium held during the meeting of the American Association for the Advancement of Science in Dallas, Texas, in December 1968

Edited by

Basil E. Eleftheriou

Staff Scientist
The Jackson Laboratory
Bar Harbor, Maine

and

John Paul Scott

Director, Center for Research on Social Behavior
Bowling Green University
Bowling Green, Ohio

Ɖ PLENUM PRESS • NEW YORK–LONDON • 1971

Library of Congress Catalog Card Number 77-164505
SBN 306-30547-X

© 1971 Plenum Press, New York
A Division of Plenum Publishing Corporation
227 West 17th Street, New York, N. Y. 10011

United Kingdom edition published by Plenum Press, London
A Division of Plenum Publishing Company, Ltd.
Davis House (4th Floor), 8 Scrubs Lane, Harlesden, NW10 6SE, England

Printed in the United States of America

PREFACE

This short volume contains papers presented at a
special symposium, "The Physiology of Aggression and
Defeat," during the AAAS meetings in Dallas, Texas, in
December, 1968.

At a time when we need to understand the basic mechanisms underlying various forms of aggression, these papers
report progress toward this goal. Although the many social,
psychologic and economic causal mechanisms contributing to
aggression have been reasonably well-understood for a
number of years, the correlated physiological, biochemical,
endocrinological and neurochemical changes taking place in
an organism that is either the aggressor or the recipient
of aggression have not been studied extensively, and the
limited available data in the past have often been in considerable conflict.

These eight papers demonstrate that complex interactions take place among the psychological, social, physiological, biochemical, endocrinological and neurochemical
factors involved in aggression and defeat. The general
indications are that while the aggressor learns to survive
and adapts readily to the fighting process, the vanquished,
if he does not die, maintains an existence highlighted by
severe and extensive changes in all physiologic and psychologic systems. We cannot make sweeping generalizations to
the human organism from the results of non-human animal
experimentation. Nevertheless, it is well-known that in
all animals, including the human, similar basic biochemical systems are involved.

We hope that the data presented in these eight papers
may contribute to the better understanding of the physiology
and psychology of the patterns of aggression and defeat in

a manner that will eventually help to reduce and eliminate the factors that contribute to the propagation of such events.

Bar Harbor, Maine 1971   B.E.E.
                                                          J.P.S.

CONTENTS

CONTRIBUTORS

PETER G. BOURNE

Director, South Central Community Mental
Health Center
Atlanta, Georgia

F. H. BRONSON

Department of Zoology
University of Texas
Austin, Texas

J. M. R. DELGADO

Professor of Physiology
Department of Psychiatry
Yale University School of Medicine
New Haven, Connecticut

C. DESJARDINS

Department of Pharmacology
Oklahoma State University
Stillwater, Oklahoma

BASIL E. ELEFTHERIOU

The Jackson Laboratory
Bar Harbor, Maine

D. MIR

Catedra de Fisiologia
Faculdad de Medicina
Avenida Sanchez Piz Juan
Seville, Spain

K. E. MOYER

Department of Psychology
Carnegie-Mellon University
Pittsburgh, Pennsylvania

R. PLOTNIK

Department of Psychology
San Diego State College
San Diego, California

BRYAN W. ROBINSON

Department of Psychology
Florida State University
Tallahassee, Florida

J. P. SCOTT

Department of Psychology
Bowling Green State University
Bowling Green, Ohio

ANNEMARIE S. WELCH

Maryland Psychiatric Research Center
Baltimore, Maryland

BRUCE L. WELCH

Chief

Psychophysiology Research
Maryland Psychiatric Research Center
and
Senior Investigator
Environmental Neurobiology
Friends of Psychiatric Research, Inc.,
Baltimore, Maryland

SYMPOSIUM: THE PHYSIOLOGY OF AGGRESSION AND DEFEAT

Introduction

Basil E. Eleftheriou and J. P. Scott

When we organized the symposium on which this volume
is based* we hoped to accomplish two things. One was to
reconcile some of the different conclusions that have been
reached by proponents of the psychophysiological and
hydraulic theories of motivation concerning aggressive behavior, and the other was to summarize our knowledge concerning the physiology of fighting and defeat in a definitive fashion. As we look over the results, we see that we
have succeeded at least partially in the first endeavor, as
the chapters by Scott and Moyer show. With respect to the
second, these papers, far from presenting final answers,
open up a whole new set of research fields concerning the
behavioral, physiological, and biochemical aspects of
fighting and defeat.

In the past, most of the physiological and behavioral
data concerning agonistic behavior have been derived from
extensive experiments with the antecedents of one behavioral
pattern belonging to this behavioral and motivational system, i.e., aggressive behavior, including fighting between
two individuals, or attacks by one individual upon another.
While this book is duly concerned with the general problem
of the causes leading to fighting, it also is concerned
with postcedent events, the internal and external <u>results</u>
of fighting. One of the latter is defeat, and it can be
shown that the physiological results of successful fighting

---

* The Physiology of Fighting and Defeat. Symposium presented at a meeting of the Animal Behavior Society and
  the American Association for the Advancement of Science
  at Dallas, Texas, December 28, 1968.

and defeat are quite different, those of defeat being both
more prolonged and more severe.

The scope of this volume further emphasizes certain
limitations of our present knowledge in this field. First,
the agonistic behavioral system includes not only fighting
but all other patterns of behavior that are adaptive in
situations of conflict. The physiological and biochemical
changes that take place during flight, passivity, and the
patterns of threat and avoidance exhibited by animals in a
dominance-subordination relationship have not been studied
by anyone. A second limitation of our current knowledge is
the small number of species on which physiological analysis
of fighting and defeat has been attempted. With one or two
exceptions, almost all physiological work has been done
with less than half a dozen species of mammals.

A much wider range of species has been studied behaviorally, but the greatest weakness of this latter work has
been physiologizing--that is, attempting to deduce physiological mechanisms from observed behavior without reference
to the known physiological mechanisms of the nervous system. Similarly, many physiologists have been guilty of the
corresponding sin of drawing conclusions regarding behavior
from their knowledge of internal changes, without bothering
to verify these through the known mechanisms of measuring
behavior. This volume reports significant advances in
techniques which directly associate the results of physiological and behavioral sciences.

Any scientist has an obligation to present the general
conclusions from his results and the facts as they then
exist, always remembering that future results may modify
these conclusions. We have not avoided this obligation,
and have tried to indicate where these findings have both
practical and theoretical applications to the human condition, always cautioning that basic physiological and biochemical mechanisms are common to mouse and man, their
overall organization to the two species is different.

The chapter by Scott presents a general introduction
to the theoretical ideas that have dominated this field of
research and shows how material in the following chapters
confirms or conflicts with these theories. He first dis-
cusses the evolutionary background of the particular
mammalian species that have been most commonly used in this

research--cats, mice, rhesus monkeys, and men. Each has evolved different adaptive functions for agonistic behavior, and hence we would expect differences in internal motivational processes and, indeed, a unique neural and hormonal organization for agonistic behavior in each species. The final assessment of the physiological basis of fighting in man therefore must rest on human data, although studies of other animals may give hints as to the possible range of motivational mechanisms.

There is wide agreement that predation and social fighting are based on different patterns of behavior and different motivational systems. Also, because fighting exists in prey animals as well as in predators, and because among predators themselves predation and fighting take quite different forms, we can conclude that social fighting cannot have evolved generally from predation. Rather, defensive fighting in reaction to injury is the most probable basic precursor of agonistic behavior. From this almost universal form of behavior, fighting has evolved into many different adaptive forms.

Scott summarizes the differences between the psychophysiological theory of motivation, based on the known facts of physiology and learning, and the hydraulic theory, derived from behavioral observation. Their most crucial points of disagreement, concerning the existence of spontaneous internal stimulation for fighting, can be partially reconciled. While there is no evidence for the existence of physiological mechanisms which stimulate fighting per se, agonistic behavior can be organized either through learning or processes of growth in relation to other motivational systems in which spontaneous internal stimulation does exist, i.e., where fighting is related to the possession of food or females. Whether or not such organization is present depends on the species involved. Consequently, a major problem in human research is the nature of the adaptive functions of agonistic behavior, and how much these are dependent upon cultural, as opposed to evolved, mechanisms.

Scott concludes that the physiological causes of fighting in man are such that we may safely work toward the reduction of external causes of fighting, and the eventual goal of an essentially non-violent world without harming the individual or interfering with his motivation for constructive activity.

Bronson and Desjardins review the central role of hormones in the physiology of aggression, both as factors which modify behavior and as substances that are in turn affected by aggression. They also review the newer and less well-known work on the role of hormones in the behavior and physiology of a defeated animal.

Recent discoveries indicate that the major male hormone, testosterone, not only has a prominent role in the expression of adult fighting behavior, but that it also plays a major part in the early organization of the nervous system. In mammals, the sex glands of males are normally stimulated to produce briefly the male hormone in the late fetal and early postnatal periods by the maternal pituitary hormones. In mice, exposure of the nervous system to the male hormone during a critical period one day after birth determines whether or not the hormone will be effective in facilitating aggressive behavior in adults. Since female offspring are normally not exposed to the male hormone, their nervous system is not affected, and remains insensitive to the male hormone when they become adults, in contrast to its positive effects on sexual behavior in both females and males. Presently, the precise mode of organizing action on the nervous system is not clear, but one possibility is that the critical period represents a time when the hormone can be received and bound in a particular brain center and thus contribute to the modification of neural organization.

In contrast to the specific role of testosterone in facilitating fighting, the prolonged experience of fighting produces significant changes on almost every part of the endocrine apparatus of an animal. These changes involve not only testosterone but also adrenocorticotropin, luteinizing hormone, thyrotropin, and adrenal glucocorticosteroids. One fact is quite significant. A trained aggressor undergoes endocrine changes in its first real fight, but if successful recovers normal hormonal levels soon after the event and does not exhibit significant hormonal changes in subsequent encounters as long as he wins. On the other hand, an animal that is defeated repeatedly exhibits hormonal changes that may last for many hours after the event. Similar changes subsequently are elicited by the mere sight of the trained aggressor, irrespective of

whether a fight actually takes place. Thus a trained
aggressor, an animal that consistently and repeatedly wins
its fight, adapts endocrinologically much more easily than
does an animal that is defeated. The defeated animals
are thus kept in a condition of chronic physiological
stress. The consequences of such stress upon physiological
health, longevity, and other forms of adaptive behavior
than fighting are as yet unknown.

Eleftheriou's chapter presents another approach to the
analysis of contrasting physiological effects on trained
aggressors and defeated animals. He presents data from
recent experiments involving ribonucleic acid ratios, total
RNA, and levels of ribonuclease, an enzyme which inacti-
vates RNA. The RNA system is currently thought to be involved in basic memory processes. The most significant
finding is that defeated animals exhibit a decline in brain
RNA. Since a number of other experiments indicate that
learning is facilitated by increases in RNA, it would be
predicted that a chronically defeated animal should not
learn as well as an undefeated one. This may be a lead to
a physiological explanation of why emotionally excited
animals appear to solve problems poorly. A tempting
analogy and one whose vitality could be tested experimentally, concerns the physiological results of the stressful
conditions of ghetto living and those produced by war in
human populations, and their possible effects on diminished
learning in these populations.

Eleftheriou speculates on a number of possible mechanisms which may bring about the phenomenon of diminished
RNA. One of the more plausible hypotheses is that increased circulation levels of adrenal glucocorticosteroids
contribute to an increased activation of ribonuclease,
with a concomitant decline in RNA. This is supported by
an experiment demonstrating that injection of corticosterone will produce a similar decline. However, extensive
additional work is necessary before the precise mechanisms can be established.

Welch and Welch present a review of another brain biochemical system that undergoes changes during fighting
behavior. This includes the substances presumably involved
in neurotransmission, the biogenic amines norepinephrine,
dopamine and serotonin. Although prolonged or intense
stress may cause these substances to disappear partially

from brain tissues, the initial effect of fighting is to
elevate simultaneously the levels of all three. The
authors suggest that this effect may reflect an accelerated
rate of transport of amines from their site of synthesis
in cell bodies toward nerve terminals, where utilization
takes place. Presumably, these changes reflect increased
brain activity during fighting.

If mice are allowed to fight for short periods each
day, both brain norepinephrine and dopamine are elevated
consistently to high levels, presumably as the animals
become adapted to chronic fighting. Furthermore, such
periodic fighting results in elevation in the levels of
epinephrine and norepinephrine produced by the adrenal
glands. Again, these changes represent adaptive changes
in the rate of biosynthesis in these amines. Other
effects include cardiac hypertrophy, and the authors
suggest that mice undergoing short periodic bouts of
fighting may provide good biological models for the study
of hypertension and cardiovascular-renal disease.

For years, laboratories in the pharmaceutical industry
have been isolating male mice for the purpose of making
them more ready to fight when placed together. Welch and
Welch show that animals treated in this way are indeed
better fighters, and are more likely to win fights than
inexperienced mice that have not been isolated. Going
along with the changes in behavior are a series of changes
in brain chemistry. There is a lower rate of biosynthesis
and utilization of the same neurotransmitters whose levels
are increased by fighting. Similarly, the substances
secreted by the adrenal cortex and medulla are reduced and
blood pressure is lowered. The precise way in which these
changes are related to increased irritability of isolated
animals is still not clear, but it provides a promising
lead toward the study of the biochemical basis of the
behavioral irritability and excitability that leads to a
greater probability of fighting.

Another major strategy for the analysis of fighting
behavior is that of brain stimulation. One of the difficulties in interpreting these results lies in the fact that
most physiologists have assumed that the results of such
stimulation reveal fundamental neural circuitry and biological organization of the brain, whereas the behavior of
the animals so stimulated could equally well reflect brain

organization based on experience. The technique introduced by Plotnik, Mir, and Delgado attacks this problem directly. Monkeys with implanted intracerebral electrodes are first given the chance to stimulate themselves. In this way, it can be determined whether the points are positively reinforced, natural, or aversive. Later, the same monkeys are placed in a free situation in a well-organized social group, and the points are stimulated by remote control. Those points that produce fighting behavior can then be determined. Essentially, only those points in the cerebrum that were aversive produced fighting, and only against those monkeys over which the stimulated animals were dominant. This latter finding confirms the importance of training in controlling the elicitation and direction of aggressive behavior and further confirms the expectation that brain stimulation reveals organization based on learning as well as that based on fundamental circuitry.

The authors distinguish between secondary aggression that follows after painful stimulation, and primary aggression that occurs and continues as brain stimulation takes place. They conclude that the aggression produced by cerebral stimulation of areas having aversive properties is the equivalent of secondary aggression, i.e., stimulation in these areas is painful. These findings relate directly to the extensive work in eliciting aggressive behavior through painful foot shock and other methods, and also to the theory proposed by Scott, that a basic adaptive function of fighting is defense against real or threatened injury.

The method has not been applied to primary aggression, defined as that which takes place while stimulation is going on. In every case, the aggression followed stimulation. It will be interesting to follow future work in which self-stimulation is used to test brain areas inducing primary aggression, i.e., to find out whether certain kinds of fighting are accompanied by pleasurable sensations. It would also be interesting to apply the method to the hypothalamus and other areas of the brain outside the cerebrum. The chapter represents a landmark in this type of work, as one of the truly rare cases where good behavioral measurements have been united with good neuroanatomical localization.

Moyer has reviewed the literature on brain stimulation,

ablation, and chemical intervention on the elicitation of
fighting behavior in man and other animals, and concludes
that there are at least 8 different kinds of behavior that
have been labeled aggressive, each based on separate neurocircuitry laid down in early development. These are predator, inter-male, fear induced, irritable, territorial,
maternal, instrumental, and sex induced aggression. Predatory aggression, as pointed out above, is very different
from all the rest in its basic adaptive function and behavior patterns as well as in its neurocircuitry.

The basic differentiating factor in Moyer's classification is the stimulus situation which elicits each kind
of response. Although some of the physiological changes
accompanying these behaviors may overlap, they are essentially different in their neural organization, and it is
possible to discriminate among them by appropriate experimental designs. Extension of this classification to aggressive behavior in man presents some difficulties, partly
because of lack of evidence, but also because the effects
of brain stimulation in corresponding areas are not consistent even between non-human animals. However, there is
a certain amount of evidence that human aggressive behavior can be elicited by brain stimulation and that certain
cases of chronic aggressive and assaultive behavior can be
alleviated by surgical interruption of various brain circuits. More evidence is needed regarding the basic circuitry involved in human aggression.

Moyer presents the theory that a particular kind of
aggression will result when a particular neural circuit is
fired and reviews factors which may facilitate, modify, or
suppress such firing. These factors include the male
hormone, heredity, blood chemistry, and organization of
behavior through learning. On this basis, he points out
certain implications for the control of undesirable aggressive behavior. An obvious method is to manipulate
the environment to minimize conditions which produce
deprivation, pain, and frustration. Second, violent and
destructive behavior can be inhibited by appropriate
training procedures. Finally, in appropriate conditions
one can internally modify physiological conditions which
facilitate various kinds of aggressive responses, using
drugs, hormones, and brain stimulations or lesions. This
suggests that an important direction for new research is
the discovery of those factors which enhance irritability

and the development of means to reduce it. The chapter
emphasizes the fact that aggression is not a unitary concept, and that consequently there is no one general solu-
tion for the problems engendered by it.

The work of Bourne demonstrates that close parallels
can exist between human physiology and that of other
animals. Although the kinds of data that can be obtained
from soldiers under combat conditions are necessarily
limited, those that can be obtained are strikingly similar
in mouse and man. Bourne measured the urine 17-hydroxi-
corticosteroid of soldiers under combat conditions in
Vietnam. Like the trained fighting mice, these men,
trained efficiently for combat conditions and reinforced
by knowledge of superiority, adapted with ease to the
combat situation. Only their officers, who were placed in
positions of responsibility for the enlisted men, showed
signs of an unusual degree of stress. This work demonstrates again the desirability of measuring human physiology in situations where actual fighting may be involved,
and also emphasizes that knowledge obtained from animal
experimentation may have real significance for human
affairs.

In conclusion, Robinson summarizes the experimental
problems raised by these chapters and points out some of
the directions for future research. He emphasizes the
fact that aggression and fighting are social behavior and
hence must be studied in animals living in groups, and
preferably a naturally formed group, if the results are to
be meaningful. He also emphasizes the fact that we need
more studies of the physiology of human aggression in
such activities as business life, sports, and hunting.
While all of these have been labeled aggression, the animal
results would indicate that they may have very different
kinds of motivation and rest on quite different neural
circuitry. He also points out the importance of pathology
as a cause of aggression, particularly in the case of what
appears to be meaningless violence, and cites the case of
the University of Texas mass murderer whose postmortem
revealed the presence of a malignant brain tumor. Finally,
Robinson argues that all aggression is not inherently bad,
that the tendency of an individual to rebel or struggle
against intolerable conditions can be healthy, helpful,
and socially desirable if channeled in the right directions. While not all of us would agree that writing a

scientific paper is a sublimated form of aggression, all
of us would support the notion that we need to find out
more about the desirable functions of agonistic behavior
as well as the means for controlling violence and
destruction.

THEORETICAL ISSUES CONCERNING THE ORIGIN AND CAUSES
OF FIGHTING

J. P. Scott

Department of Psychology
Bowling Green State University

Bowling Green, Ohio

THE EVOLUTION OF AGONISTIC BEHAVIOR

Occurrence of social fighting in the animal kingdom.
Fighting between members of the same species has only been
observed in the arthropods and the vertebrates, and not
necessarily in all of these animals. For example, it
certainly does not occur in butterflies, nor does it occur
in the order Amphibia to any great extent. These latter
animals are without teeth and claws, and have almost no
behavioral means by which they can damage an opponent.

Why does not agonistic behavior occur universally?
The answer lies in the fact that any behavior, in order to
become important, must have survival value; that is, it
must perform an adaptive function for the individuals concerned. One limitation already has been noted. Fighting
has no adaptive value where the individuals concerned lack
the motor capacity for inflicting pain or injury on each
other. More than this, social fighting is only adaptive
where the individuals are able to recognize each other as
individuals. Indiscriminate attacks on all members of the
same species, including males, females, and young, could
have only negative survival value. This probably explains
why agonistic behavior does not occur in the lower invertebrates. These animals generally have such inferior sense
organs that they cannot readily recognize and discriminate
between other individuals. Furthermore, they frequently
live in environmental situations which make visual discrim-

ination very difficult. We must conclude that agonistic
behavior is something which is relatively new in evolutionary history.

Origin of agonistic behavior. Nevertheless, we can
see in the lower invertebrates behavior which may explain
the evolutionary origin of social fighting. Almost every
species has some behavioral adaptation to meet the threat
of physical injury, whether it arises from the physical
environment, a predator, or from a species mate. There are
three common adaptive reactions: escape or avoidance, a
defensive threat, or a defensive attack. All of these reactions should be equally effective against either a predator or a species mate that has accidentally hurt the individual, and it is probable that social fighting has evolved
from this behavior. There is no need to trace back social
fighting to a common origin: this kind of behavior could
have evolved independently in many different species, from
whatever defensive or threat reactions had previously been
evolved. One might label this behavior the "cornered rat
reaction." Starting with rats and extending his experiments to other species, Ulrich (1966) has shown that defensive fighting can be evoked by pain in a great variety
of species of vertebrates. There is every reason to suspect that this response may be almost universal in this
sub-phylum with the exception of the Amphibia, the agonistic behavior of these latter animals usually being
limited to escape reactions. Therefore, we can conclude
that defensive fighting in reaction to painful stimulation
is the most basic type of social fighting and that pain is
the most basic primary eliciting stimulus ("releaser") for
fighting. We have found in the male laboratory mouse that
the only stimulus that will evoke fighting in 100% of
naive animals is an attack by another mouse. However,
defensive fighting is only the beginning of the evolutionary process.

Selective mechanisms. As Hamilton (1964) has pointed
out, natural selection is concerned with the survival of
genes, not individuals. Individual survival is important
only if it permits the individual to pass along his genes
to the next generation. I have pointed out elsewhere
(Scott, 1968) that gene survival is dependent upon a balance between selective pressures arising from genic, pre-
natal, social, biotic, and physiological environments.
These pressures do not necessarily operate to produce

effects in the same direction, and a different balance
between them may arise in every species. Therefore, we
would predict that agonistic behavior would take a different evolutionary course in every species. While general
principles may eventually be derived from the study of a
wide number of species, one cannot directly analogize from
one species to another, especially if the two are only
distantly related.

In the past, the assumption has often been made that
social and other environmental selective pressures operate
in the same direction; i.e., that fighting between individuals will result in the survival of the stronger and
that this will benefit the species in survival against
predators. This is not necessarily correct. Social selection and other selection pressures can operate in opposite
directions provided a balance is achieved which permits
survival of the species. For example, social fighting in
the various species of deer has resulted in an evolutionary tendency toward larger and larger antlers, which favor
the breeding potential of an individual involved in pushing
contests during the rutting season, but which actually
handicap the same individual in dealing with predators,
especially when the horns are in the velvet. Antlers also
involve the waste of a large expenditure of metabolic
energy, since the males shed their antlers. Social selection is thus a major factor whose importance has not been
appreciated fully in the past, and one whose results are
dependent upon interaction with other kinds of selection
pressures。

The evolution of fighting behavior in common laboratory species. The animals represented in the papers in
this symposium represent those in which most of the physiological work has been done. The anatomical, biochemical,
and electronic techniques involved are difficult and
laborious; and for that reason the list is a limited one.
It is therefore important that we have some general
appreciation of the special sorts of evolutionary tendencies seen in these animals. In the first place, they are
all mammals: the mouse, the cat, the rhesus monkey, and
man. Consequently, they should show some basic resem-
blances in physiology based on common ancestry, although
such a small sample could not be called representative of
the entire Class Mammalia.

From the ecological point of view, the sample is somewhat more satisfactory. The mouse is an omnivorous prey animal, the cat is a predator, and the rhesus monkey is neither, being largely a food-gatherer that kills very little and is not an important food species for any predator. Man living under primitive conditions can, on the other hand, be either a predator or a food-gatherer, or both, and there is no indication that man was ever an important prey species. The ecological niche of modern man is, of course extraordinarily complex.

The house mouse is a small, semi-parasitic rodent which largely lives in man's dwellings and eats his food. The importance of the species in agonistic research arises from the facts that the males can be readily induced to fight and are available in large numbers in a wide variety of genetically different strains. Laboratory mice have been derived from domesticated stocks that have been pre- sumably separate from wild stocks for many centuries. However, their behavior does not seem to have departed as widely from that of wild animals as has that of the labora- tory rat. Studies of wild mouse populations agree that mice are tolerant toward individuals with whom they have grown up, but react aggressively toward strangers (Scott, 1966). Most of the behavior toward strangers consists of mutual avoidance and, under natural conditions, escape is usually possible for an animal that is attacked. Mice are not highly territorial, being capable of defending only a small area around the nest, and not always doing this. They can develop an effective territory if the environment includes enclosures with only narrow apertures which can be effectively guarded. When placed in small enclosures, such as laboratory cages, mice are incapable of developing good dominance orders, in which all fighting is reduced to threats. The typical result in such cases is one dominant mouse that continually bites and threatens all the others, who have no dominance relationships between themselves. Thus, mice have only poorly developed behavior with re- spect to two of the most important control systems of agonistic behavior: territoriality and dominance. In a natural situation, their behavior makes it possible for mice to coexist in large numbers where a plentiful food supply is found, but it also excludes other individuals from entering such areas except when they are empty of mice. There is no fighting over females, and agonistic behavior has a general adaptive function of creating

pressure that keeps the species distributed. It may also
have the function of preventing homosexual behavior between males.

The domestic cat has been used in studies of the
physiology of fighting behavior largely because of the
lack of variation in its skull and brain and because of
its easily evoked emotional reactions and defensive threat
postures associated with agonistic behavior. As Leyhausen
(1965) has pointed out, cats are largely solitary animals
except when the female is rearing a brood of young. It is
difficult to determine the adaptive value of fighting
except as it prevents interference by one animal with
another in its hunting range. As a young animal, a cat
becomes closely attached to a particular location which
becomes the home of the individual, and the area surrounding this is used as a hunting range. No territorial
boundaries are defended, but males attack each other when-
ever they meet, with the result that they soon develop a
dominance relationship, and one flees when the other
approaches.

Fighting has some relationship to mating, although
the fighting in this case seems to be largely ritualized,
and the choice of mate is usually made by the female concerned. A new male is subjected to prolonged attack by
nearby resident males, but he will not accept defeat in
his home locality, and continues to fight until he is
either victorious or is killed. If he survives, the
males concerned establish mutually tolerant relationships.

One of the difficulties of working with cats is that
agonistic behavior forms a very prominent part of the behavioral repertory of the species and even extends into
other behavioral systems, so much so that much of the
sexual behavior of cats is very similar to agonistic behavior. Nevertheless, the patterns of predation are quite
different from those of social fighting, although some
authors have erroneously equated the two. The pattern of
rat killing is quite different from that of an attack on
another cat, and it undoubtedly has a very different
motivational and physiological basis, being more closely
related to ingestive behavior than social fighting.

In general, one may suspect that much of the agonistic behavior of cats has adaptive value only in the sense

that it appears to be the cat's way of maintaining social
contacts with its neighbors. In this way these solitary
animals are able to breed and reproduce as well as to
support themselves effectively in relatively undisturbed
hunting ranges.

Rhesus monkeys are highly social animals, and the
typical individual is born, lives, and dies within a group
of its own kind. As monkeys go, they belong to one of the
more aggressive species, and more overt fighting is seen
among them than in most other primates. Dominance organization is very important among the males, and is rigidly
enforced. Its usual effect is to keep the males spaced
out from each other, with the most dominant male near the
center of the group (Southwick, et al., 1965). As with
many species of non-human primates, agonistic behavior has
little to do with sex, and females in estrus may move from
one male to another without interference or fighting.
Dominant animals may have the choice of food in a competitive situation, although under natural conditions the wide
distribution of natural food does not bring about this
situation. Troops which unexpectedly meet may fight, but
there is no defense of territorial boundaries, the troops
ordinarily avoiding each other as they move through their
overlapping home ranges. The principal adaptive function
of fighting and the well-developed dominance order appears
to be to keep the troop distributed in a fashion which
will facilitate the protection and escape of the troop
from dangerous predators.

It is, of course, impossible at this date to say what
the agonistic behavior of human beings may have been in pre-
cultural eras. Recent discoveries of fossil remains in
Africa indicate that man and his remote ancestors have
never been physically adapted for life as predators. Judg-
ing by his small teeth and general structure, ancient man
was, like his modern descendants, an omnivorous animal,
living largely by food-gathering but occasionally able to
kill a small helpless animal, as do some of his cousins,
the chimpanzees, to this day. Man became a predator only
secondarily, with the use of tools.

Like rhesus monkeys, men are highly social animals and
normally live continuously in groups. They readily develop
behavior permitting mutual tolerance and accept dominance
and subordination. There is wide variation concerning the

importance of territoriality in primitive man, and there is
no firm evidence as to whether human territoriality is the
result of biological inheritance or is a cultural invention.
One human characteristic, as opposed to most other primates,
is long-continued consortships between adult males and
females, and it is possible that agonistic behavior has some
function with respect to sexual jealousy. Fighting can, of
course, be used instrumentally in a great variety of ways
which are not apparent in the lower animals (Scott, 1969).

Distinction between predation and social fighting. In
popular thinking there is a tendency to confuse predation,
or food-getting by carnivorous animals, with social fighting between members of the same species, and to assume that
the latter grows out of the former. Such is far from the
case. Social fighting exists in extreme forms in animals
which are never predators. In predators themselves, the
behavior patterns of prey-getting are quite different from
those employed against their own species, where the patterns are normally such that very little actual harm results. Much of their social fighting consists of threats
and vocalizations, in contrast to their well-developed
equipment for producing physical injury. While the possibility exists that a predator might, so to speak, get its
wires crossed and deliver the kind of behavior toward a
species mate which it normally uses in killing its prey,
such behavior seldom occurs. Prey-killing and social
fighting are subject to different sorts of selection
pressures and consequently have evolved in different directions.

While all hypotheses regarding the evolutionary origin
of agonistic behavior must be speculative in nature, and
while there is no reason to suppose that it arose in the
same way in every species, the most probable theory is
that social fighting originated from primitive defensive
behavior resulting from mutual interference between individuals of the same species.

Need for studies on a wide variety of species as a
basis for understanding human reactions. Most of the
physiological work on aggression and defeat has been done
on a few species of mammals which by no means represent a
broad sample of agonistic behavior in the animal kingdom
or even in the Order Mammalia. The choice of these
species has largely been dictated by economy and conven-

ience. Mice are cheap and their brains can therefore be
readily used for biochemical analysis. Cats are convenient
because their skull and brain shape is relatively uniform
and adapted for techniques of implanted electrodes.
Rhesus monkeys are one of the most readily available
species of primates. Further advances will be made when
we are able to get away from these restricted species, as
only in this way can real generalizations be established.

The problem is particularly acute when we attempt to
apply these findings to human beings. There have been a
few cases of the use of implanted electrodes in human
beings, and these have the advantage that the patients are
able to give subjective reports. However, such techniques
are justified only in pathological conditions, and the
generality of results is correspondingly limited. Biochemical tests are limited to those which can be applied
to urine or blood, the use of nervous tissues being as
yet impractical.

Consequently, most of the human studies have been
limited to hormonal reactions in simulated fighting situations. One of the exceptions to this is Bourne's paper
(this volume) on the physiology of soldiers during combat
situations. Bourne finds that physiological reactions in
human warfare are very different from those shown by
animals fighting as individuals. In short, combat between
groups is a very different kind of behavior than fighting
between individuals. If this is true, and we have every
reason to believe that it is from other sorts of evidence
(Scott, 1969), the control of human warfare is not going
to be achieved by the methods which are effective in modifying the fighting behavior of individuals.

THE INTERNAL STIMULATION OF AGONISTIC BEHAVIOR

Each behavioral system has associated with it a group
of physiological mechanisms. It is, therefore, appropriate
to look for internal stimuli as well as external ones in
the analysis of any particular system of behavior. The
particular mechanisms involved and the relative importance
of internal and external stimuli should differ in each system. This has been my own theoretical approach to the
problem of the physiological basis of agonistic behavior,
and I originally applied it in an entirely objective manner

(Scott, 1958). I accordingly summarized the results of
this investigation and recorded certain interesting and
surprising (to me) conclusions that arose from it. These
conclusions can be summarized as a psychophysiological
theory of the internal causation of agonistic behavior and
are presented in Table 1, where they are contrasted with
the older hydraulic theory. Since then a great deal of
new work has been done, much of which has been competently
reviewed by Kaada (1967). With one exception, the facts
stated in 1958 have been confirmed, and this exception has
no effect on the general conclusions. The great bulk of
this work has been done on the cat.

As indicated above, there are three major patterns of
agonistic behavior in the cat: attack, defensive threat,
and flight or escape. Of these, the defensive threat reaction has been most studied because of interest in its
obvious emotional content such as fair-fluffing, spitting,
and all of the internal reactions that go with these external expressions of the emotion of anger. A fourth
pattern, predatory attack, has sometimes been confused
with the first, but the rat-killing reaction of a cat is
obviously different from attack on another cat, both in
external form and in emotional content.

Results of ablation. The early experiments of Bard
(1950) showed that general removal of the cerebral cortex
resulted in a reaction that he called sham rage. The
symptoms are essentially those of the defense reaction,
and the unusual feature is that they can be elicited by
very minor sorts of stimulation which would ordinarily
have a neutral effect, such as merely touching the cat's
fur. This result has been confirmed by numerous other
investigators, who have shown that it will persist for
months, long after the original lesion has been healed.
It may be concluded that the cerebral cortex as a whole
has the effect of inhibiting the defensive reaction.

In other experiments Bard made extensive lesions in
the hypothalamus of cats. Such animals were sleepy and
inactive, had difficulty in maintaining a constant temperature, and were much more difficult to stimulate to agonistic behavior. However, if shown a dog or otherwise very
strongly stimulated, the defensive threat reaction could
still be elicited. The hypothalamus obviously has an
important function in producing the defensive reaction, but

Table 1

Detailed Comparison between Psychophysiological and
Hydraulic Theories of the Physiological Basis of
Agonistic Behavior

<u>Psychophysiological Theory</u>   <u>Hydraulic Theory</u>

I.   <u>Internal Processes</u>

1. Anger & Fear (the two emo-   1. Aggression-specific
   tions most directly con-   energy arises spontaneous-
   cerned with fighting) are   ly in the nervous system
   initially aroused by ex-
   ternal stimuli

2. These internal emotional   2. Aggression-specific
   processes have the function   energy is reduced by behav-
   of magnifying and prolong-   ior following external
   ing reactions to external   stimulation
   stimuli

3. Internal arousal is thus   3. Aggression-specific
   rapidly increased and main-   energy is produced at a
   tained (probably through a   uniform rate at all times
   mechanism of reverberating
   circuits) over periods of
   hours and sometimes days.
   It becomes particularly
   intense if behavior is
   blocked

4. Internal arousal eventu-   4. Aggression-specific
   ally dies out in the   energy accumulates indefi-
   absence of further external   nitely in the nervous sys-
   stimulation   tem until discharged

II. <u>External Stimulation</u>

1. Is a change to which the   1. Same
   organism attempts to adapt
   by external reactions (behavior) and internal reactions (physiology)

Table 1--cont.

2. Initiates arousal (internal processes) which maintains behavior after external stimulation ceases

2. Releases already stored aggression-specific energy in the form of behavior

3. In the absence of external stimulation, internal arousal will not occur

3. Internal arousal will occur in the absence of external stimulation

III. Behavior

1. Has function of adaptation to situation of conflict

1. Same

2. Reduces level of physiological and emotional arousal

2. Reduces level of stored aggression-specific energy

3. Successful adaptation has effect of increasing motivation to fight (or other forms of agonistic behavior) in reactions to subsequent external stimulation, through the process of reinforcement

3. Reduces motivation to fight in reaction to subsequent stimuli over short time periods; has no effect over long time periods

4. Motivation for agonistic behavior can be modified in either direction by reinforcement, either independently or in combination with emotional and physiological processes

4. Not accounted for in hydraulic theory

5. If motivation from any source or sources reaches a high level and appropriate behavior is blocked by training or other factors, inappropriate behavior is likely to occur

5. If aggression-specific energy accumulates to a high level in the absence of appropriate releasing stimuli, energy will be released by inappropriate stimuli and so di-

Table 1--cont.

	verted into other forms of behavior
6. Sublimation and cathar- sis, defined as reduction of internal arousal by behavior, are effective only when intense internal arousal has been produced by external stimulation	6. Sublimation and catharsis are effective at all times. In the absence of catharsis through overt agonistic be- havior, sublimation is essen- tial for the control of aggressive behavior

is not essential to it. Bard's final experiment was to produce hypothalamic lesions in decorticate cats. Instead of being highly irritable, it was more difficult to elicit the defense reaction in these than in normal animals. It may be concluded that the function of the hypothalamus in the expression of anger and the defense reaction is to facilitate or magnify stimulation, which then passes along to the centers of motor control in the lower brain stem.

A final question is: which part or parts of the cerebral cortex have the inhibitory function on the expres- sion of anger? Bard and Mountcastle (1948) showed that if only the neocortex is removed, the result is a remarkably placid cat, indicating that this region has an excitatory function. Their original result that removal of the amygdala produces an irritable animal like the decorticate cat has not been confirmed (Kaada, 1967). Removal of this area instead produces increased placidity and docility.

There is some evidence that ablation of the septal area in rats will cause increased irritability, but only of a transient nature. It is tempting to theorize that there normally exists a balance between excitatory and inhibitory areas of the cortex, but no sufficient basis for this exists at the present time. It must, however, be concluded that many parts of the brain are involved in the stimulation and expression of agonistic behavior. We must also conclude that agonistic behavior can be elicited by external stimuli in the absence of both the cerebral

cortex and the hypothalamus. A parsimonious explanation
of these facts is a mechanism whose action is initiated by
external stimuli which are then magnified and prolonged
by the hypothalamus, leading to prolonged behavior which
is regulated and controlled by the cerebral cortex.

Evidence from brain stimulation. As with ablation
experiments, this work has been done mostly with the cat.
I originally reviewed this material (Scott, 1958) from the
viewpoint of whether or not stimulation of any part of the
brain can produce an emotional state similar to that of
anger, and concluded that the evidence supported the conclusion that by using the correct techniques of stimulation
in rather precisely defined areas of the hypothalamus, an
experimenter can produce prolonges states of excitation,
which not only result in external behavior similar to that
of a naturally excited cat, but also produce measurable
changes of activity in the cerebral cortex similar to what
must be produced if an animal is aware of the presumed
emotional sensation that accompanies the excitation.
Kaada (1967) has reviewed the more recent literature and
comes to the same conclusion. Similar results are reported
by Delgado (1967) in the rhesus monkey also; i.e., that
stimulation in the proper areas will produce a genuine
motivational state rather than a stereotyped motor response
which persists only as long as the electrical stimulation
lasts.

Although Kaada's review indicates some disagreement
between different workers with respect to the precise
definition of responsive areas, there appear to be fairly
discrete areas in the hypothalamus which will elicit the
special behavior patterns of flight, defense attacks, and
prey-killing. Hunsperger (1956) finds that weak stimulation in a peripheral zone of the hypothalamus will elicit
flight, while somewhat stronger stimulation produces
defensive reactions. Weak stimulation in more central
areas produces defensive behavior, while stronger stimulation causes behavior to change to an attack. He and other
authors have found that both the duration and intensity of
electrical stimulation affect the kind of behavior elicited, with the result that it is possible to get different
behavior from electrodes located in the same area of the
brain. One question which these results do not answer is
that of the nature of the internal stimulation involved.
Since pain is known to be an effective elicitor of defensive

behavior, it would be expected that an electrode placed in
the area that produces the sensation of pain in the central
nervous system would lead to the same effect. Data by
Plotnik, Mir, and Delgado (this volume) bear out this expectation.

Kaada (1967) has extended the study of brain stimulation into the amygdala of the cerebral cortex and finds
that electrical stimulation will elicit either flight or
defense reactions but never attack. The areas involved
overlap each other to some extent, and the behavioral
responses are similar to those produced by stimulating the
hypothalamus. This work confirms his ablation experiments,
which indicate that without the amygdala a cat becomes a
docile and placid animal. The normal function of the
amygdala is not clear, but the fact that removing the
entire cerebral cortex produces an irritable animal leads
to the hypothesis that there are excitatory and inhibitory
areas in this organ which are normally in a state of balance
which can be disturbed by external stimulation.

Delgado (1967) and his co-workers have worked with
electrical stimulation of both cats and rhesus monkeys.
They are now concentrating on exploring the effects of
brain stimulation in animals that are living in social
groups, and in which stimulation is turned off and on by
remote radio control. This situation has many advantages
over the usual laboratory set-up in which a solitary
animal is stimulated through wires. The monkey is free to
behave in a normal fashion, and his behavior is observably
much better organized than is that of a solitary animal.
The situation has the further advantage that the significance of the behavior can be judged by its effect on other
monkeys rather than by the subjective impressions of the
experimenter. It is also possible to compare the results of
internal and external stimulation and to judge whether or
not these are identical. One very interesting result is
that monkeys and cats react differently to brain stimulation that produces aggressive behavior. Two cats that have
been previously tolerant of each other can be induced to
fight in a prolonged fashion, whereas in two monkeys having
a well-established dominance-subordination relationship
this relationship is not disturbed. On the other hand, if
two monkeys have only been together a short time, they can
be stimulated to fight (Robinson, this volume).

One of the major factors affecting fighting is training, and in Delgado's technique, it is possible to train
the animals while internal stimulation is going on. Some
reactions can be conditioned and others not. The possi-
bilities of this technique in connection with learning
studies are almost endless.

Delgado concludes that there are a large number of
brain areas that are involved in the expression of agonistic
behavior, and that there is no one central controlling area.
In an earlier paper, Delgado (1966) concluded that different
areas of the brain were involved in pain and aggression.
New data included in this volume indicates that this conclusion may need to be modified.

<u>Relationship between electrical brain stimulation and
external stimulation</u>. Most of the work with intracranial
stimulation has been measured in terms of the behavior
evoked, which is, of course, dependent in part on the environmental situation. Plotnik, Mir, and Delgado (this
volume) have made a significant technical advance, in that
they have defined the effects of such brain stimulation in
terms of both the readiness of the individual to stimulate
his own brain (thus defining whether or not the stimulation is pleasant or aversive), and by comparing the results
of such internal stimulation with external painful stimulation. For example, a monkey with implanted electrodes can
be taught to perform certain acts as a result of painful
electric shock applied to its foot. Now, if stimulation
of one of the electrodes produces the same behavior as foot
shock without additional training, it can be concluded that
the monkey is responding to a similar sensation of pain.
Likewise, if an implanted electrode stimulates fighting in
a monkey in a social situation, the monkey can be given the
opportunity to stimulate himself with the same electrode.
If he refuses to repeat this self-stimulation, this indicates that the sensation is aversive and at least unpleasant, if not painful.

Out of 174 points stimulated in the brains of several
monkeys, 35 had negative reinforcing properties and were
considered aversive. Fourteen of these stimulated aggression in a social situation. None of the rest of the points
would elicit aggression. These results emphasize the
importance of painful stimulation as an elicitor of fighting in this species.

The same authors find that in a social situation with a well-defined dominance order, only the dominant monkey can be stimulated to attack. This agrees with my own earlier attempts to elicit aggression in goats by means of frustration, where only the dominant animals fought when frustrated (Scott, 1948).

There are, however, situations in which animals appear to enjoy fighting. For example, a trained fighting mouse will attack without showing any external signs of unpleasant emotion. The technique of these authors can and should be extended to study such problems more widely.

Interaction of different brain areas. Both ablation and stimulation experiments indicate that a large number of brain areas are involved in the expression and control of agonistic behavior, beginning at the cerebral cortex and extending through the hypothalamus and mid brain to the brain stem. A major theoretical and practical problem is discovering how these different parts of the brain interact with each other in different species. Dr. Moyer (this symposium) indicates that different patterns of agonistic behavior (called by him different types of aggression) have different neurological bases. These different patterns are integrated with each other behaviorally, i.e., an animal will choose between flight, defense, and attack on the basis of the situation and the possible outcome of the behavior: is there evidence also of neurophysiological integration?

Problem of spontaneous internal stimulation. These and similar experiments with intracranial electrical stimulation have been used as a basis for arguing that spontaneous internal stimulation for aggressive behavior exists. On the face of it, the effects which are produced by internal brain stimulation are no more spontaneous than are the results of external stimuli, such as pain. Both of these have been induced by the experimenter. What these experiments do show is that internal mechanisms, concerned not only with attack but also other patterns of agonistic behavior, including flight and defensive behavior, are important. They do not give any information as to how these mechanisms for the magnification and prolongation of stimuli could be set in motion by normal internal physiological processes.

Much of the contention on this important theoretical point may have been based on mutual misunderstanding as to what is meant by spontaneity (Tinbergen, 1968). I shall therefore define what I mean by spontaneous internal stimulation. In the first place, all stimulation, whether external or internal, consists of change. An internal change that is produced by physiological or metabolic processes independently of outside stimulation is "spontaneous," and such a change which in some way activates the nervous system is "spontaneous stimulation."

That such changes do take place with respect to ingestive behavior (in the hunger and thirst mechanisms) has long been known. There is no argument on the point that internal mechanisms which magnify and prolong stimulation have effects on agonistic behavior. The point at issue is what activates these mechanisms, external stimulation or spontaneous internal changes as defined above?

A related and very important theoretical question is: if spontaneous stimulation exists, does it have a cumulative effect? As I shall show below, there are cumulative mechanisms that can affect behavior arising either from internal or external stimulation.

POSSIBLE MECHANISMS OF INTERNAL STIMULATION
AND CUMULATIVE EFFECT

There is no known physiological mechanism by which any large amount of energy can be accumulated in the nervous system. Therefore, hydraulic models of motivation (see Table 1) are chiefly valid only in that they may represent subjective interpretations of motivation; in short, how it feels to be motivated. The entire organism is, of course, a mechanism by which energy can be accumulated and stored. However, such energy is not specific to any particular kind of behavior and does not represent motivation.

There is also no evidence of metabolic changes which could result in the stimulation of fighting behavior in the same way that metabolic changes lead to the sensation of hunger and internal stimulation for ingestive behavior. Are there other possible ways in which internal stimulation for agonistic behavior could arise spontaneously, or accumulate within the nervous system?

Summation of stimuli. The physiological evidence
presented in this symposium indicates that very long lasting
emotional and physiological effects are produced by agonistic behavior could arise spontaneously, or accumulate
within the nervous system?

Summation of stimuli. The physiological evidence presented in this symposium indicates that very long lasting
emotional and physiological effects are produced by agonistic behavior, some of these measurable effects lasting at
least as long as 24 hours. This means that the same organism could be subjected within 24 hours to several external
stimuli, each of which would have the effect of stimulating
agonistic behavior before the effects of the previous stimulation had died out. It is highly likely that such stimuli
do summate, with the result that such a high degree of
internal stimulation is eventually achieved that it may
result in the breakdown of inhibitory training. Summation
effects could also result in the appearance of agonistic
behavior as a result of what appeared to be a very slight
external stimulus, as often happens in practical human
cases.

Such effects as these are basically the result of
reverberating mechanisms in the nervous system. However,
they do have a tendency to die out and do not accumulate
indefinitely. This sort of cumulative mechanism is limited
to a relatively short time period, usually of hours, and at
the most of a day or two.

Another possibility is that external stimuli eliciting
agonistic behavior may summate with arousal from other
sources. For example, if an animal is already hungry, it
is possible that under these circumstances a relatively
slight stimulus might elicit agonistic behavior. The
ethological literature (Tinbergen, 1951) is full of examples
of highly aroused animals not being able to make appropriate behavioral responses and therefore responding in
apparently unrelated ways. However, such behavior should
be most likely if there is a normal association between
agonistic behavior and another behavioral system.

Association with other behavioral systems. In ingestive
behavior, spontaneous internal stimulation is definitely important, as there are mechanisms whereby internal metabolic
changes lead to motivation for eating and drinking behavior.

If fighting is somehow tied in with ingestive behavior it should appear to be motivated in much the same way. For example, children are often more likely to fight at mealtimes than at other times of the day. Since the fighting does not get them any more food (in fact, may even delay the mealtime), it is possible that the children are responding to hunger as if it were a painful or noxious stimulation that might result from behavior of the other children.

In a still more explicit case, when fighting is directly linked with competition over food, hunger will also result in an increase in fighting. I once did an experiment with goats (Scott, 1948) in which I compared the amount of fighting over food in animals that had suffered no deprivation of food with fighting at another time when the same animals had been kept in a barn for six hours without food. As might be expected, the animals fought more when hungry. However, each pair had established a dominance relationship, and the increase in fighting was solely the result of the behavior of the dominant animal in each case. The subordinate animal simply stuck around longer and took more punishment than he would have done ordinarily. While hunger increased the amount of fighting in the group, it did so only where previous training permitted it.

Nevertheless this is a case where the spontaneous stimulation normally leading to food-seeking and eating can lead to an increase in agonistic behavior. It is also one in which the relationship between spontaneous internal stimulation and fighting is strictly determined by the situation; i.e., this is not stimulation for fighting per se.

The nature of internal stimulation in sexual behavior is still not well understood. It is obviously important in those female mammals that increase the amount of activity during the estrus period, associated with certain hormonal changes. Presumably, the sex hormones have a direct stimulating effect on the central nervous system, although how accommodation effects are prevented over a period of several hours is not clear. In male mammals where fluids tend to accumulate and cause a certain amount of pressure in the accessory sex glands, there is evidence of a mechanism which could act in a similar way to the internally accumulating stimulation that arises from metabolic changes in hunger.

There are several ways in which sexual behavior can be tied in with fighting. In those species in which males regularly fight over females, increased sexual motivation should lead to increased contacts between males as they become more attracted to females.

The same hormones which activate the accessory sex glands are also concerned in agonistic behavior, as the great majority of male mammals are more aggressive in their behavior when the male hormone is present. There is at least a faint possibility that the male hormone could produce a continuously stimulating effect on the central nervous system with respect to agonistic behavior. However, it would be difficult to explain the lack of accommodation, and the effect is more easily explained as the lowering of a treshold of stimulation.

As indicated in the first part of this paper, not all mammals compete for females. In species where this does take place, fighting occurs only in the presence of the female and not at other times. Thus, fighting is closely correlated with sexual motivation but seems to occur only where there is opportunity for sexual behavior. It is also possible that among many mammals fighting between males has the effect of preventing homosexual behavior, thus preventing the learning of maladaptive behavior that could interfere with successful reproduction. Thus, sexual motivation in males could lead to increased fighting when it leads to contacts with sexually unresponsive males, and a similar but milder effect is seen in non-receptive females.

In human beings and other higher primates, where learning plays such an important part in the development of sexual behavior, it is possible that a certain amount of "wire crossing" occurs with respect to sexual and agonistic behavior. One frequently sees inexperienced teen-aged males striking their girl friends instead of giving the appropriate courtship behavior.

Cumulative effects of reinforcement. It is well known that repeated reinforcement of either a rewarding or punishing nature will result in increased motivation. This change, while its exact biochemical and neurological nature is unknown, must be an internal one. Therefore, it is possible to cumulate motivation toward agonistic behavior as the result of experience, and the results of training ex-

periments with mice strongly bear out this expectation.
However, this is not a case of spontaneous accumulation of
energy, and the motivation only appears in connection with
specific external stimuli.

Thus, there are mechanisms by which motivation for
agonistic behavior can either be summated over short periods
of time or can be increased over long periods in specific
situations as a result of the process of reinforcement.
There are, however, no indications of spontaneous internal
stimulation specifically connected with agonistic behavior.
Spontaneous internal stimulation for ingestive and sexual
behavior can, however, be tied in with agonistic behavior
in certain special situations and thus produce apparently
spontaneous fighting.

These are, however, exceptional rather than normal conditions. It is still possible to say that there is no evidence of spontaneous internal physiological changes which
would lead to a specific need for fighting behavior. Nevertheless, the situations which elicit fighting behavior are
numerous and complex, and it would be very difficult to
entirely eliminate the causes of agonistic behavior in any
natural situation. The effect of this conclusion is to
minimize the need for sublimation of agonistic behavior and
to make possible the conclusion that it is possible for
animals and men to live for long periods without expressing
agonistic behavior and without suffering any degree of
emotional damage.

Taking the contrary viewpoint, Moyer (1968) has mar-
shalled the evidence for the existence of aggression as an
internal drive state. This is essentially a summary of the
physiological evidence for the existence of anger and other
emotional states related to agonistic behavior. There is at
the present time no argument on this point, and certainly I
have none. Moyer then goes ahead to argue that the physiological mechanisms underlying consummatory behavior are
similar to those underlying aggressive behavior, in that
they can both be influenced by similar classes of experimental procedures and other factors and processes. For
example, appropriate brain stimulation will elicit both
agonistic behavior and ingestive behavior, and learning will
modify both sorts of behavior. Again, I have no real disagreement with this viewpoint. Both agonistic behavior and
consummatory behavior are adaptive reactions of the whole

organism; i.e., both are behavior, and it is entirely appropriate to look for the same general classes of causal factors affecting all behavior. It is possible to either
stress similarities or differences among these factors.
With my background in genetics, I am interested in differences. One of the likenesses between these behavioral
systems is this: an animal can be trained to completely
suppress either ingestive or fighting behavior. The essential difference is that, in the former case, the animal
dies from starvation; in the latter case, he goes on living,
often to a ripe old age. One can place a male mouse with a
female, a situation in which no fighting takes place, and
the pair will go ahead to produce litter after litter of
offspring and show no obvious effects of deprivation of
fighting; and, if the male offspring are removed promptly
at weaning, no fighting will ever occur. Again, we have
done experiments in which the fighting of the mouse is
directly suppressed by training and then over a period of
many weeks subjected these same mice to simulated mild
attacks, which is the most effective method of eliciting
fighting. After very long periods the mouse will begin to
show mildly maladaptive behavior. In short, in the absence
of external stimulation to fight, a peaceful mouse shows no
ill effects. In the presence of external stimulation, these
effects do appear (Scott & Marston, 1953).

With respect to physiological rather than behavioral
evidence, Moyer states that a crucial experiment would be
to insert an electrode into a brain area known to stimulate
agonistic behavior, and see whether electrical currents
appear (a) in the presence of appropriate external stimulation and (b) in the absence of such stimulation. If the
latter were the case, one would have objective evidence of
spontaneous internal stimulation. Such experiments have
not yet been done, and it may be pointed out that this
would still not pinpoint the mechanism by which internal
stimulation might arise. One possible mechanism is that of
biochemical changes. In this case, an experimental demonstration should include evidence that such changes do
indeed occur and that agonistic behavior could be elicited
by bringing about such changes experimentally. Along these
lines, there is a promising lead in the experiments with
isolated animals.

Behavioral and physiological effects of isolation. It
has long been known that male mice housed together from

infancy will rarely fight, whereas if strange adults are introduced to each other there is a high probability that fighting will shortly follow the introduction. Welch & Welch (this volume) have made a systematic study of this phenomenon. From the original results it might be supposed that the animals are responding to strangeness. However, Welch & Welch have shown that mice become increasingly irritable and aggressive the longer that they are kept in isolation. Furthermore, these changes in behavior are paralleled with progressive changes in brain biochemistry. The synthesis and utilization of norepinephrine, dopamine, and serotonin are decreased. These same substances are increased as an immediate effect of fighting, although they may be exhausted after long periods. Whether or not these biochemical changes are the immediate cause of irritability and aggressiveness has not yet been established. However, we can at least conclude that the mice are emotionally disturbed by being kept separately from other mice and that this brings about measurable biochemical changes. This suggests that mice, even though they are not highly social, may still be disturbed by isolation after having lived in a social group, just as the more highly social animals, such as dogs, react to separation. At the present time we have no evidence on the effect of isolation on aggressiveness in dogs, except that fighting is much reduced in those animals that have been reared in isolation through the critical period of socialization. It would be interesting to see what the effect of rearing a mouse in isolation from birth (or at least through the socialization period) might be.

These physiological reactions to isolation may provide an explanation of the tendency of defeated mice to recover aggressiveness after isolation, which Ginsburg and Allee (1942) noted was similar to the spontaneous recovery after extinction seen in Pavlovian conditioning. However, badly defeated animals do not begin to fight even after two months in isolation (Scott & Marston, 1953).

Another commonly observed result is that mice kept in groups are more susceptible to the lethal effects of amphetamine sulfate than are those housed alone. The immediate cause of death is elevated body temperature. Welch & Welch have found that mice living in compatible groups since weaning, where there is little probability of fighting, are more resistant to amphetamine than isolated animals made hyperexcitable. Dominant animals (fighters) are more

susceptible than subordinate ones. Recently in our laboratory we have shown that fighting elevates body temperature,
with the result that fighting and amphetamine have an
additive effect on body temperature and eventually death.
Furthermore, two genetically different strains react differently to the same high dosage of amphetamine sulfate, the
BALB/c strain showing a marked rise in temperature and the
C57BL/6 a slight fall. The latter strain is, of course,
much more resistant to amphetamine poisoning. Thus, the
social and other factors which contribute to amphetamine
toxicity are highly complex; but we now have a much clearer
idea of some of the mechanisms that may be involved.

   Effects of fighting and defeat. Eleftheriou (this
volume) has shown that extensive biochemical changes occur
in the brains of animals that experience fighting and defeat. These changes begin with the release of corticosterone and are followed by a series of changes in hormones
and brain chemistry, which are part of the general stress
reaction. Restoration to normal levels takes place much
more rapidly in successful fighters than it does in repeatedly defeated animals. Changes occur selectively in different parts of the brain. For example, serotonin decreases
in the frontal cortex of defeated animals but is increased
elsewhere, whereas norepinephrine increases in this part of
the brain and decreases elsewhere. It follows that changes
in total brain content of various substances are not particularly meaningful, as results in different parts of the
brain may cancel out.

   Eleftheriou has also measured changes in RNA (ribonucleic acid) that accompany and are presumably the effect
of these other changes. Prolonged stress results in the
depletion of RNA, which suggests a mechanism for the commonly observed fact that emotional reactions interfere with
learning. This is an extremely promising lead, and final
confirmation of the hypothesis will depend upon identification of fractions of RNA definitely known to have a function
in the learning process.

   In these experiments there is abundant evidence that
major biochemical changes follow fighting and defeat, consistent with the hypothesis that internal physiological
mechanisms have the function of prolonging and magnifying
the effects of external stimulation. This view is not inconsistent with the fact that biochemical changes can also

precede fighting, presumably leading to increased irritability and modifying the probability that fighting will
occur (Welch & Welch, this volume). Both mechanisms are
possible and compatible.

    The isolation phenomenon does present an interesting
problem concerning its adaptive value under natural conditions. A mouse that became accidentally isolated under
natural conditions would not remain in a simple restricted
environment, such as a mouse cage; and we at present have
no way of knowing whether he would develop similar internal
changes. Supposing that such a wild isolated mouse did become hyperexcitable and irritable, one would expect that he
would wander around and eventually come into contact with
other mice. Presumably, he would have the tendency to
attack such mice; and being the aggressor might win and
drive them away, with some advantage to himself. However,
the behavior of mice as observed under natural conditions
indicates that under free conditions individuals are very
likely to avoid each other rather than getting into prolonged fights, nor do we know that the irritable individual
would in fact have an advantage.

    One interpretation of these results is that the isolated
mouse is accumulating fighting energy or building up a drive.
This is probably too simple an interpretation, since mice
living equally long in a social group without fighting do
not undergo these changes or build up such a drive. If this
is indeed a drive, it is something which is directly the
result of the external situation. My interpretation is that
mice, although they do not show their emotional reactions to
isolation as obviously as do dogs, are, in fact, emotionally
aroused or upset by isolation, and long periods result in
progressive internal changes. Another possible explanation
is that temperature may be affected, as isolated animals are
not as well able to maintain their bodily heat as grouped
animals. Nevertheless, these are very promising leads with
respect to understanding the neurochemistry of aggression.
Isolated mice provide an excellent opportunity to study the
behavioral and physiological causes of irritability.

    The concept of irritability. Flynn (this volume)
points out various ways in which states of prolonged physiological arousal can be produced. Decortication, various
other brain lesions, and certain biochemical treatments will
produce animals that are highly irritable and therefore re-

spond aggressively or defensively to external stimuli which
ordinarily produce no effect. There are also many human
patients with brain damage or other pathological conditions
associated with a tendency to readily fly into violent
rages.

    Rather than concentrating on the problem of the primal
cause of internal stimulation, Flynn's paper suggests that
a more fruitful direction of research would be the search
for ways in which irritability can be induced by physiological means. It would then be possible to compare states
of irritability produced by physiological intervention with
those induced by psychological factors. This in turn would
lead to the study of physiological methods by which irritability could be reduced. In this way the harmful physiological and psychological effects of prolonged states of
fear and anger could be reduced in other ways than by the
psychological methods now available.

    Development of neurophysiological organization. It has
long been known that the males and females of various species
of mammals are different from each other in aggressiveness,
the adult males being more aggressive than females in the
vast majority of cases. This difference is in some way
associated with the male hormone, the estrogenic hormones of
the female having little or no effect. This latter fact was
recognized by stock breeders before the advent of modern
physiology, as castration has been used since ancient times
to produce docility in both cattle and horses.

    If male mice are castrated as adults, the tendency to
fight can be restored by injections of the male hormone,
testosterone. Similarly treated females will respond to
testosterone injections with increased sexual behavior, but
show no change in their tendency to fight (King & Tolman,
1956).

    Bronson and Desjardins (this volume) with independent
confirmation by Edwards (1968) have shown that there is a
critical period in the mouse one or two days after birth
when the nervous system of either males or females can be
modified toward the subsequent development of an increased
capacity for aggressiveness. If young mice are castrated at
birth, an injection of male hormone will make either males
or females react with increased aggressiveness when this
hormone is again injected during adulthood. The critical

period corresponds to the time when the gonads of the young animals are temporarily stimulated into activity by the gonadotropic hormones of the mother's pituitary with the result that the adult hormones are temporarily present in fairly large quantities. Thus, there is good evidence that this is the mechanism by which the fundamental difference in aggressiveness between the two sexes is produced. In mice, at least, the male and female nervous systems are physiologically different.

This discovery opens up a whole new field of research, both with respect to the generality of this phenomenon in other mammals and in regard to the precise way in which the alteration is produced. Following up these leads may result in understanding the ways in which genetic differences within the same sex may be produced and also lead eventually to ways in which the development of aggressiveness can be modified in a practical way.

The physiological control of aggression. In a previous paper, Moyer (1968) has suggested that I have earlier placed too much emphasis on training as a method of controlling undesirable aggressive behavior, and advocates a program of research that would provide physiological methods of control. I agree that it would be an excellent idea to develop such methods. I would go farther and say that we need to develop better methods of controlling agonistic behavior on every level of organization.

On the physiological level, it would certainly be an excellent idea if one could take a pill and do away with the persistent symptoms of anger that have been aroused by an unsuccessful argument with one's boss. I can only report the result of some work with mice. In the past two years, my students and I have done some work with the effects of drugs on fighting. These experiments were designed not so much to find a cure for fighting as to discover what the general effects of drugs might be. In one series of experiments, we tested the effect of the sympathomimetic drug, amphetamine sulfate, and the ganglionic blocking agent, phenoxybenzamine, on the attack latency of mice that had been strongly trained to fight. On the positive side, amphetamine sulfate did not decrease the latency of attack, indicating that maximum efficiency of fighting had already been developed by training. On the negative, with sufficiently high dosages, attack latency was prolonged, but as

soon as the mice were physiologically able, they began to
attack again. Similar inhibitory effects were produced by
high doses of phenoxybenzamine. In short, only becoming
physically sick or disabled will have much effect on a
highly trained mouse. While drugs may do much to alleviate
emotional symptoms, we still have no drug that will selectively erase the effect of training.

SUMMARY

Agonistic behavior, or social fighting, defined as
fighting and related behavior patterns elicited by members
of the same species, has probably evolved in most cases
from the defensive responses which are almost universal reactions to pain or injury inflicted by either a predator or
a species mate. There is no evidence that social fighting
has ever evolved from predation; the behavior patterns of
predation and social fighting are quite distinct in predators, and certainly predation cannot explain the origin of
fighting in herbivorous animals. Contrary to popular
thinking, predation is particularly unimportant in man as
a possible forerunner of social fighting, as both prehis-
toric and modern man are primarily adapted for an omnivorous diet obtained by food-gathering and have become
occasional predators only secondarily with the acquisition
of tools.

Motivation for fighting depends in part upon the
direction of social evolution in any particular species
together with the resulting adaptive functions of agonistic
behavior. Where animals regularly compete for food and
females, food and sexual motivation contribute to the elicitation and duration of fighting. However, much fighting has
the simple result of keeping animals apart.

The motivational system or systems underlying fighting
are therefore similar in different species only when fighting has similar adaptive functions. In the mouse, cat, and
rhesus monkey, social fighting has the common effect of
keeping individuals apart from each other and may therefore
be presumed to have similar underlying causes. In the cat,
the species in which the most extensive neurophysiological
analyses have been made, many parts of the brain influence
the expression of agonistic behavior, the hypothalamus
being especially important as the area which produces the

emotion of anger and thereby prolongs and magnifies the
effects of stimulation originating elsewhere. There is no
evidence of "spontaneous" stimulation specific to agonistic
behavior arising in the brain itself.

However, spontaneous internal stimulation arising in
connection with ingestive and sexual behavior can contribute
to fighting under certain conditions such as those in which
fighting is related to the possession of food or females.
Such fighting ordinarily takes different forms depending on
its effects. In addition, there are general physiological
mechanisms which can result in cumulative effects on motivation to fight, particularly the summation of external
stimuli, and increased motivation resulting from repeated
reinforcement. Both cumulative effects are directly controlled by external events.

There are so many potential external causes of fighting
in man that it will never be possible to permanently eliminate all of them in any practical situation. Whether or not
"spontaneous" internal stimulation exists, the measures we
use for the control of destructive violence will be much the
same. The significance of the finding that such "spontaneous" stimulation either does not exist or at the most is
an indirect result of a tie-in with other motivational
systems, is that we can safely work toward an essentially
non-violent world, without danger of harming the individual, and with confidence that, when we fail, it is our
methods that are at fault rather than internal physiology
inherited from remote ancestors. In other words, we can
no longer excuse human violence on the basis of our biological ancestry.

From a theoretical standpoint, a scientific contro-
versy is good only if it generates data. The view which I
hold is one that I derived from the facts rather than pre-
conceived notions; and what I am interested in is not win-
ning an argument but establishing the truth. One of the
purposes of this symposium is to bring together some of the
latest facts on the physiology of fighting and defeat. I
think it will be obvious that not all the facts are in, that
the physiological mechanisms behind agonistic behavior are
still far from being completely known, and that the known
mechanisms have so far been discovered in a very small
sample of species.

REFERENCES

BARD, P. Central nervous mechanisms for the expression of
    anger in animals. In M. L. Reymart (Ed.), Feelings and
    Emotions. New York: McGraw-Hill, 1950.

BARD, P., & MOUNTCASTLE, V. B. Some forebrain mechanisms
    involved in expression of rage with special reference
    to suppression of angry behavior. Proc. Assn. Res.
    Nerv. Ment. Disease, 1948, 27, 362-404.

DELGADO, J. M. R. Aggressive behavior evoked by radio
    stimulation in monkey colonies. Am. Zoologist, 1966,
    6, 669-681.

DELGADO, J. M. R. Aggression and defense under cerebral
    radio control. In Clemente and D. B. Lindsley (eds.),
    Aggression and Defense: Neural Mechanisms and Social
    Patterns. Los Angeles: University of California
    Press, 1967, 171-193.

EDWARDS, D. A. Neonatal organization of aggressive behavior
    in mice by androgen. Am. Zoologist, 1968, 8, 749.

HAMILTON, W. D. Genetical evolution of social behavior.
    J. Theor. Biol., 1964, 7, 1-52.

HUNSPERGER, R. W. Affectreaktionen auf electrische Reizung
    im Hirnstamm de Katze. Helv. Physiol. Pharmacol. Acta,
    1956, 14, 70-92.

KAADA, B. Brain mechanisms related to aggressive behavior.
    In C. D. Clements and D. B. Lindsley (Eds.), Aggression
    and Defense: Neural Mechanisms and Social Patterns.
    Los Angeles: University of California Press, 1967.

KING, J. A., & TOLMAN, J. The effect of testosterone
    propionate on aggression in male and female C57BL/10
    mice. Brit. J. Animal Behav., 1956, 4, 147-149.

GINSBURG, B., & ALLEE, W. C. Some effects of conditioning
    on social dominance and subordination in inbred strains
    of mice. Physiol. Zool., 1942, 15, 485-506.

LEYHAUSEN, P. The communal organization of solitary
    mammals. Symp. Zool. Soc. London, 1965, No. 14,

MOYER, K. E. Aggression as an internal drive state
    (Mimeographed). Pittsburgh: Carnegie-Mellon
    University, 1968.

SCOTT, J. P. Dominance and the frustration-aggression
    hypothesis. Physiol. Zool., 1948, 21, 31-39.

SCOTT, J. P. Aggression. Chicago: University of
    Chicago Press, 1958.

SCOTT, J. P. Agonistic behavior in mice and rats. Am.
    Zoologist, 1966, 6, 683-701.

SCOTT, J. P. Evolution and domestication of the dog. In
    Th. Dobzhansky, M. K. Hecht, and W. C. Steere (Eds.),
    Evolutionary Biology. New York: Appleton-Century-
    Crofts, 1968, 2, 243-275.

SCOTT, J. P. Biological basis of human warfare. In
    M. Sheriff and C. W. Sheriff (Eds.), Interdisciplinary
    relationships in the social sciences. Chicago:
    Aldine, 1969, 121-136.

SCOTT, J. P., & MARSTON, M. V. Nonadaptive behavior result-
    ing from a series of defeats in fighting mice. J.
    Abnorm. Soc. Psychol., 1953, 48, 417-428.

SOUTHWICK, C. H., BEG, M. A., & SIDDIQUI, R. Rhesus
    monkeys in northern India. In I. DeVore (Ed.),
    Primate Behavior. New York: Holt, Rinehart, &
    Winston, 1965, 111-159.

TINBERGEN, N. The study of instinct. Oxford: Clarendon
    Press, 1951.

TINBERGEN, N. On war and peace in animals and man.
    Science, 1968, 160, 1411-1418.

ULRICH, R. Pain as a cause of aggression. Am. Zoologist,
    1966, 6, 643-662.

STEROID HORMONES AND AGGRESSIVE BEHAVIOR IN MAMMALS

F. H. Bronson and C. Desjardins

Department of Zoology, University of Texas,
Austin, and Department of Physiology and
Pharmacology, Oklahoma State University,
Stillwater, respectively

Certain steroid hormones have the ability to alter or
modulate the level of excitability in adult brain structures
that control the expression of aggression in some mammalian
species. Steroids also have been implicated recently in
the organization of these same neural tissues during critical periods of development. Conversely, concentrations of
circulating hormones in the adult animal may be altered
because of an aggressive encounter or because of stimuli
inherent in a chronic dominance-subordination social system.
The purpose of the present discussion, then, is to overview
the literature concerning these relationships. On the behavioral side, we will be interested primarily in "spontaneous"
or "inter-male" aggression (Scott, 1966 and Moyer, 1968,
respectively) with a nod of recognition to the problems
engendered by such categorization as well as by the term
aggression itself (cf., Barnett, 1969). Taxonomically,
this discussion will, by necessity, rely heavily on studies
using house mice with rats and other mammals being considered secondarily.

EFFECTS OF HORMONES ON AGGRESSION

As a generality, spontaneous aggression in most
species of mammals must be considered primarily a characteristic of adult males and usually somewhat limited to the
season of gonadal activity (Davis, 1964; also e.g.,
Bronson, 1964); thus, the early and continued interest in

43

testicular hormones (Collias, 1944). With respect to mice,
it should be noted that there may be considerable variation in frequency of spontaneous aggression among females
of the various strains. Charpentier (1969), for example,
felt that females of his stock of mice would become as
aggressive following isolation as would his males. Nevertheless, as a general rule, males of almost any strain of
mice will fight considerably more often than will females
following isolation (e.g., Lagerspetz, 1969). A working
model to explain this sexual difference and its hormonal
basis is available. There can be little doubt that androgens (or at least testosterone), occurring naturally in
physiological amounts in males but not in females, act on
the neural substrate underlying aggression to enhance both
the developmental organization of these tissues and their
level of function or responsiveness in the adult. No data
are available for circulating concentrations of androgens
in mice, but it is known that testosterone is circulating
in minute amounts in male rats throughout the period from
birth to the onset of puberty (Resko et al., 1968). Concentrations are generally less than 0.03 μg/100 ml plasma
between days 1 and 30 of life as opposed to averages between 0.1 and 0.2 μg/100 ml during adulthood. Assuming a
similar pattern of testicular activity in mice, studies on
this species have shown that: (a) the smaller amounts of
testosterone circulating early in the neonatal life of
normal males must organize some developing neural control
systems in such a manner that spontaneous attacks will be
more easily elicited in the adult (in the presence of circulating androgen) and (b) the larger amounts circulating
during adulthood act on the normally developed (i.e.,
previously androgenized) brain of the male in a manner
that enhances the possibility of an attack given appropriate behavioral stimulation. The lack of testosterone
during neonatal life, and hence the lack of both actions
of this hormone, would then result in a typical female-like
absence or low frequency of aggression.

With regard to the modulating effect of testosterone in
the normal adult male, a horde of studies have shown adequately that post-puberal castration is accompanied by a
decrease in aggressiveness and that testosterone replacement results in at least some degree of return of this behavioral pattern in mice (Uhlrich, 1938; Beeman, 1947;
Scott and Fredericson, 1951; Tollman and King, 1956; Bevan

et al., 1957; Bevan et al., 1958; Bevan et al., 1960; Yen
et al., 1962; Sigg et al., 1966; and Suchowsky et al.,
1969). Working more indirectly, Sigg (1969) has shown that
hypophysectomized male mice do not become aggressive following isolation as would be expected if the adenohypophyseal-
gonadal axis were operative. Fighting among intact males,
if it occurs, usually begins about the time of puberty as
androgen concentrations in the blood are increasing
(Fredericson, 1950; Lagerspetz, 1969). Fighting may be
induced somewhat earlier, however, by injections of testosterone (Levy and King, 1953; Lagerspetz and Talo, 1967).
Importantly, testosterone given to adult female mice does
not enhance their aggressiveness (Tollman and King, 1956)
unless these females have first been experimentally androgenized during neonatal life (Bronson & Desjardins, 1968;
Edwards, 1968).

Frequency of fighting among adult female mice may be
increased to male-like levels by giving single injections of
testosterone early in life, and then injecting the same
hormone concurrent with behavioral testing in adulthood.
Two experiments in our laboratory have shown that 83% and
96% of pairs of intact adult male C57BL/6J mice will fight
at least once in three consecutive daily encounters after
maintenance in isolation since weaning. The comparable
figures for females of this strain, treated and tested in
the same manner, are 4% and 16%. A male-like 100% of pairs
of intact females fought following a single injection of
600 μg testosterone propionate (TP) on day 0 of life and
treatment with 200 μg/day concurrent with testing in adulthood (Bronson & Desjardins, 1970). Edwards (1968) observed
fighting in over 95% ovariectomized females after they had
received 500 μg testosterone propionate on the day of their
birth, and the same dosage daily when they were being tested
for aggressiveness during adulthood. Thus, two different
laboratories were able to reverse completely the normally
large differences in aggressiveness between the sexes by
giving single injections of testosterone to females early in
life, and providing an exogenous source of the same hormone
in adulthood. Additionally, castration of males on the day
of their birth renders them unresponsive in an aggressive
situation during adulthood regardless of the presence or
absence of circulating androgen at that time (Bronson &
Desjardins, 1969). Castration on day 0 followed shortly by
a single injection of testosterone, however, results in a

relatively normal adult male with respect to his fighting
behavior (Bronson & Desjardins, op. cit.). The role of
circulating androgen as a normal organizer of some areas
of the neonatal brain that will later mediate aggression
in the adult male thus seems well established. Conversely,
the absence of androgen circulating in the normal neonatal
female would result in an absence of such organization and,
hence, the inability to respond to experimental treatment
with testosterone during adulthood (by becoming more
aggressive).

The critical period for such an organizing process is
apparently of relatively long duration, but experimental
manipulation is most easily accomplished around the day of
birth. Edwards (1969) reported a single injection of
testosterone to be more effective in this regard when given
on day 0 than when given on day 10 of life. Bronson and
Desjardins (1970) found single injections considerably more
effective on day 0 than on days 3, 6 or 12; additionally,
that single injections became ineffective sometime between
12 and 24 days of postnatal age. Daily injection for 20
days starting at 30 days of age, however, has been shown to
yield relatively good organization with respect to aggressive behavior (Edwards, 1970). The critical period of
sensitivity is thus one of relatively long duration, but
also one in which small amounts of androgen are highly
effective early in the period while massive amounts are
necessary later.

The effect of neonatal androgenization is particularly
dramatic in a chronic grouping situation as opposed to the
more typical procedure for the assessment of aggression in
mice, i.e., short daily encounters which are stopped when a
fight is initiated. Bronson and Desjardins (1968) paired
neonatally androgenized females with males for 18 hours and
found considerable wounding and occasional death among the
males. The strength of the neonatal organization process
is obvious in a recent experiment in which females were
given oil, 10 μg, 100 μg, or 400 μg testosterone propionate
on the day of birth, ovariectomized on days 24-26, and then
isolated until 70-75 days of age. Adults treated in this
manner were then chronically administered testosterone
propionate and grouped 4 or 5 per cage. Seven days of
grouping resulted in no wounding among the groups receiving
oil neonatally (Table 1). Some wounding was observed among
those receiving 10 μg TP neonatally while 69% of those

TABLE I

Incidence of wounding and death among females given oil
or one of 3 doses of testosterone propionate on day
of birth, injected with testosterone during adulthood,
and then grouped for 7 days

Neonatal Injection	No. Females	Severity of Wounding*				No. Dead	% Wounded or Dead
		0	1	2	3		
Oil	18	18	0	0	0	0	0
10 μg TP	34	28	6	0	0	0	18
100 μg TP	34	26	3	3	0	2	24
400 μg TP	36	11	2	7	10	6	69

*Severity of wounding on a 0-3 scale where 0 = no wounds
and 1-3 indicates a range from a few minor wounds on tail
and rump to a condition where tails and sometimes hind feet
were bitten off and where, in all cases, the skin on the
back and rump was solidly adhered to underlying tissues.

receiving 400 μg on the day of birth were wounded (6 of 36
females had been killed). It should be emphasized that 69%
is close to the expected maximum. It is normal for previously isolated, intact males of this strain to fight
vigorously when grouped until one unwounded dominant per
group emerges while the subordinates are often wounded to
varying degrees or occasionally killed (Bronson, 1967).
Such strong hierarchy formation may be presumed for the
females receiving 400 μg TP neonatally since 7 of 8 cages
had a single unwounded female in each (presumably the dominant) while the ninth cage contained only unwounded animals.
A similar experiment (Bronson & Desjardins, 1970) used the
same design as that shown in Table 1 except females receiving either oil or TP in adulthood prior to grouping.
Fighting was observed only among neonatally androgenized
females that were given androgen prior to grouping; any
other combination of injections, including TP early and oil
before testing, resulted in no fighting.

Questions concerning the parts of the neonatal brain
that are being organized, what actually is meant, chemically

and/or morphologically, by the term "organization," and how
testosterone can modulate the action of specific units in
the adult brain in such a manner that aggression is more
easily elicited are largely unexplored. If studies on
adult monkeys can be generalized (Delgado, 1966), it is
possibly meaningless to look for an effect of testosterone
on a specific nucleus controlling aggression. Such a line
of research has proven fruitful for the hypothalamus and
sexual behavior in several species (e.g., Nadler, 1968).
Certainly, the effects of testosterone on the hypothalamus
followed by the amygdala and other pertinent structures
will be of interest in future aggression research. Regardless of the neural location(s) where testosterone is·flu-
encing aggression, it seems realistic to view such effects
at the level of the genome and as reflected by specific
protein synthesis in nerve cells. Experimental evidence is
accumulating slowly on this point. Neonatal androgen administration in rats has been shown to result in new
species of RNA being synthesized in the brain. Shimada and
Gorbman (1970) using DNA-RNA-hybridization techniques showed
long-lasting effects of early testosterone treatment on RNA
synthsis in the forebrains but not in the midbrain-hind-
brain area of rats killed at 47 days of age. Clayton et al.
(1970) have demonstrated changes in RNA metabolism in the
amygdala and anterior hypothalamus of newborn rats following testosterone administration. Using the absence of ovulation during adulthood as an index of the effectiveness of
neonatal androgen administration, Kobayashi and Gorski
(1970) have blocked the effect of early androgen treatment
with both actinomycin-D and puromycin (DNA-dependent RNA
and protein synthesis inhibitors, respectively). Thus the
neuronal genome as well as the intracellular biochemical
processes of RNA and protein synthesis have been implicated
in the mechanism by which early androgen administration
masculinizes the female brain. At this point, it should be
noted that any mouse, male or female, will fight back if
given a sufficiently painful stimulus such as pinching
their tails. Female mice also will fight with relatively
high frequency if suckling young (Scott, 1966). In addition, Edwards (1969), employing what he called a "bully
test," found that androgen was not a necessary prerequisite
either neonatally or in adulthood for an attack on a much
smaller, prepuberal male mouse, Thus, it is obvious that
the neural substrate necessary for spontaneous attack,
whether considered at the molecular or at the tissue level,
is present in both sexes, but is markedly less responsive

in the adult female unless she has had an exogenous source
of androgen both neonatally and in adulthood. The effects
of early androgenization, then, can hardly be explained on
the basis of creating linkages between specific neural
units which would not otherwise have occurred. It is more
probable that early androgenization results in an alteration in the rate of synthesis of specific enzyme systems
that will later function in the adult, function by becoming
more (or less?) active given the presence of circulating
androgen. Following this line of thought, Ladosky and
Gaziri (1970) have shown sex-dependent chronological
changes in serotonin concentration in whole brains of neonatal rats. Importantly, such changes were predictably
altered by both neonatal castration and androgen administration. Thus, concentrations of at least one neurotransmitter
are known to be influenced by neonatal androgen treatment
and, presumably, so are one or more of the enzyme systems
associated with its metabolism. Early treatment with testosterone has broad influences on ovulation, cyclicity, and
sex behavior as well as on aggression; hence, none, some,
or all of the above may be pertinent directly to the organization of aggression. Nevertheless, implicating the
neuronal genome, RNA and enzyme synthesis, and neurotransmitter concentrations in the early androgen syndrome certainly points the way for future and exciting research in
this area.

Three additional aspects of the effects of hormones on
aggression bear discussion: (a) the utility of the model
presented above for species other than mice, (b) the effect
of hormones other than testosterone on spontaneous aggression, and (c) the relative importance of hormones in determining aggressiveness when compared to the host of other
natural or experimental factors known to influence this
behavior.

The utility of the dual-action testosterone-aggression
model for species other than mice is largely unknown. There
can be little doubt that the relative importance of the neonatal organizing and adult modulating actions of testosterone or other androgens varies probably with both the type
of aggression being examined and with the species being
considered. In only one species, the rat, have these
functions been examined at all closely. Sexual differences
in aggressiveness in favor of the male apparently are normal
in this species, particularly in wild animals (Barnett,

1958). Like mice, male rats do not begin fighting until
puberty (Seward, 1945) while castration and testosterone
replacement in adult males have their expected effects
(Beach, 1945). Importantly, early androgenization of
female rats has been reported to increase adult aggressiveness in two studies concerned primarily with sex behavior
(Feder, 1967; Gerall, 1967). Additionally, Conner and
Levine (1969) have examined both the adult and neonatal
actions of testosterone in shock-induced defensive fighting
in rats. Males respond more frequently by fighting when
given foot shock than do females and castration depresses
this response (see also Hutchinson et al., 1965). The
success of androgen therapy upon fighting in response to
shock during adulthood, as reported by Conner and Levine,
is dependent upon age at which males are castrated; adult
testosterone injections increase effectively fighting in
males castrated as weanlings, but not in males castrated
just after birth. Thus, the implication of a neonatal
organizing role for androgen, with respect to aggression,
certainly is present in this species. In non-murids, Goy
(1966) reported that early play-behavior of rhesus monkeys
that were androgenized as fetuses seemed more masculine and
aggressive than that usually observed in normal females.
Finally, it is known that sexual differentiation of the
neural control of the temporal pattern of luteinizing hormone secretion and of sexual behavior is dependent upon the
presence or absence of androgen early in life in several
species; e.g., guinea pigs, rats, rhesus monkeys, cats (reviewed by Gorski, 1966; Levine & Mullins, 1966; Valenstein,
1969). It seems not unreasonable, then, to expect that the
dual function of androgen relative to aggressiveness would
also show an equally broad phylogenetic effect in mammals.

With regard to the second problem, the effect of hormones other than testosterone on aggression, surprisingly
little experimental work actually has been done. Two types
of studies may be visualized: those directed to a normal
role played by a steroid occurring naturally in an animal and
pharmacological studies where a steroid foreign to the animal (at least in physiological amounts) is evaluated. With
respect to the first type of study, another testicular
androgen, androstenedione, is present in the testes of neonatal rats, but undetectable in the plasma until the
approach of puberty (Resko et al., 1968). It is not known
in any species whether or not this androgen could function
in either an organizing role or in the enhancement of

aggression in the normal adult male. Suchowsky et al.
(1969) reported methyltestosterone as well as testosterone
effective in restoring aggressiveness in isolated castrated
male mice. In a particularly interesting study, Bevan et
al. (1957) reported androsterone and dihydroisoandrosterone
effective in increasing aggressiveness in castrate males at
doses too low to show good seminal vesicle effects, but
that these hormones as well as testosterone actually suppressed aggression at higher (possibly anesthetic?) doses.
Finally, it should be remembered, in all experiments dealing with hormones, that metabolism of the injected hormone
can yield another hormone that is actually the effective
form at the level of the cellular nucleus. Thus Bruchovsky
and Wilson (1968) among others have shown the conversion of
testosterone to dihydrotestosterone which is actively bound
in the nucleus and is, apparently, the active hormone in
this regard.

A possible role for estrogens and/or progesterone in
female aggressiveness has not been studied sufficiently to
permit any good generalizations. Ovariectomy in mice is
without apparent effect on their spontaneous aggression
(Levy, 1954) nor is an estrogen effective in influencing
aggression in adult females of the same species (Gustafson
& Winokur, 1960). On the other hand, there are reports
that estrogen increases aggressiveness in female monkeys
(Birch & Clark, 1946; see also Michael, 1969) and hamsters
(Kislak & Beach, 1945); the latter, a species in which
female aggressiveness is pronounced. Of particularly
intriguing interest is the report that both testosterone
and estradiol will support aggressive behavior in castrated
male hamsters (Vandenbergh, in press). Before leaving the
gonadal hormones, it should be noted that no attempts
(other than the negative effect of castration) have been
made in mammals to look for a direct relationship between
gonadotropins, particularly LH, and aggression as has been
demonstrated in starlings (cf., Davis, 1964).

The adrenal cortex, because it is also a steroidogenic
organ, has been frequently suggested as a possible influence
on aggressiveness. Sigg et al. (1966) and Sigg (1969), however, could find no direct relationship between adrenalectomy and isolation-induced aggressiveness in male mice. In
addition, an extensive study in our laboratory was unsuccessful in its attempt to influence frequency of spontaneous
aggression in intact, previously isolated, adult C57BL/6J

mice employing both physiological and pharmacological doses
of ACTH (Bronson, unpublished). It could probably be said
as a generality that any hormone, such as thyroid hormones,
affecting general function, metabolism, or growth of brain
or other tissues should have their effect, possibly subtly,
on this behavior (see chapter by Welch & Welch). It is
interesting to note in this context that one developmental
action of testosterone is to increase body size (see
Valenstein, 1969), an effect that could indirectly influence either the initiation or the outcome of an aggressive
encounter. The magnitude of this effect can be relatively
large. Single injections of testosterone in neonatal
females any time between 0 and 6 days of age result in an
increase in body weight during adulthood that is on the
order of 15% in mice (Bronson & Desjardins, unpublished).

     With respect to pharmacological studies, Suchowsky et
al. (1969) found that estradiol (completely) and progesterone (partially) depressed aggressiveness in previously isolated intact male mice. Whether these two hormones were
operating directly on the brain or via a depression of the
pituitary-testicular axis is unknown. It is known that
estradiol, when given as a single injection to intact neonatal mice, results in about a 50% reduction in their
adult aggressiveness, but that this effect is accompanied
by much smaller testes and sex accessories than normal
(Bronson & Desjardins, 1968).

     Finally, a hormonal basis for aggression must be
viewed in perspective with other causative factors; i.e.,
presence or absence of hormones is not the sole determi-
nant of the behavior. More so, depending upon the species,
it might not even be a relatively important factor. In
general, we may expect both the organizing and adult-modu-
lating roles of testosterone to be important in any
species in which there exists a reasonable sexual difference in aggressiveness in favor of the male. Even in such
species, however, the effects of testosterone must be re-
garded as acting permissively, allowing the elicitation of
an attack by social stimuli, and set within a framework of
modification of the CNS by past experiences. Bevan et al.
(1960), for example, examined the relative importance of
testosterone and pre-test fightin experience on fighting
in adult male mice, and concluded that the latter factor
was more important than androgen status. Sigg (1969)
reports the overriding effect of isolation vs. grouping on

aggression in male mice regardless of gonadal status. Castration in the above studies, however, was done long after the testes would have played their early brain-differentiating role, and this action could be, by far, the most important effect of androgen in that it establishes the neuro-biochemical substrate upon which hormones will later act in the adult. It should not be considered inconceivable (even if possibly improbable) that there could be species in which early brain organization or differentiation by androgen was paramount but in which hormones would play a relatively minor role in modulating the expression of aggressiveness in the normal adult.

EFFECTS OF AGGRESSION ON HORMONES

This type of steroid hormone-aggression relationship will not be extensively discussed since the subject has been adequately reviewed in the recent past (Christian & Davis, 1964; Christian et al., 1969; Bronson, 1967; Archer, 1969). It is of general knowledge now that activities connected with high population density, defeat, and/or chronic subordination, are a rich source of adrenal-exciting stimuli in several species. For instance, in mice, repeated short daily defeats by a trained fighter cause the adrenal glands of the defeated mouse to increase in size in proportion to body length and to increase the level of circulating corticosterone (Bronson & Eleftheriou, 1964, 1965a). In such defeated mice, plasma corticosterone concentrations reach a peak within one hour after fighting, and may remain high in excess of 24 hours after the first defeat. These observations indicate that some aspect of the experience of defeat may continue to act on the hypothalamo-hypophyseal axis to elicit release of adrenocorticotropic hormone for a considerable period of time after an attack actually has taken place. A dominant mouse or a trained fighter is apparently little affected by such activities as assessed by changes in adrenal weight (Bronson, 1967). More recently, Bronson and Eleftheriou (1965b) demonstrated that actual physical contact between the fighter and the defeated mouse was not necessary. The simple presence of a trained fighter evoked an increase in plasma corticosterone in mice that previously had experienced physical defeat, an increase that was comparable to that found at the end of an actual fight. These findings suggest that threat of attack alone is sufficiently stimulating to trigger pituitary corticotropin release in a defeat-experienced mouse.

Once we depart from the easily controlled experimental situation involving a trained fighter and a naive mouse, however, the relationships between adrenocortical steroids and aggression become considerably more variable. This probably is not because of a change in the basic effect of stimuli associated with defeat on ACTH secretion, but more probably because of the interacting effects of other stimuli, and the modifying effect of the many past experiences associated with a chronic social system. In a simple two mouse dominant-subordinate system, for example, plasma concentrations of corticosterone in subordinate mice may not be significantly different from those of dominants as measured (at one instant in time) after a 7-day period--implying a certain amount of adaptation on the part of the subordinate (Chapman, Desjardins & Bronson, 1969). Nevertheless, the application of an additional stress at that time, such as that associated with exposure to an open field, revealed marked differences between dominant and subordinate mice. Such exposure resulted in a significantly greater increase in plasma corticosterone on the part of subordinate males than it did in dominant males or in paired males which had not fought to establish social rank. Thus, there is a suggestion that studies involving adrenal function and aggression and/or social status probably reveal minimal differences between treatments when examined over a longer period of time and only within the confines of an animal's "home" environment.

As noted above, the basic relationship between defeat and/or subordination and ACTH secretion has been well established (at least in laboratory experiments) and will not be further documented here except to point to a large volume of literature concerning grouping and adrenal function mostly by Christian, Davis, and their associates (e.g., Christian et al., 1969). Considerably more work is needed on several related lines of interest; for example: (a) the effect of an attack or a defeat or of chronic dominance or subordination on hormones other than ACTH and the adrenocortical steroids, (b) a description of the precise stimuli involved and their mediating sensory systems, (c) investigations designed to yield testable models about patterns of hormone secretion under conditions of interacting specific stimuli associated with aggression (i.e., an approach to

field problems), and (d) what such changes in steroids and
pituitary hormones have to do with brain function and later
manifested behavior (aggressive or otherwise). Only in the
first of these possible lines of investigation has much
work been done with regard to steroid and protein hormones
(see chapter by Welch & Welch).

Sufficient evidence certainly is on hand to indicate
that thyroid and gonadal function may be altered by stimuli
that evoke ACTH synthesis and release. If wild rats,
Rattus norvegicus, are attacked by a member of the same
species, some may die in a few hours without much evidence
of being wounded (Barnett, 1958). Among the animals that
survive such attack, marked changes in thyroid glands have
been noted (Barnett & Evans, 1966). Barnett observed an
inhibition in the release of I^{131} from the thyroid glands
in wild rats exposed to fighters whereas exposure to an
empty cage failed to inhibit I^{131} release. Thyroid inhibition lasted for as long as 59 hours after exposure to a
single attack. The failure to observe a continual release
of I^{131} from the thyroid glands of defeated rats may have
been due to a reduction in the secretion of thyroid stimulating hormone (TSH). In contrast to these observations
in wild rats, studies in mice exposed to acute defeat for
2, 4, 8, and 16 days showed a significant increase in plasma
TSH concentrations and a continual rise in pituitary TSH
levels indicating that exposure to repeated defeat may increase the synthesis, release, and storage of TSH
(Eleftheriou et al., 1968). These observations with mice
coincide with previous studies in wild rabbits following
capture (Eickhoff, 1949, and Kracht & Kracht, 1952) who
report intense overactivity of the pituitary-thyroid system
coupled with autonomic instability within a few weeks after
capture. Exposure of captive wild rabbits to their predators (ferrets, dogs, and man) is also a sufficient stimulus
to elicit a thyrotoxic response. In addition, Kracht and
Kracht (1952) and Bansi et al.(1953) noted that the response
to predators could be abolished by either removing the
thyroid or inhibiting the secretion of thyroid hormones with
thiouracil. The observations with wild rabbits point to the
fact that the psychological threat of injury might, in some
case, lead to unrestrained secretion of TSH and it may be
caused by the failure of adrenocortical steroids to inhibit
TSH secretion (Harris & Woods, 1958).

The basic depressive effect of defeat or subordination
on gonadal function seems well documented at least in simple

laboratory situations. Testicular function of subordinates
is less than dominant or isolated males as indicated indirectly by sex accessory weights (see Christian et al.,
1969) or by seminal vesicle fructose (Chapman et al., 1969).
No meaningful work in this context has been done measuring
the gonadal steroids themselves or gonadotropins in the
blood. In general, it can be said that the relationship
between gonadal function and acute defeat, chronic subordination, etc. is more variable than that usually observed
when using an adrenal measure (given the same degree of
environmental control). For example, Eleftheriou and Church
(1967) noted significant increases in the concentration of
luteinizing hormone in the plasma of defeated male mice
rather than the opposite effect. Furthermore, repeated
exposure to a trained fighter produced a significant reduction in luteinizing hormone releasing factor (LH-RF) in the
hypothalamus. The decline in LH-RF was apparent 2 days
after exposure to aggression and was maximal 8-16 days after
defeat. In contrast to the defeated mice, the LH-RF of
fighter males declined up to the 5th day after fighting,
but thereafter the level of LH-RF increased and returned to
control levels within 16 days of continuous fighting. These
findings imply that aggressive or socially dominant mice may
be capable of neurohumoral adaptation, whereas mice that are
defeated continually in their daily encounters lack such
adaptability.

In summary, then, it is well documented that stimuli
associated with defeat or subordination, though poorly
defined, are capable of altering the neural mechanisms involved in regulating ACTH, TSH, and LH secretion in males.
Considerable confusion exists relative to the precise
nature of such stimuli, their mediating sensory systems,
the interaction between relevant stimuli (e.g., between
general gonadotropin depressing "stressors" and gonado-
tropin-releasing social pheromones) and what any of this
has to do with shaping future behavior. It is tempting to
speculate that a number of sensory systems are involved in
receiving the external signals that are eventually converted
into a variety of physiological responses. Little can be
said beyond this other than, at the present time, the available evidence certainly suggests that the hypothalamo-hypophyseal neuroendocrine unit is the final common path for
mediating altered titers of trophic hormones and, hence,
circulating steroids.

REFERENCES

ARCHER, J. E. Effects of population density on behavior in rodents. In J. H. Crook (Ed.), Determinants of Social Behavior. New York: Academic Press, 1969.

BANSI, J. W., KRACHT, J., KRACHT, U., & MEISSNER, J. Zur Entastehung des Marhus Basedow. Deut. med. Wochschr., 1953, 78, 256.

BARNETT, S. A. Grouping and dispersive behavior among wild rats. In S. Grarattini and E. B. Sigg (Eds.), Aggressive Behavior. Amsterdam: Excerpta Medica Monograph, 1969.

BARNETT, S. A. Physiological effects of "social stress" in wild rats. I. The adrenal cortex. J. Psychosomat. Res., 1958, 3, 1-11.

BARNETT, S. A., & EVANS, C. S. Physiological effects of fighting in mice. Gen. Comp. Endocrinol., 1966, 4, 9-14.

BARRACLOUGH, C. A. Personal communication, 1968.

BEACH, F. A. Bisexual mating behavior in the male rat - effects of castration and hormone administration. Physiol. Zool., 1945, 18, 195.

BEEMAN, E. A. The effect of male hormone on aggressive behavior in mice. Physiol. Zool., 1947, 20, 373.

BEVAN, J. M., BEVAN, W., & WILLIAMS, B. F. Spontaneous aggressiveness in young castrate C3H male mice treated with three dose levels of testosterone. Physiol. Zool., 1958, 31, 284-288.

BEVAN, W. D., DAVES, W. F., & LEVY, F. W. The relation of castration, androgen therapy, and pre-test fighting experience to competitive aggression in male C57BL/10 mice. Anim. Behav., 1960, 8, 6-12.

BEVAN, W., LEVY, G. W., WHITEHOUSE, J. M., & BEVAN, J. M. Spontaneous aggression in two strains of mice castrated and treated with one of three androgens. Physiol. Zool., 1957, 30, 341-349.

BIRCH, J. G., & CLARK, G. Hormonal modification of social
    behavior, II: The effects of sex-hormone administra-
    tion on the social dominance status of the female-cas-
    trate chimpanzee. Psychosom. Med., 1946, 8(5),
    320-331.
BRONSON, F. J. Agonistic behavior in woodchucks. Anim.
    Behav., 1964, 12, 470-478.

BRONSON, F. H. Effects of social stimulation on adrenal
    and reproductive physiology of rodents. In M. L.
    Conalty (Ed.), Husbandry of Laboratory Animals.
    London: Academic Press, 1967.

BRONSON, F. H., & DESJARDINS, C. Aggression in adult mice:
    modification by neonatal injections of gonadal hor-
    mones. Science, 1968, 161, 705-706.

BRONSON, F. H., & DESJARDINS, C. Aggressive behavior and
    seminal vesicle function in mice: differential sensi-
    tivity to androgen given neonatally. Endocrinology,
    85, 971-974.

BRONSON, F. H., & DESJARDINS, C. Neonatal androgen adminis-
    tration and adult aggressiveness in female mice. Gen.
    Comp. Endocrinol., 1970, in press.

BRONSON, F. H., & ELEFTHERIOU, B. E. Chronic physiological
    effects of fighting in mice. Gen. Comp. Endocrinol.,
    1964, 4, 9-14.

BRONSON, F. H., & ELEFTHERIOU, B. E. Relative effects of
    fighting on bound and unbound corticosterone in mice.
    Proc. Soc. Exp. Biol. Med., 1965a, 118, 146-149.

BRONSON, F. H., & ELEFTHERIOU, B. E. Adrenal resppnse to
    fighting in mice: separation of physical and psycho-
    logical causes. Science, 1965b, 147, 627-628.

BRUCHOVSKY, N., & WILSON, J. D. Conversion of testosterone
    to 5α-androstan-17-ol-3-one by rat prostate in vivo
    and in vitro. J. Bio. Chem., 1968, 243, 2021-2027.

CHAPMAN, V. M., DESJARDINS, C., & BRONSON, F. H. Social
    rank in male mice and adrenocortical response to open
    field exposure. Proc. Soc. Exp. Biol. Med., 1969,
    130, 624-627.

CHARPENTIER, J. Analysis and measurement of aggressive
    behavior in mice. In S. Garattini and E. B. Sigg
    (Eds.), Aggressive Behavior. Amsterdam: Excerpta
    Medica Monograph, 1969.

CHRISTIAN, J. J., & DAVIS, D. E. Endocrines, behavior,
    and population. Science, 1964, 146, 550-560.

CHRISTIAN, J. J., LLOYD, J. F., & DAVIS, D. E. The role
    of endocrines in the self-regulation of mammalian
    populations. Rec. Progr. Hormone Res., 1969, 14,
    501-578.

CLAYTON, R. B., KOGURA, J., & KRAEMER, H. C. Sexual
    differentiation of the brain: effects of testosterone
    on brain RNA metabolism in new-born female rats.
    Nature, 1970, 226, 810-812.

COLLIAS, N. E. Aggressive behavior among vertebrate
    animals. Physiol. Zool., 1944, 17, 83.

CONNER, R. L., & LEVINE, S. Hormonal influences on aggres-
    sive behavior. In S. Garattini and E. B. Sigg (Eds.),
    Aggressive Behavior. Amsterdam: Excerpta Medica
    Monograph, 1969.

DAVIS, D. E. The physiological analysis of aggressive
    behavior. In Social Behavior and Organization Among
    Vertebrates, p. 53. Chicago: Univ. of Chicago Press.

DELGADO, J. M. R. Aggressive behavior evoked by radio
    stimulation in monkey colonies. Amer. Zool., 1966,
    6, 669-681.

EDWARDS, D. E. Mice: Fighting by neonatally androgenized
    females. Science, 1968, 1027-1028.

EDWARDS, D. E. Early androgen stimulation and aggressive
    behavior in male and female mice. Physiol. Behav.,
    1969, 4, 333-338.

EDWARDS, D. E. Post-neonatal androgenization and adult
    aggressive behavior in female mice. Physiol. Behav.,

60 F. H. BRONSON AND C. DESJARDINS

EICKHOFF, W. Schildruse und Basedow. Stuttgart: George
Thieme, 1949.

ELEFTHERIOU, B. E. & CHURCH, R. L. Effects of repeated exposure to aggression and defeat on plasma and pituitary levels of leutinizing hormone in C57BL/6J mice.
Gen. Comp. Endocrinol., 1967, 9, 263-266.

ELEFTHERIOU, B. E., CHURCH, R. L., NORMAN, R. L., PATTISON,
M., & ZOLOVICK, A. J. Effect of repeated exposure to
aggression and defeat on plasma and pituitary levels
of thyrotropin. Physiol. Behav., 1968, 3, 467-469.

FEDER, H. H. Specificity of testosterone and estradiol in
the differentiating neonatal rat. Anat. Rec., 1967,
157, 79.

FREDERICSON, E. The effects of food deprivation upon
competitive and spontaneous combat in C57 black mice.
J. Psychol., 1950, 29, 89.

GERALL, A. A. Effects of early post-natal androgen and
estrogen injections on the estrous activity cycles
and mating behavior of rats. Anat. Rec., 1967, 157, 97.

GOY, R. W. Role of androgens in the establishment and regulation of behavioral sex differences in mammals. J.
Anim. Sci., 1966, 25 (Suppl.), 21-48.

GORSKI, R. A. Localization and sexual differentiation of
the nervous system structures which regulate ovulation.
J. Reprod. Fertil. Suppl., 1966, 1, 67-88.

GUSTAFSON, J. E. & WINOKUR, G. The effect of sexual satiation and female hormone upon aggressivity in an inbred
mouse strain. J. Neuropsychiat., 1960, 1, 182-184.

HARRIS, G. W., & WOODS, J. W. The effect of electrical
stimulation of the hypothalamus or pituitary gland on
thyroid activity. J. Physiol., 1958, 143, 246.

HUTCHINSON, R. R., ELRICH, R. E., & AZRIN, N. H. Effects of
age and related factors on the pain-aggression reaction. J. Comp. Physiol. Psychol., 1965, 59, 365.

KISLAK, J. W., & BEACH, F. A.   Inhibition of aggressiveness
   by ovarian hormones. Endocrinology, 1955, 56, 684-692.

KOBAYASHI, R., & GORSKI, R. A.   Effects of antibiotics on
   androgenization of the neonatal female rat. Endoci-
   nology, 1969, 86, 285-289.

KRACHT, J., & KRACHT, U.   Zur Histopathologie und Therapie
   der Schreckthyreotoxikose des Wildkaninches. Arch.
   Pathol. Anat. u. Physiol., Virchow's, 1952, 321, 238.

LADOSKY, W., & GAZIRI, L. C. J.   Brain serotonin and sexual
   differentiation of the nervous system. Neuroendocrinology, 1969, 6, 168-174.

LAGERSPETZ, K. M. J.   Aggression and aggressiveness in
   laboratory mice. In S. Garattini and E. B. Sigg,
   (Eds.), Aggressive Behavior. Amsterdam: Excerpta
   Medica Monograph, 1969.

LAGERSPETZ, K. M. J., & TALO, S.   Maturation of aggressive
   behaviour in young mice. Rep. Psychol. Inst. Univ.
   Turku, 1967, 28, 1.

LEVINE, S., & MULLINS, R. F., JR.   Hormonal influences on
   brain organization in infant rats. Science, 1966,
   152, 1585-1592.

LEVY, I. V., & KING, I. A.   The effects of testosterone
   propionate on fighting behavior in young male
   C57BL/10 mice. Anat. Rec., 1953, 117, 562.

LEVY, J. F.   The effects of testosterone propionate on
   fighting behavior in C57BL/10 young female mice
   (Abstract). Proc. West Virginia Acad. Sci., 1954,
   26, 14.

MICHAEL, R. P.   Effects of gonadal hormones on displaced
   and direct aggression in rhesus monkeys of opposite
   sex. In S. Garattini and E. B. Sigg (Eds.), Aggressive Behavior. Amsterdam: Excerpta Medica Monograph,
   1969.

MOYER, K. E.   Kinds of aggression and their physiological
   bases. Comm. Behav. Biol., 1968, 2, 65-87.

NADLER, R. D. Masculinization of female rats by intra-
    cranial implantation of androgen in infance. J. Comp.
    Physiol. Psychol., 1968, 66, 157-167.

RESKO, J. A., FEDER, H. H., & GOY, R. W. Androgen concen-
    trations of plasma and testis of developing rats. J.
    Endocrinol., 1968, 40, 485-491.

SCOTT, J. P. Agonistic behavior of mice and rats. A
    review. Amer. Zool., 1966, 6, 683.

SCOTT, J. P., & FREDERICSON, E. The causes of fighting in
    mice and rats. Physiol. Zool., 1951, 24, 273.

SEWARD, J. P. Aggressive behavior in the rat: I. General
    characteristics, age and sex differences. J. Comp.
    Psychol., 1945, 38, 175.

SHIMADA, H., & GORBMAN, A. Long lasting changes in RNA
    synthesis in the forebrains of female rats treated
    with testosterone soon after birth. Biochem. Biophys.
    Res. Comm., 1945, 38, 423-430.

SIGG, E. B., DAY, C. A., & COLUMBO, C. Endocrine factors in
    isolation-induced aggressiveness in rodents. Endocri-
    nology, 1966, 78, 679.

SIGG, E. B. Relationship of aggressive behavior to adrenal
    and gonadal function in male mice. In S. Garattini
    and E. B. Sigg (Eds.), Aggressive Behavior. Amsterdam:
    Excerpta Medica Monograph, 1969.

SUCHOWSKY, G. K., PEGRASSI, L., & BONSIGNORI, A. The effect
    of steroids on aggressive behaviour in isolated male
    mice. In S. Garattini and E. B. Sigg (Eds.), Aggres-
    sive Behavior. Amsterdam: Excerpta Medica Monograph,
    1969.

TOLLMAN, J., & KING, J. A. The effects of testosterone
    propionate on aggression in male and female C57BL/10
    mice. Brit. J. Anim. Behav., 1956, 4, 147.

UHLRICH, J. The social hierarchy in albino mice. J. Comp.
    Psychol., 1938, 25, 373.

VALENSTEIN, E. S.   Steroid hormones and the neuropsychology
    of development.   In R. L. Isaacson (Ed.), The Neuro-
    psychology of Development.   New York: John Wiley and
    Sons, Inc., 1969.

VANDENBERGH, J. G.   Personal communication, 1970.

YEN, H. C. Y., DAY, D. A., & E. B. SIGG.   Influence of
    endocrine factors on development of fighting behavior
    in rodents.   Pharmacologist, 1962, 4, 173.

EFFECTS OF AGGRESSION AND DEFEAT ON BRAIN MACROMOLECULES

Basil E. Eleftheriou

The Jackson Laboratory

Bar Harbor, Maine

Aggression in animals can be induced and/or modified by diverse methods such as simple isolation-frustration (Elul, 1966; Yeu, Stanger & Millman, 1959), frontal lobectomy (Karli, 1955), destruction of olfactory bulbs (Vergnes & Karli, 1965), olfactory lesions and destruction of prepyriform cortex (Karli & Vergnes, 1963), lesions of septal nuclei which produce septal irritability (Brady & Nauta, 1953), electric foot shock (Miller, 1948; O'Kelly & Steckle, 1938; Ulrich, Hutchinson & Azrin, 1965), and by several pharmacologic agents (Brown, 1960; Everett, 1961; Reinhard, Plekss & Scudi, 1960).

For the past seven years, aggression and defeat have been studied in our laboratory utilizing the training method of Scott, 1946. We have studied specifically the effects of exposure to agonistic behavior for measured periods of time, and the mode of endocrine and neurochemical adaptation of the combatant mice, especially of the repeatedly defeated mice.

Our data indicate generally a trend toward earlier development of systemic endocrine adaptation in the aggressor mice than in defeated mice. The surprising finding is the lack of neurochemical adaptation in the frontal cortex, amygdala, and hypothalamus of defeated mice. Thus, when we measured levels of biogenic amines such as serotonin and norepinephrine (Eleftheriou & Church, 1968) in these brain areas, we found a persistent effect of the exposure to

65

TABLE I

Mean levels (SD) of serotonin and norepinephrine (μg/g) in the amygdala, hypothalamus and frontal cortex of "naive" mice exposed to trained fighters for two 5-min. periods/day 0, 2, 4, 8, and 16 days

No. of days of 2 fights/day	Serotonin			Norepinephrine		
	Amygdala	Hypothalamus	Frontal Cortex	Amygdala	Hypothalamus	Frontal Cortex
Unfought Control (0)	0.477(0.02)	0.637(0.05)	0.640(0.09)	0.660(0.07)	1.215(0.02)	0.306(0.04)
2	0.419(0.02)	0.440(0.02)	0.458(0.06)	0.741(0.03)	1.832(0.02)	0.529(0.02)
4	0.932(0.13)	0.890(0.11)	0.420(0.02)	0.310(0.09)	0.946(0.09)	0.591(0.07)
8	1.062(0.11)	0.862(0.09)	0.446(0.07)	0.398(0.04)	0.989(0.09)	0.602(0.03)
16	0.864(0.08)	0.903(0.03)	0.380(0.07)	0.306(0.02)	0.876(0.06)	0.662(0.09)

Adapted from Eleftheriou & Church, 1968.

aggression (Table 1), which was evident up to 16 days of exposure, a time limit at which systemic adrenal-pituitary
adaptation has occurred (Bronson & Eleftheriou, 1965a,
1965b). Correlating somewhat to these findings are our
findings on regional brain activities of 5-hydroxytryptophan
decarboxylase (Eleftheriou & Church, 1968) and monoamine
oxidase (Eleftheriou & Boehlke, 1967). Both enzymes exhibit
an inconsistent waning and waxing of activity with exposure
to aggression and defeat.

    An additional problem in interpreting some of the bio-
chemical data on aggression arises as a result of the different techniques used to induce the aggressive or defeated behavior. Although aggression, as a behavioral phenomenon,
can be induced by a number of drugs, physiological and/or
psychological stimuli, no one has attempted to classify the
different types of aggression in relation to the physiologic
or neurochemical responses which they elicit. However, it
appears that exposure to aggression and defeat as performed
by the method of Scott (1946) produces significant changes
in brain serotonin (Eleftheriou & Church, 1968), while
aggression induced by isolation does not produce any changes
in brain serotonin, although it produces significant changes
in brain 5-hydroxyindole acetic acid (Garattini, Giacolone &
Valzelli, 1967). These findings indicate that aggressive
behavior induced by different experimental techniques may
produce different effects on synthetic and inactivating reactions involving the biogenic amines. In short, we may
have a graded neurochemical response dependent directly on
the degree of neural stimulation produced by various states
of the aggressive or defeat pattern. Generally, the biochemical data we have obtained tend to support the original
conclusions of Scott that there is no centrally arising
stimulation for fighting or defeat behavior, but rather that
the central mechanisms serve to enlarge and prolong the
effects of external stimuli.

    Our general findings tend also to support Moyer's con-
cept that different kinds of aggression elicit different
kinds of physiological responses. Conversely, however, it
should be pointed out that since isolation per se induces a
degree of emotional irritability, and since our initial
treatment is accompanied by isolation of about 40 days, our
particular neurochemical data may be the result of compound-
ing emotional distress due to isolation and emotional distress due to the "defeat" process. This may help to explain

some of the seemingly inconsistent results found by us and
by other workers.

We felt that we had only two possible alternatives in
finding the mode of mediation of the aggressive or defeat
pattern: (1) psychological, through various behavioral
tests and situations, and (2) biochemical, at the molecular
level.   It was felt that, ultimately, the most satisfactory
answer will be given by data arising from regional brain
analyses of ribonucleic acids and related components.   Thus,
we observed the effects of exposure to aggression and defeat on regional brain levels of ribonuclease (RNA-ase),
total ribonucleic acid (RNA), and base percents and ratios
(AMP, CMP, GMP, UMP).

This orientation in our research was reinforced by a
number of previous experiments in which it was found that
moderate stimuli alter the content of RNA in the brain
(Vladimirov, Baranov, Prevzner & Tsyn-Yan, 1961; Baranov &
Prevzner, 1963; Attardi, 1957; Talwar, Sadasivudu & Chitre,
1961).   Furthermore, overstimulation or overexcitation of
the nervous system results in fatigue and exhaustion accompanied by a general decline in RNA; presumably because its
synthesis is much slower than its utilization (Talwar et al.
1961; Noach et al., 1962).   The induction of overstimulation
has varied from simple electroshock (Noach et al., 1962;
Mihailovic et al., 1958) to drug-induced convulsions (Talwar
et al., 1961).   It is agreed that exposure to aggression and
defeat are "stressful" stimuli.   Thus, the general objec-
tives of our recent studies have been to utilize aggression
and defeat as a generalized nervous stimulus, and to study
its effect on regional brain RNA balances.   The results
presented here are far from complete, but they represent the
background to more systematic studies which are now in progress in our laboratory.

PROCEDURES

In all our experiments, we used 70-day-old C57BL/6J
mice which had been isolated at weaning (21 days), and
handled experimentally according to the training method of
Scott (1946).   The defeated or "naive" mice were never
trained to fight.   Animals were fought for 5-minute
periods/day with at least 6 hours of rest allowed between
any two fights, and were exposed to actual fighting for
1, 2, 4, 8, or 16 days of 2 daily fights.   All animals were

sacrificed 20 minutes after their last fight, brain areas
removed and immersed in liquid nitrogen until the time of
their respective biochemical analyses. In some experiments,
the control animals transferred from their home cage to the
fighter's cage, without the presence of the fighter. The
treatment, however, did not change the measurements, and
therefore was omitted in some of the later experiments.
Early fighters is a designation of mice at the 7th day of
their training period, while late fighters are mice that
have completed successfully their training period and have
defeated repeatedly "naive" mice in at least 16 days of 1
daily fight.

Analyses for brain ribonuclease activity were conducted
according to previously reported techniques (McLeod, King &
Hollander, 1963; Zimmerman & Sandeen, 1965), and protein was
estimated by a standard method (Lowry, et al., 1951). The
radioactive RNA used in this assay was prepared in our
laboratory by using mouse embryo tissue cultures and supple-
menting the Eagle's medium with H^3-uridine ($1\mu C$/ml of medium).
The H^3-RNA was isolated from the tissue culture monolayers by
phenol extraction, alcohol precipitation, deoxyribonuclease
treatment and a number of chloroform extractions.

In addition, a number of groups of animals were injected
daily, for 5 days, with the following hormones: dopamine
(200 μg/day), corticosterone (200 μg/day), serotonin (50
μg/day), testosterone (100 μg/day) and estrogen (100 μg/day).
These hormone treatments were instituted in an attempt to
obtain some insight into the effects of these hormones on
brain macromolecules, and by comparison with effects of
fighting experience to make inferences on the role of hormones in aggression and defeat. The data are summarized in
Table 2.

Effects of aggression and defeat on brain ribonuclease
(RNA-ase). Since this is the first attempt at correlating
the effects of aggression and defeat on regional brain
RNA-ase activity, the significance of the findings is not
totally clear at this time. The implications, however, are
of great importance. To date, we do not have any information regarding endogenous brain RNA-ase activity pertaining
to behavioral manipulations. Data are available, however,
which indicate that certain membrane transport systems are
dependent on RNA since surface positive components of
dendritic potentials are enhanced after topical application

TABLE II

Ribonuclease (RNA-ase) activity, in cpm/μg protein, in frontal cortex, cerebellum, hypothalamus and amygdala of male C57BL/6J mice after exposure to practice in aggression, defeat, and hormone treatment (SD)

Treatment	Frontal Cortex	Cerebellum	Hypothalamus	Amygdala
Unfought control	39.6 (5.6)	32.1 (7.6)	54.6 (8.5)	43.2 (4.0)
Day 1 (2 fights/day)	38.6 (6.7)	31.2 (6.9)	129.8 (4.3)	55.2 (3.2)
Day 2 (2 fights/day)	33.6 (6.3)	31.0 (3.4)	86.3 (6.9)	61.6 (3.4)
Day 4 (2 fights/day)	60.8 (9.7)	51.7 (3.5)	70.3 (3.7)	76.4 (5.7)
Day 8 (2 fights/day)	66.8 (10.9)	46.1 (7.5)	97.9 (3.4)	104.3 (5.4)
Day 16 (2 fights/day)	35.8 (7.3)	32.2 (2.6)	63.8 (6.9)	69.0 (3.2)
Early fighters	38.8 (3.5)	33.5 (6.4)	70.5 (2.9)	70.1 (3.6)
Late fighters	38.6 (3.3)	28.8 (3.1)	24.5 (8.1)	19.0 (3.9)
Dopamine (200 μg)	61.8 (2.6)	36.4 (7.4)	63.2 (4.4)	60.6 (3.3)
Corticosterone (200 μg)	39.5 (6.6)	30.0 (4.2)	70.2 (1.8)	42.8 (5.6)
Serotonin (50 μg)	44.0 (4.4)	45.0 (3.7)	82.8 (4.9)	58.5 (2.5)
Testosterone (100 μg)	39.0 (9.5)	20.0 (5.3)	44.2 (4.3)	47.2 (4.6)
Estrogen (100 μg)	30.3 (2.6)	26.4 (4.9)	23.2 (3.8)	22.4 (3.9)

of RNA-ase to the cortex (Shtark, 1965). In addition, data available from conditioning experiments indicate that the presence of exogenous ribonuclease interferes with transfer of information in regenerating cells (Corning & John, 1961). Although some degree of caution must be used in generalizing from these data, nevertheless, the possibility that learning and memory are enhanced with increases in RNA resulting from decreases in RNA-ase cannot be totally discounted without further exhaustive studies (Kral & Sved, 1963). Disruptive effects on the retention or transfer of learning or memory after RNA-ase injections might be due to effective interference of a feedback loop previously established.

In aggression and defeat, the significant increases in hypothalamic and amygdaloid RNA-ase activity between day 1 and day 16 of exposure may interfere with proper neural function, probably resulting from a decline in total neural RNA as seen in Table 3. It is most interesting to point to the finding that fighters during their early training period also exhibit similar changes in RNA-ase which, however, become reversed after their training period has been completed. Thus, the "aggressor" mouse is enhanced endogenously and more specifically neurally, by low RNA-ase activity in learning to be a "winner" in all aggressive encounters. How this change from early to later adaptation occurs in the fighters that are being trained is not clear. It also is not clear whether or not this "learning" on the part of the aggressor has, in fact, a hormonal component.

From some of the previous experiments (Bronson & Eleftheriou, 1965a, b), it is known that systemic hormonal levels adapt within a short period of time in aggressor-mice, but remain high in continually-defeated mice. The hormonal and neurohumoral data on RNA-ase (Table 2) is suggestive. Indeed, it may well be that such hormones as dopamine, norepinephrine, serotonin and corticosterone, all of which have been found to be high in defeated mice, contribute to significant increases in brain RNA-ase which leads to decreases in brain RNA, that ultimately contributes to an enhancement and enlargement of the stressful effects of external stimuli. By pure observation, as some of my colleagues may confirm, the defeated mouse, as tested by the method of Scott, certainly never learns anything very well, and even a simple avoidance of the fighter is learned poorly as evidenced by the initial and repeated extensive wounding. Although addi-

TABLE III

Levels of ribonucleic acid (RNA) in μg/100 mg of tissue in the frontal cortex, cerebellum, hypothalamus, and amygdala of male C57BL/6J mice exposed to defeat, practice in aggression and in mice injected with various hormones (SD)

Treatment	Frontal Cortex	Cerebellum	Hypothalamus	Amygdala
Unfought control	128.0 (6.9)	160.1 (3.9)	144.4 (5.9)	160.3 (5.4)
Day 1 (2 fights/day)	120.6 (9.1)	155.1 (6.3)	100.3 (3.2)	125.1 (6.3)
Day 2 (2 fights/day)	160.1 (9.6)	130.0 (9.1)	128.8 (7.2)	106.3 (8.7)
Day 4 (2 fights/day)	117.8 (7.0)	104.4 (2.5)	114.9 (9.2)	101.3 (10.3)
Day 8 (2 fights/day)	104.2 (4.9)	167.3 (4.4)	111.3 (3.2)	96.1 (9.0)
Day 16 (2 fights/day)	143.5 (3.9)	164.0 (5.8)	164.0 (5.8)	105.6 (4.2)
Early fighters	133.1 (9.2)	151.4 (3.2)	120.6 (4.5)	120.6 (2.5)
Late fighters	165.7 (7.0)	161.1 (2.6)	165.0 (6.1)	131.6 (7.5)
Dopamine (200 μg)	191.9 (5.6)	167.0 (4.5)	161.9 (5.7)	151.7 (4.7)
Corticosterone (200 μg)	191.0 (6.9)	226.1 (10.9)	179.4 (7.6)	176.1 (3.4)
Serotonin (50 μg)	162.5 (5.1)	153.9 (3.7)	166.0 (8.8)	171.8 (6.4)
Testosterone (100 μg)	183.3 (2.6)	148.4 (9.6)	154.3 (5.0)	182.4 (8.9)
Estrogen (100 μg)	148.3 (2.6)	170.3 (4.2)	165.4 (3.6)	155.6 (4.2)

tional data are necessary for establishing unequivocally the exact role of RNA-ase, and the relationship of hormones in this phenomenon, nevertheless, the present findings, I believe, open extensive avenues for serious thought and future research.

Indeed, based on our molecular and biochemical data, it appears that we have corroborative neurochemical evidence for the well-known finding that emotions and emotional disturbances interfere biochemically with aspects of avoidance-learning.

Effects of aggression and defeat on ribonucleic acid (RNA). Because of the profound effects of aggression and defeat on RNA-ase, we repeated our initial experiment, under identical conditions, and we analyzed these brain areas for their total content of RNA. In order to obtain sufficient RNA to supplement our studies on RNA base analyses, for each analysis we pooled ten identical brain areas from mice treated identically. Analyses for total RNA, extraction, and determination were conducted according to acceptable techniques (Santeen & Agranoff, 1963; Ledig et al., 1963; Schneider, 1957; Schmidt & Thannhauser, 1945). The data are summarized in Table 3.

The data on regional brain RNA content tend to support our findings with RNA-ase. Generally, a persistent and significant decline in total RNA is exhibited uniformly in the hypothalamus and amygdala of repeatedly defeated mice as well as of fighters during the early part of their training experience. It is unfortunate that we do not have additional information on RNA turnover rates, RNA-polymerase activity and similar events. However, since we are at the embryonic stage of our studies on aggression, defeat and macromolecules, we hope that in the future we will have the additional necessary information. At this time, however, we must rely, to a degree, on some speculation and supportive evidence from other types of behavioral experiments, especially those dealing with memory and learning.

At first, we must review briefly the function of various neurons under varying degrees of stimulation and their RNA content. It is agreed that physiological stimulation in the form of proprioceptive vestibular impulses (Allardi, 1957; Zemp, Wilson & Glassman, 1967, light

(Bratgaard, 1952; Rasch, Swift & Chow, 1961), and behavior-
al-physiological conditioning in the form of auditory stimulation (Smirnov, 1964), or even diversified alternatives to
imprinting (Eiduson, Geller & Beckwith, 1961) are accompanied by significant increases in neuronal RNA. In contrast
to this situation, the absence of these stimuli and the
presence of stressful stimuli lead to significant decreases
in neuronal RNA (Attardi, 1957; Baranov & Prevzner, 1963;
Mihailovic, et al., 1958; Talwar et al., 1961) in a number
of varied experimental designs.

From previous knowledge that exposure to repeated
aggression and defeat as well as early training to become a
fighter both are stressful, the significant decline in RNA
in the hypothalamus and the amygdala is in agreement regarding the disposition of RNA levels during or immediately
after stress. By day 16 of exposure to aggression and by
the attainment of competence to be aggressive, the hypothalamic RNA has returned to normal levels, the amygdala
remains below normal possibly indicating lack of adaptive
neural responses. Generally, the frontal cortex and
cerebellum exhibit transient changes, but these are not
of the magnitude occurring in the other two areas.

The hormone treatment, although it did produce some
changes in RNA-ase, did not produce a decline in total RNA.
Thus, the nature of the systemic increases in these hormones and their effects on RNA remains obscure. A possible
explanation, however, may be that the extent of RNA turnover in defeat is far too great to be compensated by any
increases in RNA resulting from increases in the systemic or
neural hormones. We still need information on nuclear RNA
polymerase in order to permit overall generalizations regarding RNA synthesis and utilization equilibria. Unfortu-
nately, our efforts to determine nuclear RNA polymerase in
brain areas have met with failure due to the need for large
quantities of tissue.

Time does not permit us to discuss extensively the
large amount of available data on learning and RNA. It is
possible, however, that RNA changes may not be the critical
mechanism. It is not totally inappropriate to mention that
learning is facilitated generally by increases in neuronal
RNA, and substances which interfere with synthesis of
nucleoproteins or nucleotides result in loss or failure to
retain learned tasks. Thus, it is not surprising that inter-

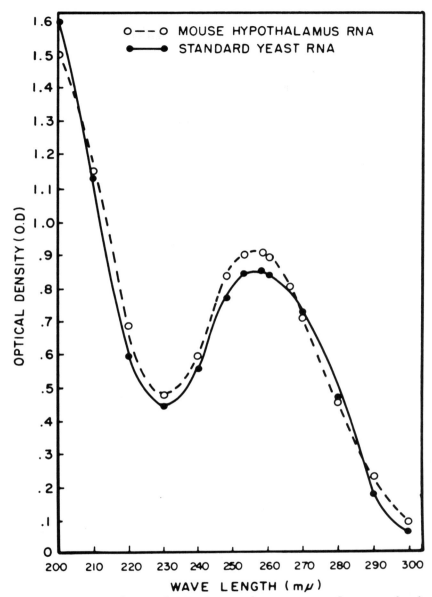

Fig. 1.   Comparison of UV absorption curves of a standard
RNA preparation (yeast) and RNA extracted from mouse brain
(hypothalamus).   Low reading at 234 mμ and high reading at
258 mμ.

ference with efficient avoidance-learning is exhibited by
the continually defeated mice which exhibit only a "weak"
escape response. Whatever may be the endogenous mechanism
for enhancing the neuronal disturbances leading to persistent decline in hypothalamic and amygdaloid RNA, certainly it must be very effective.

Effects of aggression and defeat on brain RNA base
ratios. Following the determination of total RNA, analyses
were carried out on the RNA base percent and base ratios.
The procedure followed for the isolation of regional brain
RNA was a modification of the technique originally used by
Kirby (1965). Confirmation analyses for purity of RNA and
its bases were conducted with the use of column chromatography (Mandell & Hershey, 1960; Sueoka & Cheng, 1961)
utilizing methylated albumin kieselguhr (MAK). Results
obtained from various brain areas indicated that the RNA
isolated from the brain presented an absorption curve
typical of nucleic acids with maximal absorption curve
peak at 258 mμ and minimal absorption at 230 mU. The 280
mμ/260 mμ ratio was equal to 0.486, thus demonstrating the
purity of the product (Fig. 1). The results agreed well
with those reported previously (Popa, Cruceanu & Lacatus,
1967) for mouse brains. Further confirmatory data are
presented in Fig. 2.

The technique employed for base ratio analyses was
that of Katz and Comb (1963). Calculations for the bases,
uridine-monophosphate (UMP), guanosine-monophosphate (GMP),
adenine-monophosphate (AMP), and cytidine-monophosphate
(CMP), were conducted according to an equation established
previously (Loring, Chargaff & Davidson, 1955). Statistical treatment of all data included the estimation of
standard deviation, a two-way analysis of variance and the
rank order interaction test of Newman-Kules (Winer, 1962)
was employed to determine which base was affected the most
within groups of the various experimental treatments. The
data of the base percentages and ratios are summarized in
Tables 4 - 7.

In comparing the various treatments, the two-way
analysis of variance indicates that all treatments had a
significant effect on the base ratios in all the brain
areas examined. Based on an overall analysis, it appears
that AMP and GMP proportions changed most, CMP changed

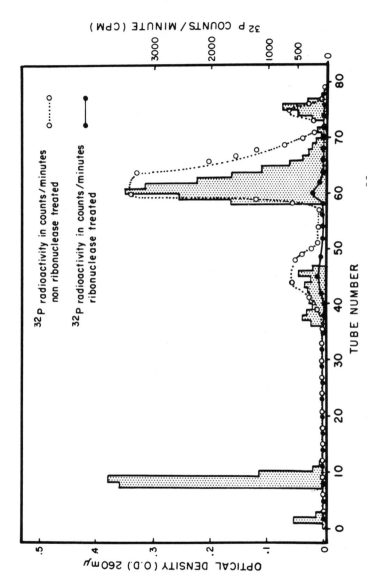

Fig. 2. Results of MAK column chromatography. Extracted P³² labelled RNA was separated by the column and 5 ml fractions collected. Fractions were divided into two equal portions with one set receiving RNA-ase (25 μg/ml), the other receiving no RNA-ase. RNA was reprecipitated with TCA on separate membrane filters and the cpm recorded. Optical density for each fraction was read at 260 mμ and plotted.

less, and UMP changes least. All brain areas, including
the cerebellum, exhibited significant changes in RNA composition during some period of exposure to the various treatments. Aggression and defeat had the most persistent
effect upon the RNA of hypothalamus and amygdala.

With the exception of the cerebellum, all the other
three brain areas exhibited a significant decline in the
G+C/A+U ratio. Based on previous work (Hyden & Egyhazi,
1964), we must assume that this change in the ratio indicates the increased synthesis of messenger-type of RNA. In
contrast to this situation, the reversal of this ratio in
the cerebellum indicates that for the latter area, the
synthesis of RNA was primarily of the ribosomal type. Although isolation and measurement of the various types of
RNA were not made in this study, the changes in the nucleo-
tide ratio are usually a reliable estimate of the changes
in the synthesis of various types of RNA. The decrease in
total RNA must be assumed to be due to increased utilization and turnover rates which we did not measure in this
study. Thus, the demand for RNA in the aggressive and defeated mouse must be very high. The RNA that is synthesized
appears to be rich in AMP and CMP with an almost constant
proportion of UMP.

The possibility exists that, on comparison with results
obtained from chromosomal RNA, exposure to aggression and defeat resulted in stimulation of the genome of the neurons.
Certainly, the significant changes in RNA base composition
must indicate an acute situation with no precedence in the
animal's life history which acts as a genomic stimulator,
thus resulting in the production of highly specific RNA
rich in AMP. This appears to be the initial case with the
hypothalamus, amygdala, and frontal cortex, but not with
the cerebellum. By day 16 of exposure to aggression and
defeat, the base ratios in the hypothalamus and amygdala
appear to have attained their original, unfought control-
type of relationships although the frontal cortex appears
to be at a reduced level indicating certain degree of turnover probably due to m-RNA. In contrast, the cerebellum
exhibits the optimum increase, rather than a decrease, in
the G+C/A+U ratio on day 16.

The situation in the RNA base relationship of the
various brain areas in the early and late fighters seems
somewhat inconsistent and difficult to interpret. It

TABLE IV

Effects of exposure to defeat, practice in aggression and hormonal
injection on regional brain RNA base ratios
in C57BL/6J mice (SD)

HYPOTHALAMUS

Treatment	adenine monophosphate	cytidine monophosphate	guanosine monophosphate	uridine monophosphate	G+C/A+U
Unfought Control	18.97 (1.4)	14.56 (1.6)	53.99 (2.8)	12.48 (0.8)	2.17
Day 1 (2 fights/day)	33.73 (0.8)	22.96 (0.8)	29.90 (2.1)	13.40 (0.9)	1.12
Day 4 (2 fights/day)	26.34 (0.6)	17.54 (0.4)	43.56 (0.6)	12.55 (0.4)	1.57
Day 8 (2 fights/day)	23.93 (0.6)	14.54 (0.3)	49.39 (0.6)	12.12 (0.3)	1.77
Day 16 (2 fights/day)	22.53 (1.5)	16.64 (1.7)	50.18 (2.1)	10.64 (0.9)	2.01
Early fighters	19.80 (0.2)	17.40 (0.4)	51.80 (0.4)	10.94 (0.2)	2.25
Late fighters	25.98 (1.6)	14.05 (2.3)	47.49 (3.4)	12.48 (1.5)	1.60
Dopamine (200 µg)	26.61 (0.8)	15.57 (0.3)	45.97 (0.8)	11.83 (0.6)	1.60
Corticosterone (200 µg)	28.02 (2.2)	15.34 (0.8)	42.99 (1.8)	13.64 (1.6)	1.40
Serotonin (50 µg)	29.20 (1.2)	17.26 (1.2)	38.23 (0.9)	13.29 (0.8)	1.30

TABLE V

Effects of exposure to defeat, practice in aggression and hormonal
injection on regional brain RNA base ratios
in C57BL/6J mice (SD)

AMYGDALA

Treatment	adenine monophosphate	cytidine monophosphate	guanosine monophosphate	uridine monophosphate	G+C/A+U
Unfought Control	16.36 (0.8)	13.02 (1.6)	53.93 (0.9)	10.60 (0.8)	2.48
Day 1 (2 fights/day)	25.06 (0.8)	16.40 (0.8)	44.68 (0.8)	13.86 (0.6)	1.56
Day 4 (2 fights/day)	25.05 (0.6)	16.56 (0.4)	42.53 (0.6)	15.81 (0.2)	1.44
Day 8 (2 fights/day)	24.87 (0.4)	19.54 (0.4)	44.29 (0.6)	11.28 (0.3)	1.76
Day 16 (2 fights/day)	21.95 (0.8)	16.00 (3.2)	52.20 (0.8)	9.85 (1.8)	2.14
Early fighters	21.71 (0.6)	14.03 (0.4)	49.47 (0.2)	14.77 (0.2)	1.74
Late fighters	28.86 (1.1)	15.89 (1.3)	41.80 (1.3)	13.45 (1.0)	1.36
Dopamine (200 µg)	25.07 (0.5)	17.89 (0.6)	42.39 (0.5)	14.46 (0.6)	1.51
Corticosterone (200 µg)	29.53 (1.2)	16.46 (2.0)	41.56 (2.1)	12.45 (0.6)	1.38
Serotonin (50 µg)	27.98 (1.2)	19.75 (0.9)	39.67 (0.9)	12.59 (0.7)	1.46

TABLE VI

Effects of exposure to defeat, practice in aggression and hormonal
injection on regional brain RNA base ratios
in C57BL/6J mice (SD)

FRONTAL CORTEX

Treatment	adenine monophosphate	cytidine monophosphate	guanosine monophosphate	uridine monophosphate	G+C/A+U
Unfought Control	20.50 (0.7)	14.61 (1.7)	54.57 (0.9)	10.32 (1.7)	2.24
Day 1 (2 fights/day)	31.62 (0.9)	20.72 (1.2)	34.37 (0.9)	13.28 (0.8)	1.22
Day 4 (2 fights/day)	24.33 (0.4)	17.00 (0.2)	38.26 (0.4)	20.40 (0.2)	1.23
Day 8 (2 fights/day)	25.23 (0.4)	18.83 (0.6)	41.68 (0.2)	14.24 (0.4)	1.53
Day 16 (2 fights/day)	27.08 (0.7)	16.11 (1.3)	44.39 (2.6)	12.42 (1.2)	1.52
Early fighters	21.96 (0.4)	19.44 (0.6)	37.62 (0.4)	20.96 (0.4)	1.32
Late fighters	26.36 (1.4)	16.85 (0.4)	45.88 (0.7)	10.91 (1.7)	1.95
Dopamine (200 μg)	26.34 (0.3)	17.98 (0.4)	41.29 (0.4)	15.93 (0.5)	1.40
Corticosterone (200 μg)	26.66 (1.1)	18.23 (1.2)	44.25 (1.8)	10.85 (1.4)	1.66
Serotonin (50 μg)	26.92 (0.6)	17.59 (0.9)	43.84 (0.9)	11.64 (1.2)	1.59

TABLE VII

Effects of exposure to defeat, practice in aggression and hormonal
injection on regional brain RNA base ratios
in C57BL/6J mice (SD)

CEREBELLUM

Treatment	adenine monophosphate	cytidine monophosphate	guanosine monophosphate	uridine monophosphate	G+C/A+U
Unfought Control	30.37 (0.8)	9.70 (0.9)	38.74 (1.1)	18.10 (0.9)	0.99
Day 1 (2 fights/day)	34.47 (2.7)	13.09 (1.5)	36.17 (0.8)	16.28 (2.4)	0.97
Day 4 (2 fights/day)	24.40 (0.2)	18.96 (0.4)	43.45 (0.5)	13.17 (0.6)	1.66
Day 8 (2 fights/day)	23.12 (0.4)	15.79 (0.3)	44.79 (0.4)	16.29 (0.4)	1.53
Day 16 (2 fights/day)	19.95 (1.5)	18.89 (1.4)	47.62 (0.7)	13.53 (1.3)	1.98
Early fighters	22.27 (0.4)	21.54 (0.4)	37.31 (0.4)	18.87 (0.4)	1.43
Late fighters	26.47 (0.8)	8.94 (0.6)	47.41 (0.8)	17.18 (2.1)	1.29
Dopamine (200 µg)	22.19 (0.5)	17.98 (0.4)	42.46 (0.5)	17.36 (1.2)	1.52
Corticosterone (200 µg)	31.23 (1.6)	11.36 (0.9)	43.04 (1.3)	14.37 (2.1)	1.19
Serotonin (50 µg)	29.20 (0.8)	23.45 (0.8)	31.42 (0.9)	16.71 (1.2)	1.19

appears that the G+C/A+U ratio in the hypothalamus and
amygdala of early fighters is not as low as it is in the
late fighters, indicating a more active synthesis of m-RNA
in the late fighters than in the early fighters. The
frontal cortical ratio, however, is significantly the low-
est in the early fighters. We must assume that the differential changes in these brain areas reflect different types
of on-going phenomena associated endogenously with the
various types of behavioral responses. The significance
of these changes is not clear at this time. Although the
hormone injections appear to have produced base RNA ratio
changes in the same direction as fighting stress, any
assumptions attempted here would be very dangerous and
rather unfounded.

     Theoretical assumptions. This is the first attempt at
correlating this type of macromolecular data with exposure
to aggression and defeat. Because we need specific additional information on the types of RNA changed specifically, turnover rates and RNA polymerase, any assumptions regarding the significance of the data would be mere conjec-
tures.

     In a number of earlier works on learning, memory and
acquisition of certain tasks (Albert, 1966; Briggs & Kitto,
1962; Hyden & Egyhasi, 1962, 1963; Hyden & Lange, 1967;
John, 1967), significant differences in base ratios were
found in RNA, containing proportionately higher adenine
and lower uracil, in animals that had their learning experience enhanced. The various interpretations proposed indicated that learning may act as a genomic stimulation or
that learning results in changes in DNA and/or RNA which
result in alternation of membrane proteins in certain
nerve cells (Elul, 1966).

     Our present findings indicate that exposure to aggres-
sion and defeat increases ribonuclease activity and is
accompanied by regional reduction in brain RNA. The base
ratio analysis indicates that the increase is in messenger
type of RNA. Since the utilization and demand for RNA is
very high, synthesis does not, for a time, keep up with
utilization, and, thus, there is a general initial decline
in RNA in the areas we analyzed. The manner by which
these molecular changes in the brain are brought about is
not clear. We may speculate and propose that initial
fighting stress causes the systemic hormones such as

corticosterone to rise, followed by increase in these
hormones passing the blood-brain barrier. At this level,
the hormones increase RNA-ase which then initiates the
changes that one sees in the present data. Thus, the
generalization and enhancement of the "stress" stimulus
may be propagated centrally in this or an analogous
manner. Once the hormone or particular neurohumor returns
to within normal plasma levels, its effect on RNA-ase
"wears off" and neuronal readjustment occurs in RNA and
associated components.

An alternative explanation may be made based on
previous work with learning (Briggs & Kitto, 1962). For
example, it well may be that with increased exposure to
aggression mice which are inflicted with defeat "stress,"
exhibit an ever-increasing demand for endogenous neurotransmitters to the point where the endogenous stores are
depleted. This depletion, with accompanying changes in
gradients, may alter precursor levels in such a way as to
create a situation which is analogous to enzyme induction.
These changes feeding back on the DNA in the nuclei of
various neurons produce inhibitions on repressor sites on
the DNA, and permit the synthesis of new RNA which, in
turn, will make greater amounts of neurotransmitter substances that are demanded by the particular situation.

Whatever the mechanism of mediation of these changes,
it certainly escapes us at this time. Additional information now is being gathered regarding the type of RNA
changing during the exposure to aggression and defeat.
However, the present data indicate that the phenomenon of
fighting-stress is capable of producing specific profound
effects in the brain at the molecular level.

ACKNOWLEDGMENTS

Sincere thanks are expressed to Dr. R. A. Consigli of
the Division of Biology, Kansas State University, Man-
hattan, for his invaluable advice in various phases of
these studies. Special thanks are due some of my former
graduate students for their untiring and enthusiastic
support of various aspects of this research. They are:
Mr. M. L. Pattison, Mrs. M. E. Lenz, Miss M. A. Hamlet
and Mr. R. L. Norman.

Supported by Grant AM 11195 from the Endocrine
Section, National Institute of Arthritis and Metabolic
Diseases, National Institutes of Health, Bethesda,
Maryland.

Due to illness of the author, this paper was not
presented at the symposium. At that time, the author was
on the faculty of Kansas State University. However, work
presented herein was conducted in both institutions.

REFERENCES

ALBERT, D. J. Memory in mammals: evidence for a system
involving nuclear ribonucleic acid. Neuropsychologia,
1966, 4, 79-92.

ATTARDI, G. Quantitative behaviour of cytoplasmic RNA in
rat Purkinje cells following prolonged physiological
stimulation. Exp. Cell Res., Suppl., 1957, 4, 25-53.

BARANOV, M. N., & PEVZNER, L. Z. Microchemical and micro-
spectrophotometric studies on the intralaminar distribution of nucleic acids in the brain cortex under
various experimental conditions. J. Neurochem., 1963,
10, 279-283.

BRADY, Y. V., & NAUTA, W. S. H. Subcortical mechanisms in
emotional behavior affective changes following septal
forebrain lesions in the albino rat. J. Comp.
Physiol. Psychol., 1953, 46, 239-244.

BRATGAARD, S. O. RNA increase in ganglion cells of retina
after stimulation by light. Acta Radiol. Suppl.,
1952, 96, 80-101.

BRIGGS, M. H., & KITTO, G. B. The molecular basis of
memory and learning. Psychol. Rev., 1962, 69-537-541.

BRONSON, F. H., & ELEFTHERIOU, B. E. Relative effects of
fighting on bound and unbound corticosterone in mice.
Proc. Soc. Exp. Biol. Med., 1965a, 118, 146-149.

BRONSON, F. H., & ELEFTHERIOU, B. E. Adrenal responses to
fighting in mice: separation of physical and psychological causes. Science, 1965b, 147, 627-628.

BROWN, B. B. CNS-drug action and interaction in mice.
    Arch. Internat. Pharmacodynamie, 1960, 128, 391-395.

CORNING, W. C., & JOHN, E. R. Effect of ribonuclease on
    retention of response in regenerated planarians.
    Science, 1961, 134, 1363-1365.

EIDUSON, S., GELLER, E., & BECKWITH, W. Some biochemical
    correlates of imprinting. Fed. Proc., 1961, 20, 345.

ELEFTHERIOU, B. E., & BOEHLKE, K. W. Brain monoamine
    oxidase in mice after exposure to aggression and
    defeat. Science, 1967, 155, 1693-1694.

ELEFTHERIOU, B. E., & CHURCH, R. L. Brain levels of
    serotonin and norepinephrine in mice after exposure
    to aggression and defeat. Physiol. Behav., 1968,
    3, 977-980.

ELEFTHERIOU, B. E., & CHURCH, R. L. Brain 5-hydroxytrypto-
    phan decarboxylase in mice after exposure to aggression
    and defeat. Physiol. Behav. 1968, 3, 323-325.

ELUL, R. Dependence of synaptic transmission on protein
    metabolism of nerve cells - a possible electrokinetic
    mechanism of learning. Nature, 1966, 210, 1127.

EVERETT, G. M. Some electrophysiological and biochemical
    correlation of motor activity and aggressive behavior.
    Neuropharmacology, Vol. 2, Amsterdam: Elsevier
    Press, 1961, Pp. 479.

GARATTINI, S., GIACALONE, E., & VALZELLI, L. Isolation,
    aggressiveness and brain serotonin turnover. J.
    Pharm. Pharmacol., 1967, 19, 338-339.

HYDEN, H., & EGYHAZI, E. Nuclear RNA changes of nerve cells
    during a learning experiment in rats. Proc. Nat. Sci.,
    1962, 48, 1366-1373.

HYDEN, H., & EGYHAZI, E. Glial RNA changes during a learn-
    ing experiment with rats. Proc. Nat. Acad. Sci.,
    1963, 49, 618-624.

HYDEN, H., & EGYHAZI, E.   Changes in RNA content and base
    composition in cortical neurons of rats in a learning
    experiment involving transfer of handedness.   Proc.
    Nat. Acad. Sci., 1964, 52, 1030-1035.

HYDEN, H., & LANGE, P. W.   A differentiation in RNA response
    in neurons early and late during learning.   Proc. Nat.
    Acad. Sci., 1967, 53, 946-952.

JOHN, E. ROY.   Mechanisms of Memory.   New York: Academic
    Press, 1967.

KARLI, O.   Effects de lesions experimentales des noyau
    amygdaliens et du lobe frontal sur le comportement
    d'aggression du rat vis-a-vis de la souris.   Comp.
    Rend. Soc. Biol. (Paris), 1955, 149, 2227-2231.

KARLI, P., & VERGNES, M.   Declenchement du comportement
    d'aggression interspecifique rat-souris par des
    lesions experimentales de la bandalette olfactive
    laterale et du cortex praepyriform.   Comp. Rend. Soc.
    Biol. (Paris), 1963, 157, 372-375.

KATZ, S., & COMB, G.   A new method for the determination of
    the base composition of ribonucleic acid.   J. Biol.
    Chem., 1963, 238, 3065-3067.

KIRBY, K.   A new method for the isolation of ribonucleic
    acids from mammalian tissues.   Biochem. J., 1965,
    64, 405-408.

KRAL, V. A., & SVED, S.   Midwest Psychol. Assoc. Meet. Symp.
    Nucleic Acids Behavior, 1963.

LEDIG, M., FEIGENBAUM, H., & MANDELL, P.   Sur la nature des
    phosphopeptides qui contaminent la fraction ribonucleo-
    tidique an cours du dosage d'acides nucleiques selon.
    Bioch. Bioph. Acta, 1963, 72, 332-334.

LORING, H., CHARGAFF, E., & DAVIDSON, J.   The Nucleic Acids.
    Vol. 1, New York: Academic Press, Inc., 1955, p. 201.

LOWRY, O. H., ROSENBROUGH, N. S., FARR, A., L., & RANDALL,
    R. J.   Measurement with the Folin phenol reagent.
    J. Biol. Chem., 1951, 193, 265-275.

MANDELL, J., & HERSHEY, H. A fractionating column for the analysis of nucleic acids. Anal. Biochem., 1960, 1, 66-77.

MACLEOD, R. M., KING, C. E., & HOLLANDER, V. P. Effect of corticosteroids on ribonuclease and nucleic acid content in lymphosarcoma P1798. Cancer Res., 1963, 23, 1045-1050.

MIHAILOVIC, L. J., JANKOVIC, B. D., PETROVIC, M., & ISAKOVIC, K. Effect of electroshock upon nucleic acid concentrations in various parts of cat brain. Experientia, 1958, 14, 144-146.

MILLER, W. E. Theory and experiment relating psychoanalytic displacement to stimulus-response generalization. J. Abnorm. Psychol., 1948, 43, 155-160.

NOACH, E. L., JOOSTING, B. J., & WIJLING, A. Influence of electroshock and phenobarbital on nucleic acid content of rat brain cortex. Acta Physiol. Neerl., 1962, 11, 54-59.

O'KELLY, L. T., & STECKLE, L. C. A note on long-enduring emotional responses in the rat. J. Psychol., 1938, 8, 125-126.

POPA, L., CRUCEANU, A., & LACATUS, V. Some physiochemical properties of mouse brain RNA. Rev. Roum. Biochem., 1967, 4, 137-142.

RASCH, E., SWIFT, H., & CHOW, K. L. Altered structure and composition of retinal cells in dark reared mammals. Exptl. Cell Res., 1961, 25, 348-363.

REINHARD, J. F., PLEKSS, O. J., & SCUDI, J. V. Some pharmacological actions of amphetamines. Proc. Soc. Exp. Biol. Med., 1960, 104, 480-483.

SANTEEN, R. J., & AGRANOFF, B. W. Studies on the estimation of deoxyribonucleic acid in rat brain. Biochem. Biophys. Acta, 1963, 72, 251-262.

SCHMIDT, G., & THANNHAUSER, S. J. A method for the determination of desoxyribonucleic acid, nucleic acids and phosphoproteins in animal tissues. J. Biol. Chem., 1945, 161, 83-89.

SCHNEIDER, W. C. Determination of Nucleic Acids in Tissues by Pentose Analysis. In S. P. Colowick and N. O. Kalpan (Eds.) Methods in Enzymology, Vol. 3. New York: Academic Press, 1957, Pp. 680-684.

SCOTT, J. P. Incomplete adjustment caused by frustration of untrained fighting mice. J. Comp. Psychol., 1946, 39, 379-390.

SHTARK, M. B. Participation of nucleic acids metabolism in formation of electrical properties of apical dendrites of cerebral cortex. Bull. Exptl. Biol. USSR, 1965, 59, 230-296.

SMIRNOV, A. A. Dokl. Akad. Nauk. SSSR. 105, 185, 195. Cited by PALLADIN, A. V. In Problems of the Biochemistry of the Central Nervous System. New York: Macmillan (Pergamon), 1964, Pp. 311-312.

SUEOKA, N., & CHENG, T. Fractionation of nucleic acids with the methylated albumin column. J. Mol. Biol., 4, 161-172.

TALWAR, G. P., SADASIVUDU, B., & CHITRE, V. S. Changes in pentose-nucleic acid content of sub-cellular fractions of the brain of the rat during "metrazol" convulsions. Nature, 1961, 191, 1007-1008.

ULRICH, R. E., HUTCHINSON, E. R., & AZRIN, N. H. Pain elicited aggression. The Psychol. Rec., 1965, 15, 111.

VERGNES, M., & KARLI, P. Déclenchement du comportement d'aggression interspecifique rat-souris par ablation bilatérale des bulbes olfactives. Action de l'hydrazine sur cette aggressivité provoquée. Comp. Rend. Soc. Biol. (Paris), 1965, 157, 1061-1066.

VLADIMIROV, G. E., BARANOV, M. N., PREVZNER, L. Z., & TSYNYAN, W. On differences in metabolism existing in some areas and layers of brain cortex. In S. S. Kety and J. Elkes, Regional Neurochemistry. Proc. 4th Internat. Neurochem. Symp. Oxford: Pergamon Press, 1961.

WINER, B. J.   Statistical Principles in Experimental
    Design. New York: McGraw-Hill, 1962. P. 75.

YEU, C. Y., STANGER, R. L., & MILLMAN, N.   Ataractic
    suppression of isolation-induced aggressive behavior.
    Arch. Internat. Pharmacodynamie, 1959, 123, 179-182.

ZEMP, J. W., WILSON, J. E., & GLASSMAN, E.   Brain function
    and macromolecules II. Site of increased labelling
    of RNA in brains of mice during a short term training
    experience. Proc. Nat. Acad. Sci. U. S., 1967, 58,
    1120-1125.

ZIMMERMAN, S. B., & SANDEEN, G.   A sensitive assay for
    pancreatic ribonuclease. Anal. Biochem., 1965, 10,
    444-449.

ISOLATION, REACTIVITY AND AGGRESSION: EVIDENCE FOR AN INVOLVEMENT OF BRAIN CATECHOLAMINES AND SEROTONIN

Annemarie S. Welch and Bruce L. Welch

Maryland Psychiatric Research Center

Baltimore, Maryland

Animals that live in environments having different mean levels of environmental stimulation metabolize various brain neurochemicals at different rates. Norepinephrine (NE), dopamine (DA), serotonin (5-hydroxytryptamine (5-HT), 5-hydroxyindoleacetic acid (5-HIAA), aspartic acid, N-acetyl aspartic acid, glutamic acid, glutamine, gamma-aminobutyric acid, and the enzymes acetylcholinesterase and cholinesterase, are among the neurochemicals that have been shown either to occur in different concentrations or to turnover at different rates in animals that live in, or are placed into, different environmental situations (Agrawal, Fox & Himwich, 1967; Bennett et al., 1964; Garattini, Giacalone & Valzelli, 1967; Giacalone et al., 1968; Krech, Rosenzweig & Bennett, 1966; Marcucci et al., 1968; Valzelli & Garattini, 1968; Welch, 1967; Welch & Welch, 1968a, 1968c, 1968e).

In this paper we will review some of the experiments demonstrating that the environment may affect the normal metabolism and rate of turnover of the three amines NE, DA, and 5-HT in the brain. Next, we will present evidence that the same environmental differences that alter brain amine metabolism also result in differences in reactivity to a number of stressors, to drugs, and to other animals, the latter being associated with a change in aggressiveness and a shifting potential for dominance or subordinance in the social hierarchy. Subsequently, we will describe recent experiments that show some of the changes

91

in brain amine metabolism that occur when male mice that
have been made hyperexcitable by long-term isolation are
paired suddenly with others of their kind and allowed to
fight. And, finally, we will describe the effects of
short (5-10 min) daily fights upon mice that live for the
major part of the day in isolation.

We have chosen to focus our attention on the catecholamines NE and DA, and the indoleamine 5-HT, because
they are believed to serve as neurotransmitters or modula-
tors of neurotransmission in specific neuronal systems in
the brain. They have been localized histologically within
specific neurons and the pathways of major neuronal systems
that contain them have recently been traced by fluorescence
histochemical techniques (Anden et al., 1966a; Fuxe, 1965;
Hillarp, Fuxe & Dahlstrom, 1966). Because deviations in
the normal metabolism of these amines have been widely
implicated in the development or persistence of abnormal
affective states (for recent reviews see Acheson, 1966;
Garattini & Shore, 1968; Himwich, Kety & Smythies, 1967;
Schildkraut & Kety, 19661; Woolley, 1962a), changes in the
metabolism of these neurochemicals that can be produced by
environmental manipulation, and subsequently correlated
with changes in behavior, have seemed to us to be of particular interest.

EARLIER STUDIES IMPLICATING THE CATECHOLAMINES
OR SEROTONIN IN AGGRESSIVENESS

There have been several reports that strains of mice
with low levels of brain 5-HT are more aggressive than
other strains with higher levels. Thus, Bourgault et al.
found that an aggressive mouse strain (SC-1) had lower
levels of 5-HT and NE in the brain, a shorter electroshock
latency, and a greater resistance to tranquilizers than
the less aggressive C57B1 strain (Bourgault, Karczmar &
Scudder, 1963). Karczmar and Scudder (1967) continued
these strain comparisons and concluded that strains containing relatively low levels of catecholamines and 5-HT
are more aggressive, engage in more exploratory activity,
exhibit less stereotyped behavior, have shorter electroshock latencies and have lower electroshock thresholds
than strains or genera with higher amine levels. They
suggested that the catecholamines and 5-HT are involved in
inhibitory circuits in the forebrain and limbic system
Karczmar & Scudder, 1967; Scudder et al., 1966).

Langerspetz bred mice for aggressiveness for 13-15 generations; the aggressive strain was found to have lower 5-HT in the forebrain, but there were no differences in brainstem levels of 5-HT. Brainstem NE was higher in the aggressive strain, and their adrenals contained slightly more epinephrine (Lagerspetz, Tirri & Lagerspetz, 1967). It was not clear, however, whether or how recently the animals had fought before being killed, and as we will show later this has an important effect upon these measures.

Maas compared C57Bl and BALB/c mice. He found the C57Bl strain to be more aggressive, more active in several types of motor activity tests and to have lower levels of brainstem 5-HT; this difference in 5-HT, however, could not be detected simply by measuring levels in whole brain. The aggressive strain was also less emotional in open field tests (Maas, 1962). Similarly, "Maudsley reactive" rats had higher levels of brain 5-HT than their nonreactive, more aggressive counterparts (Sudak & Maas, 1964).

More recently, Karli has demonstrated that the 5-HT biosynthesis inhibitor, parachlorophenylalanine, can potentiate the development of mouse-killing (muricide) behavior in rats that is induced by olfactory deafferentation; moreover, he found it to induce muricide behavior in many animals that were not subjected to the operation (Karli, 1969). Other investigators, however, have induced muricide behavior in rats through the use of the catecholamine biosynthesis inhibitor α-methylparatyrosine, and they suggested that the catecholamines may be important in the control of muricide activity (Leaf, 1969).

Individual caging has been employed in the pharmaceutical industry for many years to make laboratory mice aggressive for use in pharmacological screening (Valzelli, 1967; Yen, Stagner & Millman, 1959). Both the development of aggressiveness in these animals and the amelioration of aggressiveness after they are returned to group living are time-dependent processes (Welch & Welch, 1966. It is possible that the changes in the metabolism of the catecholamines and serotonin that occur during isolation may be related in some functional way to the behavioral changes that occur, although there seems no reason to suggest that amines bear a direct and specific relation to any specific behavior (Welch & Welch, 1969).

SUMMARY OF METHODS

All studies that are reported here were carried out
with male white Swiss mice unless otherwise noted. The
mice were weaned at 3-4 weeks of age; all mice in each experiment were born within a 2 day period and were within
1-2 g of the same body weight. A few days after weaning
the mice were randomly distributed to group (6-8 mice) or
individual caging. The mice were housed in opaque solid-
bottomed cages 7 x 11.5 x 5 inches in a room maintained at
25-27°C. The animal room contained only the mice used in
these experiments. The isolated mice presumably could hear
and smell the other mice, but they could not see, touch, or
otherwise interact with them. In some experiments the
grouped mice were color-coded for ease in identification,
and daily observations were made of aggressive interactions.

When groups were constituted shortly after weaning
there was little or no obvious fighting, and mice seldom
bore scars. If the mice were pre-isolated for several weeks
before they were grouped a great deal more fighting took
place, the dominance-subordinance hierarchy was usually
quite evident and the subordinate animals often bore scars
on their tails and rumps.

In the fighting experiments that are reported here,
pre-isolated mice were removed from their home cages at zero
time and placed gently into a clean strange cage either in
pairs or in groups of 4-5. The mice briefly explored their
new environment, and in the process noted the presence of
one or several strangers. Fighting usually began within
5-60 sec. Fighting was more intense and there were fewer
pauses between flurries when the mice were placed into
groups of 4 rather than in pairs, an observation that also
has been made by Valzelli (1969).

In all experiments we rotated systematically from one
treatment to another at 5 or 7 min intervals in all aspects
of the animal experimentation in order to minimize bias due
to the diurnal variability that occurs in behavior, drug
response, and tissue levels of brain and adrenal amines
(Davis, 1962; Friedman & Walker, 1968; Halberg et al., 1958;
Schering et al., 1968a, 1968b; Woolley & Timiras, 1962b).
The mice were decapitated; the brain and other organs were
quickly removed, trimmed, weighed, and frozen on dry ice.
Our chemical methods for the analysis of brain and adrenal

amines have been described elsewhere (Welch & Welch, 1968e,
1968g). Statistical comparisons were made by analysis of
variance.

A NOTE ON THE BIOCHEMISTRY OF THE CATECHOLAMINES
AND SEROTONIN

          This brief section is intended only for those who are
not already conversant with the biochemistry of these amines;
it is not complete, but it will provide background information necessary for understanding the data presented in the
remainder of the paper.

          All three brain amines, and also the adrenal hormone
epinephrine (E), are derived from essential amino acids.
The catecholamines, NE, DA, and E, are derived from tyrosine,
and 5-HT is derived from tryptophane. In general the amines
are thought to penetrate the brain only to a small extent;
their passage is prevented by a poorly understood "blood-
brain barrier" that prevents direct access of circulating
amines to nervous tissue. They are synthesized within the
neurons of the brain from precursor amino acids that themselves pass readily into the brain, probably by active
transport. For catecholamine synthesis, the steps are as
follows: tyrosine--------->dihydroxyphenylalanine (DOPA)-
--------->dopamine--------->norepinephrine--------->epineph-
rine. The first step is carried out by the enzyme tyrosine
hydroxylase which is believed to be the rate limiting step
in the pathway. Alpha-methyl-para-tyrosine (α-MT) is a drug
that is widely used experimentally to block this first
synthetic step. The disappearance of NE or DA from nervous
tissue after the administration of α-MT is thought to be due
to the release of the amines from nerve endings. After
release, NE and DA may be taken back up into the neuron and
rebound or they may be catabolized extra-neuronally by the
enzyme catechol-O-methyltransferase. Inside the neuron unbound (and therefore unprotected) amines are rapidly catabolized by the mitochondrial enzyme monoamine oxidase (MAO);
widely used MAO inhibitors (MAOI) are pargyline, iproniazid,
and tranylcypromine. After MAOI the levels of the three
brain monoamines, NE, DA, and 5-HT, all increase very rapidly; initially the rate of accumulation is probably indicative
of the rate of synthesis, although after awhile it is possible that the accumulating amines act to repress the rate-
limiting enzyme and thereby slow their own rate of synthesis
(Acheson, 1966; Anden, Fuxe & Hokfelt, 1966b; Baldessarini &

Kopin, 1966; Dahlstrom & Fuxe, 1965a, 1965b; Iverson, 1967; Spector et al., 1967).

Serotonin is synthesized from tryptophane through the following steps: tryptophane------->5-hydroxytryptophane (5-HTP)--------->serotonin (5-HT)--------->5-HIAA. Tryptophane and 5-HTP pass readily into the brain, but 5-HT does not. 5-HIAA is the major oxidative catabolite of 5-HT; it is removed from the brain by an active transport process. Unlike in the case of the catecholamines, there is no convenient distinction between an intraneuronal and an extraneuronal breakdown of 5-HT, although it is generally assumed that 5-HT is released extraneuronally. The same MAO inhibitors that cause an accumulation of the catecholamines also cause an intraneuronal accumulation of 5-HT (Aghafanian, Rosecrans & sheard, 1969; Chase, Broese & Kopin, 1967; Garattini & Shore, 1968; Werdinius, 1967).

EVIDENCE RELATING THE CATECHOLAMINES AND SEROTONIN TO CNS ACTIVATION AND REACTIVITY

These amines seem to have a primary role in determing the level of activation and reactivity of the central nervous system (CNS). Thus, when their rate of flow from neurons is increased, CNS activation is increased; this may be demonstrated by forcibly accelerating the release of the amines by administering precursor amino acids (DOPA or 5-HTP) either alone or in combination with a MAO inhibitor, or by a MAO inhibitor alone. D-amphetamine, an excitatory drug that is thought to act indirectly by prolonging the effects of catecholamines that are released from nerve endings, has a similar facilitating effect on CNS activation. Up to a point increased activation facilitates many behaviors, including fighting, but beyond that point it causes disorganizing overactivation and coordinated behaviors are severely impaired (Sheard, 1967; Welch & Welch, 1969; Welch & Welch, 1968d). On the other hand, when the supply of available catecholamines is diminished by inhibiting their biosynthesis with α-MT, animals become somewhat sedated and behavioral performance degenerates; normal levels of activation and performance may then be reinstated by the intraventricular injection of NE (Wise & Stein, 1969) or the intraperitoneal administration of its precursor DOPA (Corrodi, Fuxe & Hokfelt, 1966). The excitatory effects of d-amphetamine may also be prevented by inhibiting catecholamine biosynthesis, and they may also be reinstated by administering DOPA

(Corrodi, Fuxe & Hokfelt, 1966). The excitatory effects of
d-amphetamine may also be prevented by inhibiting catecholamine biosynthesis, and they may also be reinstated by
administering DOPA (Weissman, Koe & Tenen, 1966). Thus the
evidence suggests that the catecholamines are necessary for
the maintenance of alert behavior; they are present in many
neurons of the reticular formation of the brain-stem
(Dahlstrom & Fuxe, 1965a; Fuxe, 1965), an activating system
which has been shown to play an important role in the maintenance of the waking state (Magoun, 1963), and possibly
these NE-containing neurons may contribute to behavioral
arousal and alerting.

DEMONSTRATION OF ENVIRONMENTAL EFFECTS ON SEROTONIN AND CATECHOLAMINE METABOLISM

Over the past decade a number of physiological and
endocrine differences have been demonstrated between
grouped and isolated rodents. Thus, mice, rats and rabbits
living in small groups or in isolation have been found to
have smaller adrenals than controls living in larger groups
or populations (Christian, Lloyd & Davis, 1965; Welch, 1965;
Welch & Welch, 1966); the reduced size of the adrenal in
animals living under low levels of environmental stimulation
appears to be associated with a lower basal level of adrenal
cortical activity (Barrett & Stockham, 1963; Bronson, 1967).
The adrenals of isolates also contain smaller stores of the
adrenal catecholamines, especially epinephrine (Welch, 1965,
1967), and they appear to release these stores into the
plasma more slowly (Welch & Welch, 1968c). In view of the
well-known role of circulating plasma epinephrine in the
mobilization of lipid depots, the recent data of Garattini
and co-workers which shows that isolated mice have lower
levels of plasma free fatty acids than grouped mice
(Valzelli & Garattini, 1968) offer additional support for
the belief that isolates exist under a lower level of
peripheral sympathetic activation than their grouped
controls.

Figure 1 demonstrates one kind of evidence that isolated
mice metabolize the catecholamines more slowly than mice that
live under the higher level of environmental stimulation
provided by grouping. In this experiment the tyrosine
hydroxylase inhibitor α-MT was given to grouped and isolated
mice, and the animals were then returned to their home cages
for 6.5 hr. The grouped mice showed a significantly greater

reduction in brain NE and DA stores, and also in adrenal
epinephrine, during the period between drug administration
and sacrifice than did their isolated littermates, suggest-
ing that the grouped animals experienced a faster rate of
synthesis, release, and turnover of these amines (Welch &
Welch, 1968c). Indeed, in view of the fact that in this
experiment the grouped mice became mildly sedated and
reduced their activity earlier than the isolates, the
differences that we observed were probably minimal esti-
mates of the differences that actually occurred in the
rates of catecholamine release and turnover in their brains
and adrenals. These biochemical results are in good agreement with the observations of Pirch and Rech (1968a, 1968b)
who found that α-MT caused less behavioral depression in
isolated than in grouped rats, and less synchronization of
the electrocorticogram; since neuronal release of NE is
probably essential for the maintenance of EEG activity,
this would be expected as a result of a slower rate of NE
depletion in the isolated animals.

The differences in the rates of turnover of these
amines appear to be graded according to the level of environmental stimulation under which the animals live. Thus
Figure 2 shows graded differences in the amounts of brain
amines accumulated within a few hours after the quick-acting
MAO inhibitor pargyline was administered to mice that had
lived in isolation or in groups of 2, 5, or 10 for 14
months. Again, these data suggest that grouped mice experience a faster rate of synthesis and turnover of these brain
amines than isolates and, furthermore, that these effects
are graded in response to the mean level of stimulation
provided by the group in which the anima lives (Welch, 1965).

Garattini and his colleagues also have offered evidence
that 5-HT turnover is faster in grouped mice. They reported
similar findings in the rate of increase of 5-HT in grouped
and isolated mice after the MAOI tranylcypromine (Garattini,
Giacalone & Valzelli, 1967; Giacalone et al., 1968). They
also noted that 5-HIAA concentrations were consistently
lower in isolated (aggressive) mice, and that the turnover
time of 5-HT was slower. We were subsequently able to confirm their observations on the reduced levels of 5-HIAA in
isolated mice (Welch & Welch, 1968a).

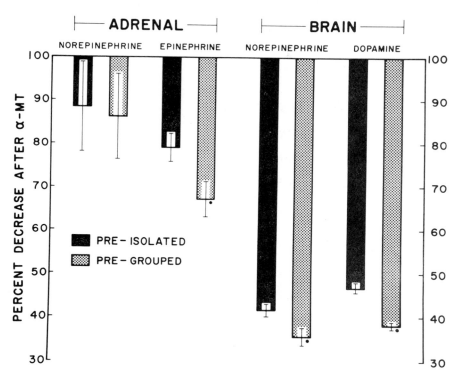

Figure 1. Differential lowering of brain and adrenal catecholamines after α-methyltyrosine in grouped and isolated
mice.

Male mice that had lived in groups of 8 or in isolation for
14 weeks were injected with 80 mg/kg of α-MT, i.p., or with
saline, and returned to their home cages for 6.5 hr until
sacrifice. Percentage changes are based on saline control
values. A black dot signifies group-isolate differences
significant at the 0.01 level or better by a two-tailed
t-test. N = 15 saline, 15 drug for each housing condition.
The s.e.m. is indicated on each bar. Adapted from Welch
and Welch, 1968c.

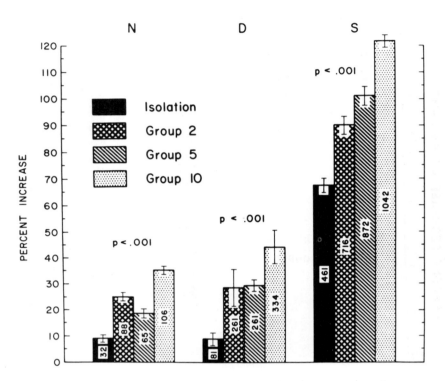

Figure 2. Differential elevation of brain amines after pargyline in mice housed in isolation and in varying sized groups for 14 months.

Male mice that had lived in isolation or in groups of 2, 5, or 10 for 14 months were administered saline or pargyline· HCl, 40 mg/kg, i.p., and then isolated for 2.5 hr during the period of drug effect. Percentage changes are based on saline control values; the s.e.m. and the absolute change in ng/gm are indicated on each bar. N = 25 saline, 25 drug for each housing condition. Abbreviations: N = norepinephrine, D = dopamine and S = serotonin.

DEMONSTRATION OF ENVIRONMENTAL EFFECTS
ON DRUG RESPONSE

It has long been known that grouped mice are more
sensitive to the sympathomimetic d-amphetamine than
isolated mice (Gunn & Gurd, 1940), but it has not been
generally recognized that this is an <u>acute</u> effect; that is,
in the bulk of studies, colony housed (pre-grouped) mice
were treated with amphetamine and then deliberately crowded
(agregated) or placed into isolation. Under these circumstances d-amphetamine is definitely more lethal to the
aggregated mice, and a large number of other sympathomimetic
drugs have similarly been shown to have an increased toxicity
for aggregated mice (Greenblatt & Osterberg, 1961). However, when drug toxicity and effectiveness were compared in
mice that had been differentially housed for several weeks
in groups or in isolation, amphetamine was found to be more
toxic to pre-isolated animals (Consolo, Garattini & Valzelli,
1965a; Welch, 1965; Welch & Welch, 1966), whereas the tranquilizers reserpine and chlorpromazine have been reported to
have greater effect upon grouped animals (Brown, 1960;
Consolo, Garattini & Valzelli, 1965b).

Figure 3 shows the differential response to d-amphetamine in an experiment in which mice were grouped or isolated for 5 weeks, and then injected with a lethal dose of
this drug and placed into isolation until death in order to
avoid the "aggregation effect." The number of minutes until
death was the parameter measured. This experiment illustrates two very important points. First, the mean dying
time of the pre-grouped mice was nearly twice that of the
pre-isolated mice. Secondly, the pre-isolated mice reacted
much more uniformly to the drug than did the pre-grouped
mice; the mean, maximal and minimal dying times were very
similar for pre-isolated mice, but very variable for the pre-
grouped mice. On the whole the grouped mice were far less
sensitive to the drug; indeed, in some experiments it has
been difficult to kill some of the grouped mice with this
central excitatory agent. In other experiments we have
studied the causes of this variability. We have found that
it is the subordinate mice that are so very insensitive to
this drug; survivors of doses that are toxic to most other
animals invariably turn out to be low in social rank.
Dominants, on the other hand, are more like isolates; they
are more sensitive to d-amphetamine, and they die faster
than the mean dying time of their group (Welch & Welch, 1966).

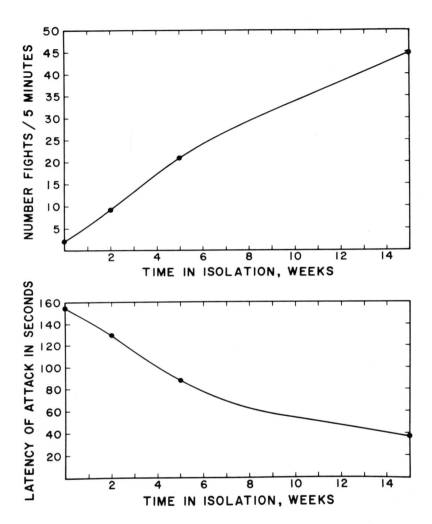

Figure 3.   Effect of time in isolation on aggressivity.

Male mice were removed from groups of 10 and housed in
isolation for 2, 5, or 15 weeks before termination of the
experiment.   Relative aggressivity was estimated by pairing
mice from the same prior treatment condition together in a
cage strange to both and recording (1) the number of sec
before the first attack and (2) the number of attacks during
the ensuing 5 min period. ·Adapted from Welch, 1967.

Even in the most sensitive experiment we could devise, in which forty sets of 6 littermates each were compared after being housed in isolation, in littermate pairs, or in bisexual littermate pairs from weaning, the isolates were still the most sensitive to d-amphetamine (Welch & Welch, 1966). In this group situation of "maximal compatibility" paired animals were affected by the drug and by the stimulation of living in pairs in a manner similar to that which we had come to expect for grouped mice, i.e., paired males had enlarged adrenals and they were less sensitive to d-amphetamine than were their isolated littermates. Thus the effects of grouping and isolation appear to be very subtle indeed.

DIFFERENTIAL RESPONSIVITY TO ENVIRONMENTAL STIMULI

Isolated mice are hypersensitive to all sorts of environmental stimuli, including handling (King, Lee & Visscher, 1955), noise (Barrett & Stockham, 1963; Chance, 1947), and electroshock (Kimbrell, 1968). Figure 4 shows data from an experiment using restraint stress; the pre-isolated mice were more responsive than the pre-grouped mice to the mild stress of being gently restrained with tape on the bottom of a plastic cage for 2.5 hr before sacrifice, and they showed a much greater accumulation of brain amines in response to this stress than did their less excitable pre-grouped littermates (Welch & Welch, 1968a). This differential neurochemical response to stress may be a factor in the greater excitability of isolates in response to stress may be a factor in the greater excitability of isolates in response to many forms of environmental stimuli.

Isolated mice are also more sensitive to the presence of other animals. Figure 5 graphically demonstrates the increasing aggressivity of mice with increasing time spent in individual housing (Welch, 1967). The top section of the figure shows the number of fights observed per five min observation period when mice that had been maintained in isolation for 2, 5, or 15 weeks were paired with another mouse from the same treatment condition. The lower section shows the latency in sec before the first fight occurred. It can be seen that the latency before the first attack was dramatically reduced as the time spent in isolation increased, whereas the number of attacks per observation

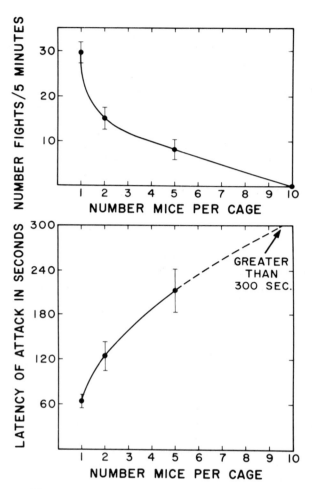

Figure 4. Effect of group size on aggressivity.

Male mice were housed in isolation or in groups of 2, 5, or
10 for 5 weeks. Relative aggressivity was estimated by
pairing mice from the same prior treatment condition (but
from different groups) in a cage strange to both. The mice
were observed for at least 5 min, and the latency before
the first attack was measured in seconds; if there was an
attack during the first 5 min, the number of attacks during
the ensuing 5 min was also recorded. N = 25 pairings for
each prior housing condition. Each animal was tested only
once. Adapted from Welch and Welch, 1968b.

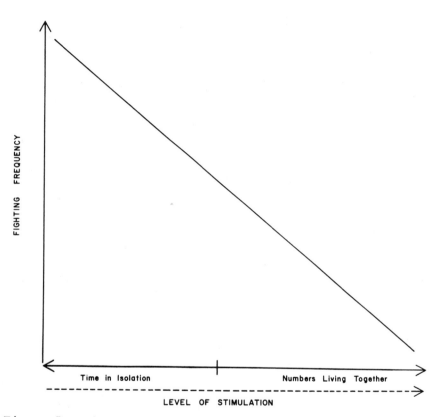

Figure 5. Diagramatic representation of the effects of isolation and grouping on aggressivity as estimated by the
methods described in Figure 3 and Figure 4. Aggressivity
increases in a time-dependent manner with length of time in
isolation and decreases with increasing numbers of animals
living together, and in a time-dependent manner with increasing time of residence in a group.

period markedly increased. Thus, the tendency to fight, as measured by these two parameters, is directly related to the time spent in isolation; similar observations have been made with other strains of mice (Bourgault et al., 1963; Valzelli, 1969).

Conversely, mice become less aggressive with increasing size of the group in which they are housed. In the experiment shown in Figure 6, mice were housed for 5 weeks in isolation, or in groups of 2, 5, or 10. At the end of the 5 weeks of differential housing they were paired in a strange cage with a mouse from a different cage (i.e., not a cagemate) but from the same sized group, and the latency before the first aggressive encounter was measured with a stopwatch (Welch & Welch, 1966). The mice that had been isolated for 5 weeks attacked within 68 ± 11 sec, but the mice that had been housed in groups of 10 did not attack at all within the 300 sec period of observation. In this case, the number of fights per 5 min observation period was inversely related to the number of animals living together.

Thus we can say that these mice become increasingly aggressive with time spent in isolation, or less aggressive with increasing group size. The differences are related both to group size and to the length of time spent under a given level of environmental stimulation. Figure 7 diagrams this concept.

EFFECT OF ENVIRONMENTAL MANIPULATION ON SOCIAL RANK: PREDISPOSITION TO SOCIAL DOMINANCE BY ISOLATION

Not only does isolation make mice aggressive; it also increases the chance that mice will become dominant in a social group, and it can even turn a previously subordinate mouse into a dominant. If at weaning mice are randomly allotted to isolation or to living in a group for several weeks and then are placed into pairs, each pair containing one pre-isolate and one pre-grouped mouse, a very high proportion of the pre-isolated mice assume dominant positions in the hierarchy. In one experiment we made systematic observations daily over a five-day period after permanently pairing mice that previously had been isolated or grouped for five weeks post-weaning; in 71 pairings where we were able to make clear distinctions between dominants and subordinants, 78% of the dominants were mice that had previously been housed in isolation.

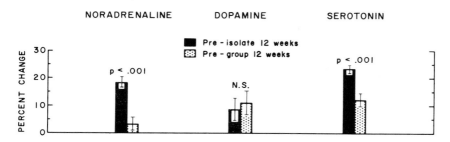

Figure 6. Differential neurochemical responsivity of
grouped and isolated mice to restraint stress.

Male mice that had lived in isolation or in groups of 8
were restrained gently with tape for 2.5 hr before sacrifice. Results are presented as percentage changes from
undisturbed grouped or isolated controls; the s.e.m. is
presented on each bar. N = 22 for each treatment.
Adapted from Welch and Welch, 1968a.

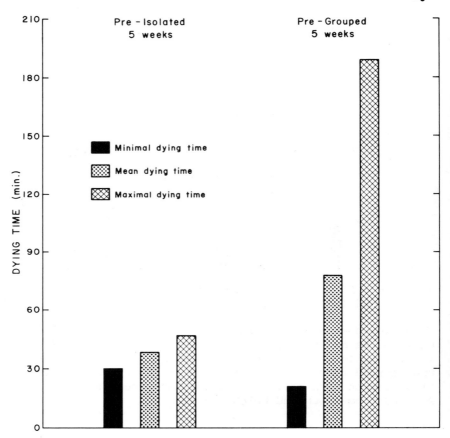

Figure 7. Differential responsivity to d-amphetamine.

Male mice that had lived in isolation or in a group of 10
for five weeks were administered 45 mg/kg d-amphetamine
sulfate and placed into individual cages during the period
of drug effect. The bars represent the minimal, mean, and
maximal dying times. Adapted from Welch, 1965.

Mr. Robert Eskay in our laboratory has conducted
other relevant experiments (in preparation). In his experiments, previously isolated mice became dominant in 53%
of the instances where they were paired with known dominants from existing pairs (16/30 pairings). Previously
isolated mice became dominant in 73% of the instances where
isolates were paired with known subordinates from existing
pairs (22/30 pairings); in 5 pairs dominants and subordinates could not be clearly distinguished and isolates,
therefore, were dominant in 88% of the pairs in which a
distinction could be made (22/25 pairings).

When subordinate mice were isolated for 5 weeks while
their dominants were grouped, after reconstitution of the
original pairs 56% of the mice that were originally subordinate were able to reverse their social rank and become
dominant over the mouse that had previously dominated them;
thus 18 of 32 subordinates were able to reverse their
social rank after only 5 weeks of isolation. If both the
subordinate and the dominant mice were isolated for 5 weeks,
however, 77% of the original dominants reclaimed their
original dominant status when the pairs were reconstituted.

Clearly, isolation not only increases the tendency to
fight, but it increases the probability that mice will establish themselves in socially dominant positions. Isolation has previously been used together with confidence
training to elevate mice and chickens in the social hierarchy (Allee, 1942; Ginsburg & Allee, 1942; Guhl, 1961),
but to the best of our knowledge this is the first time
that isolation alone has been shown to be determinative
for social dominance.

It is apparent that male mice inherit a tendency to
fight other male mice in certain situations, and when they
are given the chance they do so with vigor and with highly
characteristic behavioral patterns. However, the generalization should not be made that isolation will predispose
animals of all species to become dominant in conflict
situations. This is clearly not the case, although isolation does make all species of higher animals that have been
carefully studied hyperexcitable. The important point is
that different environmental conditions do produce differences, probably in the set-point of basic neuroendocrine
mechanisms, that may override the biasing effect of training and experience and have important determinative effects

upon social behavior.

PHYSIOLOGICAL SIMILARITIES OF PRE-ISOLATED AND DOMINANT ANIMALS

Not only can isolation or grouping predispose a mouse to a position of social dominance or subordination, but also the rates of turnover of amines in the brains of dominants and subordinants show certain similarities to the differences obtained between grouped and isolated mice. Figure 8 shows the differential response to the MAOI pargyline in mice that had been determined to be dominants or subordinates within their groups after a long period of daily behavioral observations. As in Figure 2, the mice were placed in isolation during the period of drug effect; hence, the differences observed are thought to be due to differences in the normal rates of synthesis and turnover of the brain monoamines. It can be seen that both NE and DA accumulated more rapidly in the subordinate animals than they did in the dominants. As in the amphetamine toxicity studies this would again suggest that subordinate mice tend to be more like grouped mice, while dominants are more like isolates in their response.

Adrenal catecholamines have been found to follow a similar pattern; in mice that have lived together long enough for adaptive changes to occur, we consistently find high levels of epinephrine in the adrenals of grouped mice and of subordinate mice, and lower levels in the adrenals of isolated mice and socially dominant mice (Welch, 1965; 1967).

ACUTE EFFECTS OF FIGHTING ON BRAIN AND ADRENAL AMINES

The availability of hyperreactive mice that will predictably fight when they are removed from isolation and placed into a cage with another strange mouse has provided us with a tool for studying the changes in brain amine metabolism that occur under conditions of natural physiological stress. The intensity of the fighting may be varied by varying the length of the time that the mice are pre-isolated (Figure 5) or by varying the number of animals that are placed together (Valzelli, 1969).

When the degree of conflict is especially severe,

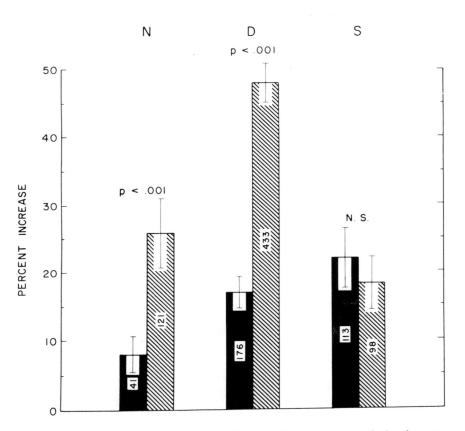

Figure 8. Differential neurochemical response of dominant
and subordinate mice to pargyline.

Dominant and subordinate mice, as determined by several
weeks of behavioral observations, were administered saline
or pargyline·HCl, 15 mg/kg i.p., and placed into individual
cages during the 1 hr period of drug effect. Whole brains
were analyzed for norepinephrine (N), dopamine (D), and
serotonin (S). N = 16 per treatment; the s.e.m. and the
absolute change in ng/gm are indicated on each bar. Mr.
Robert Eskay made the behavioral observations. Solid
bars indicate dominant mice and cross-hatched bars indicate subordinate mice.

brain catecholamines may be lowered, but in most cases whole brain amines have been found to be elevated; in exception to this, NE, which has the slowest rate of biosynthesis of the three amines, is occasionally left unchanged. The elevation in NE, DA, and 5-HT are about 1/3 to 1/2 as great as those which can be brought about in a similar period of time by the quick acting MAO inhibitor pargyline is given to mice and they are then allowed to fight, the fighting potentiates the elevation induced by the pargyline but the effects of the drug and of the physical stimulation are not additive as might be expected if the elevations were due to mechanisms that were not related, such as a combination of increased biosynthesis plus MAO inhibition. After a careful analysis of results from several related experiments we have speculated that the stimulus of fighting may bring about a natural partial inhibition of monoamine oxidase, probably as a result of reduced oxygen tension in the tissue during the period of increased stress; the resulting increase in amine levels in neurons occurs at a time when the amines are presumably most needed for release and utilization (Welch & Welch, 1968b) and we consider this an important form of neuronal adaptation.

Figure 9 shows that fighting for one hour, as might be expected, does lead to intense peripheral sympathetic activation; this is exemplified by a contraction of the spleen and a 47% reduction in the level of adrenal epinephrine; modest changes occurred in adrenal norepinephrine but these were not significant. Vogt, in her investigations of a number of central excitatory drugs (1954), reported a high degree of correlation between peripheral sympathetic activation, the reduction of adrenal catecholamines, and the simultaneous lowering of brain norepinephrine, so we initially expected to find reduced levels of brain amines in the fighting animals. In most experiments, however, this did not turn out to be the case.

In the first experiment brain tissues were sampled from mice that had been allowed to fight for 10, 30, 60, or 120 min (Figure 10). Fighting caused each of the three amines to be elevated at each of the four time periods. Within only 10 min after the commencement of fighting the two catecholamines were significantly elevated and the elevation of 5-HT approached statistical significance. The maximal elevations caused by fighting were approxi-

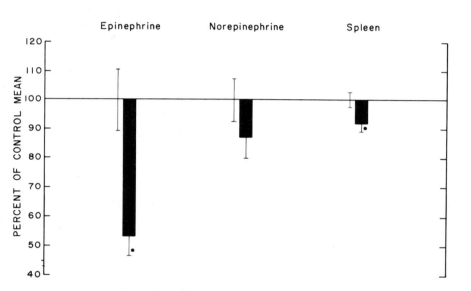

Figure 9. Acute effects of a single episode of intense fighting upon spleen weight and adrenal catecholamines.

Pre-isolated male mice were allowed to fight in groups of four for 1 hr. Means and s.e.m. are presented as percentages of non-fighting controls; a black dot indicates individual means that differ significantly from controls (at least p <.05 by two-tailed t-test).

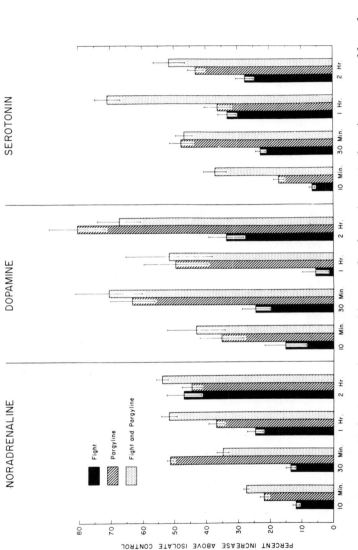

Figure 10. Effect of fighting and pargyline on brain amines. Male mice were allowed to fight for 10 min, 30 min, 1 hr, or 2 hr. Other mice were treated with 40 mg/kg pargyline·HCl for the same time periods. Some mice received pargyline and also were allowed to fight. All values are expressed as a percentage of non-fighting saline controls; the s.e.m. is indicated on each bar. N = 24 for each treatment.

mately 47% for NE at 2 hr, 34% for DA at 2 hr, and 33% for
5-HT at 1 hr; for each amine the overall increases that
were induced by fighting were highly significant. Overall,
these fighting-induced elevations of brain amines were
similar to, but somewhat smaller than, the elevations produced in non-fighting control mice by pargyline. In non-
fighting mice pargyline elevated all three brain amines by
about 20% within only 10 min, and it caused greater elevations at each longer period of time.

When pre-isolated BALB/c mice were allowed to fight
for 45 min, both 5-HT and 5-HIAA were found to be elevated
(Table 1). These mice fought very vigorously in groups of
4, instead of in pairs, and this may explain the comparatively modest elevation of brain 5-HT in this experiment
(note that after 2 hr 5-HT was declining in the experiment
in Figure 10). Although 5-HT was somewhat elevated during
the fighting, the 5-HIAA was also elevated, and this
suggests that 5-HT was being released and oxidized at an
accelerated rate during this period of intense stimulation.
The elevated 5-HIAA could, however, be due partly to a decreased rate of removal from the brain, since its removal
is known to be dependent upon an active transport process
(Werdinius, 1967).

TABLE I

Effect of fighting upon brain serotonin and
5-HIAA in male BALB/c mice

	Pre-isolated Non-Fight	Pre-isolated Fight 45 min	$p <$
Serotonin (ng/gm)	911 ± 29.5	982 ± 40.8	.05
5-HIAA (ng/gm)	327 ± 7.9	418 ± 18.9	.001

N = 14 per treatment. Values are means ± s.e.m. Prior
isolation was 24 weeks. The mice fought in groups of four.

When pre-isolated females were similarly grouped they did not fight, but they sniffed and explored one another vigorously, and ran about excitedly. This increased activity and excitation were accompanied by modest but non-significant increases in all three brain amines (Table 2).

TABLE II

Elevation of brain amines in female mice grouped in 4's after 13 weeks of isolation. They did not fight.

	Isolated	Grouped 2 hours
Norepinephrine (ng/gm)	335 ± 33.5	356 ± 23.7
Dopamine (ng/gm)	884 ± 29.6	964 ± 49.7
Serotonin (ng/gm)	1055 ± 62.6	1118 ± 46.9

$N = 18$ per treatment.   Values are means ± s.e.m.

In Figure 6 we showed that pre-isolated mice are hyperreactive to restraint stress. The even milder "stress" of allowing these excitable mice to hear (and smell?) fighting going on in a neighboring cage can also cause a measurable elevation of brain amines (Table 3).

Thus in four different experiments, and in others that are not reported here, both mild social or psychological stimulus and also actual fighting have been found to elevate brain amines; in experiments where all three amines have been measured, all three are usually found to be elevated. When the effects of fighting and pargyline were combined (Figure 10), fighting slightly enhanced the accumulation of brain amines that was caused by pargyline, but the effects were not always necessarily additive, as might be the case if the effects of the drug and fighting were due to unrelated mechanisms.

Increases in brain amine levels resulting from various forms of stimulation or stress are frequently interpreted as resulting from an increased rate of biosynthesis in

TABLE III

Psychological effects of fighting: elevation of
brain norepinephrine and serotonin in isolated
mice that could hear fighting, but did not fight

	Controls	Hear fighting 1 hr	p<
Norepinephrine (ng/gm)	276 ± 17.6	317 ± 9.8	.05
Serotonin (ng/gm)	758 ± 22.1	1038 ± 101.4	.01

Hypersensitive pre-isolated (18 wk) mice were located within
a few feet of cages containing 8 pre-isolates that were
fighting vigorously. N = 5 per treatment. Values are
means ± s.e.m.

response to an increased rate of release and turnover. However, even if de-repression of the rate-limiting enzyme
tyrosine hydroxylase, brought about by an increased rate of
catecholamine release and utilization, resulted in increased
synthesis of DA and NE, no similar explanation exists to
account for the simultaneous increase in brain 5-HT. The
5-HT increases induced both by pargyline and by fighting
(and also restraint stress in Figure 6) were of approximately the same relative magnitude as those of the catecholamines.

In the absence of biosynthesis, as when biosynthetic
pathways are blocked by specific inhibitors (α-MT for the
catecholamines, p-chlorophenylalanine for 5-HT), stress
causes no accumulation of amines, but neither is there
necessarily an acceleration of the rate of their depletion
(Welch & Welch, 1968a; 1968e). Indeed, stress, including
fighting, may actually retard the rate of depletion of
these amines following biosynthesis inhibition (Welch &
Welch, 1968f), just as MAO inhibitors may retard the depletion caused by biosynthesis inhibition (Moore & Rech, 1967).

Since all three brain amines are rapidly elevated
within only a few minutes after the initiation of many forms

of stress, including fighting, it does not seem likely to us that the mechanism is a rapid increase in amine biosynthesis, even though it certainly depends on a continuation of on-going synthesis. There are several reasons for this belief. First, the rate limiting enzymes in the biosynthetic pathways are oxygenases, and as such are very sensitive to tissue oxygen tensions. Hence, during periods of stress tissue pO_2 levels are likely to be reduced (Davies & Bronk, 1957), and such a reduction should slow the rate of biosynthesis. On the other hand, mitochondrial MAO is also an oxygenase and as such is also exquisitely sensitive to oxygen tension (Novick, 1966), and if its activity were abruptly decreased at the initiation of stress a prompt reduction in the rate of breakdown of these presumed neurotransmitters would induce their rapid accumulation within the neuron, and would thereby make them available to satisfy the increased demands for their release and utilization that occur during the period of stress. Additional factors which might contribute to a reduction of MAO activity during periods of intense activation are the structural modifications of the mitochondria that occur during stress. Mitochondria are known to be extremely susceptible to osmotic changes that favor shrinking or swelling (Lehninger, 1967), and the vast changes in intraneuronal ionic concentration that occur during intense nervous stimulation would favor structural modifications that undoubtedly alter the activities of the contained enzymes (Aebi, 1962). Thus stress may indirectly bring about a natural inhibition of mitochondrial monoamine oxidase. An ability to instantaneously decrease intraneuronal catabolism when stress is initiated would provide the neuron with a means of rapidly increasing and conserving neurotransmitters when they are most needed. This model would suggest that the activity of mitochondrial MAO is continuously modulated by stimulus, and that this modulation provides a fine control over the amount of neurotransmitter available in the functional pool for release by nerve stimulation.

Although this or another mechanism may be active to conserve transmitter amines during periods of stress, at times the compensatory mechanism is inadequate, and stress may lower brain amines (Maynert & Levi, 1964). Figure 11 shows the results from an experiment in which pre-isolated mice were grouped to fight in groups of four; under these conditions, as we noted above, fighting is somewhat more intense than it is in pairs, and pauses between flurries of

attacks are less frequent. Within only 30 min there was a
slight but significant reduction in brain NE and a non-significant lowering of brain DA. However, in animals that
received 5 mg/kg d-amphetamine sulfate before being grouped
to fight, the fighting resulted in a marked lowering of
both amines; whole brain NE was lowered approximately 26%
(p <.001) and dopamine was lowered about 17% (p <.01). In
other experiments, d-amphetamine has been found to have a
biphasic effect, elevating brain amines at low doses or at
short time periods and lowering them at higher doses or
longer time periods (Welch & Welch, 1969). The results
from this experiment clearly demonstrate that intense
natural nervous stimulation may accelerate the depletion
of both brain NE and brain DA by d-amphetamine, and they
may be interpreted as evidence that utilization of these
amines, presumably for maintaining neurotransmission, was
increased by the increase in nervous activity that occurred
during fighting.

In other experiments we have dissected the brain into
telencephalon (including basal ganglia), diencephalon-mesen-
cephalon, and pons and medulla oblongata; the cerebellum,
which contains only very low stores of amines, has been discarded. Figure 12 shows that when these different parts of
the brain were examined for changes in amine levels during
fighting, we found that the changes do not occur uniformly
throughout the brain. In general we have found that reductions in brain catecholamines occur first in the brainstem,
and they may become progressively greater with passing time.
These findings are similar to those of Reis and Gunne who
have found reduced concentrations of NE in the brainstem of
cats following "rage" reactions induced either by electrical
stimulation of the amygdala or lateral hypothalamus or by
high decerebration. Low decerebration which did not cause
a rage reaction also did not affect brain catecholamine
levels. They also found reductions of adrenal epinephrine
of up to 44% after rage reactions, which would agree well
with our experiment presented in Figure 9, in which 1 hr of
fighting caused a 47% lowering of adrenal epinephrine (Reis
& Gunne, 1965; Feis et al., 1967).

In Figure 12 two separate experiments are combined for
simplicity of presentation. When male mice were allowed to
fight in groups of four for 5, 45, or 150 min there was a
significant loss of NE in the pons-medulla oblongata over
the shorter time periods measured, accompanied by a slight

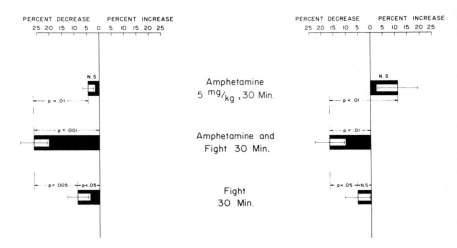

Figure 11.   Effect of fighting and amphetamine on brain amines.

Pre-isolated male mice were injected at zero time with saline or with d-amphetamine sulfate, 5 mg/k. Half of the mice were returned to their home cages and half were paired with a similar mouse and allowed to fight for 30 min. Results are presented as percentage changes from non-fighting saline controls; the s.e.m. is indicated on each bar. N = 10 per treatment.

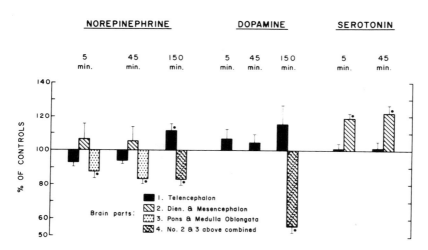

Figure 12. Preferential lowering of brainstem catechol-amines during fighting.

Male mice were allowed to fight in groups of four for 5 or 45 min (Expt. 1) or 120 min (Expt. 2). In Expt. 1 (5 and 45 min) there were 54 mice, with 18 in each of three treat-ments; brain parts were analyzed separately except that the pons and medulla oblongata were pooled in pairs for analysis. In Expt. 2 (150 min) there were 50 mice; tissues from 2 mice were pooled for analysis. The mean and s.e.m. are presented as percentages of their mean undisturbed, isolated controls. Black dots designate individual values that differ significantly from controls by the t-test.

accumulation of NE in the upper brainstem; after 150 min
of fighting NE in the combined brainstem (medulla oblong-
ata-diencephalon) was reduced by 18%. DA followed a
similar pattern with a significant loss of amine in the
subcortex accompanied by modest increases in the telencephalon. 5-HT was not reduced at the time periods
measured, but significant increases were found only in the
upper brainstem; they were similar in magnitude at both
the time periods measured.

The marked changes in catecholamine concentration produced in the brainstem become particularly interesting when
it is realized that the recent fluorescence histochemical
studies have localized the cell bodies of the catecholamine
containing neurons in the mesencephalon (DA) and the rhomb-
encephalon (NE) (Dahlstrom & Fuxe, 1965a; Fuxe, 1965;
Hillarp, Fuxe & Dahlstrom, 1966). The regional differences
observed in the effect of fighting upon these presumed
neurotransmitters suggest that the amines were reduced
primarily in the areas containing the neuronal cell bodies,
whereas they were slightly increased in the areas containing predominately nerve terminals. Thus, DA was reduced to
59% of its control value in the brainstem, while the telencephalon showed no sign of a loss, and indeed tended tended
to show a modest increase in concentration at all time
periods measured. Likewise, NE followed a similar pattern
with losses primarily in the pons and medulla oblongata,
where the noradrenergic neurones originate, accompanied by
modest increases in the upper brainstem; after 150 min of
fighting the brainstem showed an 15% loss in NE content,
whereas at this time there was a slight increase in
telencephalic NE.

Similar reductions of NE in the lower brainstem have
been observed in parallel experiments in which pre-isolated
hyperexcitable males were not allowed to fight, but rather
were suspended in a wire basket over a cage that contained
other mice fighting in groups of 4-5 (Welch & Welch, 1968g).
In this experiment the mere psychological impact of observing fighting among the other animals resulted in a 32% reduction of NE in the pons and medulla oblongata (Figure 13).
Control mice that were simply suspended over an empty
strange cage for the same period of time explored the
wire-mesh suspension cage and then rested quietly or went
to sleep, whereas the mice exposed to the excitement of
fighting remained alert and activated and pawed at their

confining wire barrier in an apparent attempt to join the
action going on below. The fighting mice paid no attention
to the suspended mouse, for they were totally occupied with
one another. This experiment is thought to be the first
clear demonstration of an effect on brain biochemistry of
a purely psychological event, namely, observation of the
sights, sounds, and smells of fighting without an opportunity to engage in the actual stresses and strains of the
fight. At the very least, the effects of actual physical
contact were eliminated. In a somewhat similar experiment,
except that there was no barrier present, Bliss and
Zwangziger have shown that "submissive" mice exposed to
a trained fighter experienced a lowering of brainstem NE
even though they were rescued before they were actually
injured (Bliss & Zwanziger, 1966).

The behavioral arousal observed in the mice involved
in or witnessing fighting fits well with an assumed activation of the reticular formation of the brainstem, since
noradrenergic neurons originating in the pons and medulla
have been shown to be functional components of this important activating system of the brain (Fuxe, 1965; Magoun,
1963) and NE has been shown to have a definite role in CNS
activation (Corrodi et al., 1966; Wise & Stein, 1969).

The amine granules are known to be transported distally
to the nerve terminals by axoplasmic flow (Dahlstrom &
Haggendal, 1966; Kapeller & Mayor, 1967; Laduron & Belpaire,
1968). Hence, this pattern of loss of catecholamines from
the area of the brain where the nerve cell bodies are
located, with lesser reductions or even increases in concentration in the regions containing the nerve terminals,
suggests to us that the intense activation caused by fighting may have accelerated the movement of catecholamine-con-
taining granules from the cell bodies where they are synthesized towards the nerve terminals where presumably the
amines are released at an increased rate during periods of
intense activation. The increases in catecholamines in the
telencephalon during fighting could also have been due in
part to a reduced rate of intraneuronal amine oxidation by
MAO, as discussed above. Possibly related to these findings are the observations of Fuxe and his colleagues who
have found that conditioned avoidance responding (CAR) in
rats caused an increased rate of disappearance of the
catecholamines in the metencephalon of rats pretreated with

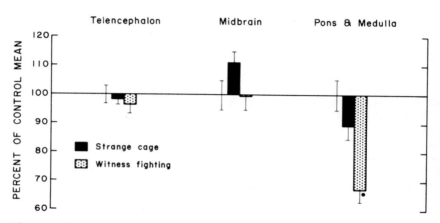

Figure 13. Disappearance of norepinephrine in the pons and medulla oblongata in mice that observed fighting but were not themselves involved in the fighting.

Male mice that had lived in isolation for 10 weeks were suspended in wire-mesh baskets above a cage containing fighting mice for 75 min. Other mice were suspended above an empty strange cage for the same period of time. The mean and s.e.m. are expressed as percentage changes from undisturbed controls. N = 20 for each treatment. Brain parts from individual animals were analyzed separately for NE. Figure adapted from Welch & Welch, 1968g.

α-MT. Although CAR did not cause a visible decrease in
fluorescence intensity in the subcortical areas of saline
treated control rats, it did cause an increase in the
number and intensity of NE nerve terminals in the telencephalon (Fuxe & Hanson, 1967). This histochemical evidence of an increase in telencephalic NE in response to
stimulus offers a further indication of the generality of
this response.

This speculation of an increased rate of proximo-distal
transport of amine granules in response to stimulus is
compatible with the observation of Kerkut (1967) who has
measured an increased rate of transport of a neurotransmitter from the ganglionic nerve cell body to the nerve ter-
minal in response to electrical stimulation in Helix, but
it is not compatible with the recent reports of Geffen and
co-workers who have been unable to find a measurable increase in the rate of NE granule transport in the peripheral
nervous system in response to stimulation of the splenic
nerve (L. B. Geffen, personal communication).

CHRONIC EFFECTS OF FIGHTING: LASTING EFFECTS OF
SHORT DAILY FIGHTS ON HEART, ADRENAL AND
SPLEEN WEIGHTS, AND BRAIN AND ADRENAL AMINE CONTENT

Isolation-induced fighting in male mice provides a
simple natural method for accelerating central and peripheral catecholamine and adrenal cortical metabolism, and
when it is used under standard conditions it may provide
a convenient model system for exploring the effects of
short periods of natural stress on the adaptation of
various neuroendocrine systems, and on the functioning of
the cardiovascular and renal systems as well. In this
section we will describe recent experiments which suggest
that brief stressful experiences may have profound long-
lasting effects on the heart, the spleen, the adrenal,
and the brain.

Figures 14 and 15 show the combined results of two
separate experiments. In the first, pre-isolated males
were paired for 10 min/day for 14 days; they were compared
with undisturbed littermate controls that had been grouped
or isolated for a similar period of time (4 mo). In a
repetition of this experiment, the mice were paired for
only 5 min/day, and they were allowed to fight daily for

either 5 days or 10 days before sacrifice. The mice were
sacrificed 24 hr after the last fight. The changes found
are plotted as percent increases or decreases in tissue
weights or in tissue amine concentrations as compared with
undisturbed isolate controls.

Figure 14 shows that daily fighting for 14 days caused
an elevation of about 10% in both of the brain catecholamines, and that daily fighting for only 10 days caused a
significant elevation in brain DA. The mice that lived in
groups did not differ significantly from their isolated
controls in brain amine concentration, although presumably
experiments of the sort described in the first section of
this paper would have shown that turnover rates of the
amines were faster. Although the slight differences in
5-HT levels were not statistically significant in our
experiments, Eleftheriou has found 5-HT to be reduced in
some parts of the brain when isolated C57B1 males were
exposed 2-5 min/day for 2, 4, 8, and 16 days to trained
fighters. In his experiment he also found both elevations
and reductions in tissue NE levels depending on the number
of days of fighting exposure (Eleftheriou & Church, 1969).
Our experiments and Eleftheriou's, however, cannot be
directly compared due to the fact that he killed his mice
20 min after the last exposure and we killed ours 24 hr
after the last exposure to fighting.

Other investigators have also found elevated tissue
concentrations of NE after daily stimulation for a period
of several days or weeks. Kety et al. (1967) have shown
this effect when rats were administered electroconvulsive
shock (ECS) twice a day for 7 days, and Nielson and
Fleming have found both NE and DA elevated after daily
ECS or cold stress (Kety et al., 1967; Nielson & Fleming,
1968). Since the acute effect of intense fighting may be
to lower NE and DA, at least in the brainstem, it is
apparent that adaptive compensations of some kind occurred.
The nature of these changes and their relative importance
in different parts of the brain, however, remain to be
determined.

Figure 15 shows that although daily fighting did not
significantly affect body weight in these mice, it did
affect almost everything else that was measured. Grouped
mice had enlarged spleens (+68%) and adrenals (+20%), and

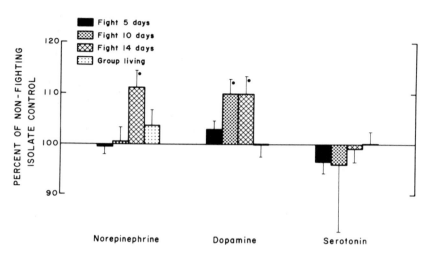

Figure 14. Lasting effects of short daily fights: elevation of brain catecholamines in mice allowed to fight for
5-10 min daily for 5, 10, or 14 days.

Results of two experiments are presented. In the first
experiment, male mice (DUB/ICR) were housed in isolation
or in groups of eight for 4 1/2 months. During the last
14 days of the experiment, isolated mice were paired and
allowed to fight for 10 min each day; they were then
returned to their home cages. In the second experiment
male mice (CD-1) were housed in isolation for 2 months,
after which they were placed together in pairs and
allowed to fight for 5 min each day for 5 or for 10 days;
controls were left undisturbed in their individual cages.
All mice were killed by decapitation 24 hr after the last
fight. Means and s.e.m. are presented as percentage
changes from the undisturbed isolated controls. Black
dots indicate individual means that differ significantly
from controls (at least p <.05 by two-tailed t-test).
N = 34 per treatment in experiment 1 and N = 11 per
treatment in experiment 2.

somewhat shrunken kidneys (-10%); notably, however, their
hearts were not enlarged. Adrenal epinephrine was significantly elevated (+36%) but NE was not. The elevated
adrenal E in the grouped mice agrees with out previous
findings on group-isolate differences, and as we have
previously suggested it probably represents an adaptation
to an increased rate of epinephrine release and utilization (see Figure 1). Blood pressures of our grouped mice
have been measured and reported by Henry et al. (1967);
even when the heart was not enlarged the blood pressures
of the grouped mice were higher than those of isolated
mice. The kidneys of mature grouped mice are usually
contracted and shrunken, and after 10-14 months they show
clear histological evidence of glomerular hyalinisation
and nephritis, similar to findings in human cardiovascular-
renal disease (in preparation).

    Short daily fights cause even more dramatic effects on
peripheral organs and endocrines than simple group living;
although group living allows virtually infinite opportunity
for fighting, comparatively little fighting actually occurs
(see Figure 4). The adrenal, heart, and spleen were all
enlarged by fighting, and the adrenal content of both NE
and E were elevated. These are the first experiments in
which we have found significant elevations of adrenal NE;
after only 5 days of fighting, adrenal E was not elevated,
but by 10 and 14 days it was elevated 63% and 56% respectively. The time dynamics of the elevations of NE and E
in the adrenal medulla agree with reports of earlier
workers who found that NE was the first amine replenished
in exhausted adrenals, whereas E reappeared much more
slowly (Butterworth & Mann, 1957). Since an acute episode
of fighting can cause a considerable reduction in adrenal
epinephrine, these large increases in adrenal stores after
10 and 14 days probably indicate that the adrenal medulla
had undergone adaptive changes in its capacity for synthesis and storage.

    The consistent enlargement of the heart in the fight-
ing mice agrees with the recent observations of Henry and
co-workers who have found that when previously isolated
male mice are forced to live together there was a great
deal of strife, a marked elevation of blood pressure and
a 10% enlargement of the heart (personal communication).
Such observations are also in agreement with our previous
report of enlarged hearts of subordinate mice that are

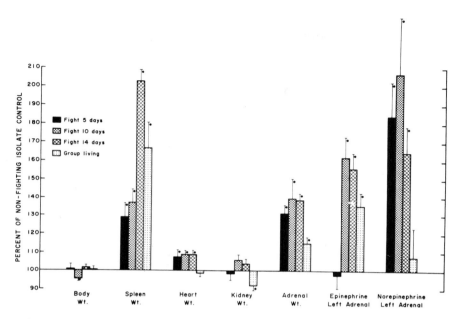

Figure 15. Lasting effects of short daily fights on body, adrenal, heart, kidney, and spleen weights, and upon adrenal catecholamines.

Results of two experiments are presented. In the first experiment, male mice (DUB/ICR) were housed in isolation or in groups of eight for 4 1/2 months. During the last 14 days of the experiment, isolated mice were paired and allowed to fight for 10 min each day; they were then returned to their home cages. In the second experiment male mice (CD-1) were housed in isolation for 2 months, after which they were placed together in pairs and allowed to fight for 5 min each day for 5 or for 10 days; controls were left undisturbed in their individual cages. All mice were killed by decapitation 24 hr after the last fight. Means and s.e.m. are presented as percentage changes from the undisturbed isolated controls. Black dots indicate individual means that differ significantly from controls (at least p <.05 by two-tailed t-test). N = 34 per treatment in experiment 1 and N = 11 per treatment in experiment 2.

frequent recipients of attack by dominants (Welch, 1967).

Enlargement of the spleen as a consequence of periodic fighting and group housing has been previously reported (Clarke, 1953) and histologically it has been said to
reflect an increased extramedullary hematopoiesis (Rapp &
Christian, 1963).

The dramatic enlargements of the adrenal glands that
were caused by fighting probably reflect an intense activation of the anterior pituitary-adrenal cortical axis.
Short episodes of daily fighting have been previously
shown to elevate plasma corticosterone (Bronson, 1967), to
cause sustained enlargements of the adrenals of mice
(Bronson, 1967; Christian et al., 1965), and to produce
distinct histological changes in the adrenals of rats
(Barnett, 1964).

Animals that live under the relatively low stimulus
levels of individual housing are hyperexcitable and dis-
turbing them causes exaggerated elevations of plasma corticosterone; further the levels remain high for hours after a
single short-lasting disturbance (Barrett & Stockham,
1963). Such elevations can be expected to have wide-rang-
ing effects on many systems of the body, including alterations in protein metabolism leading to a negative nitrogen
balance and muscle wasting; changes in electrolyte balance
and muscle wasting; osteoporosis; changes in electrolyte
balance that result in elevated blood pressures and altered
neuromuscular (and cardiac) irritability; altered erythro-
poiesis; and a suppression of normal immune response. The
changes in carbohydrate and lipid metabolism may also have
serious deleterious effects.

Short intermittent periods of stress probably approxi-
mate the conditions experienced in the real world of nature
more nearly than do prolonged periods. Fighting of male
mice provides a relatively natural form of physiological
stress that may be used as a tool for studying normal
mechanisms of neuroendocrine adaptation and control, and
it may also be useful in providing a model system for the
study of hypertension and cardiovascular-renal disease.
Since at least some components of this stress are probably
psychological, it may be useful also in gaining a better
understanding of the importance of emotional stresses in
the pathological processes discussed above.

The growing evidence that very short-lasting social
stresses have profound long-lasting physiological effects
provides support for the hypothesis that psychophysiological mechanisms may play an important role in our
response to the physical and emotional environment, and
that this response may be very important in the maintenance of health or in the development of disease.

SUMMARY

Male mice can be made aggressive simply by housing
them individually for several weeks. This also results in
a reduction in the rates of biosynthesis and utilization
of the presumed neurotransmitters norepinephrine, dopamine,
and serotonin in the brain; in a reduction in the basal
levels of secretion of the adrenal cortex and of the
adrenal medulla; and, after a period of time, in the
maintenance of lower blood pressures. It is not yet clear
to what extent these changes in brain biogenic amines may
be functionally related to the changes in aggressiveness
and excitability or to the changes in endocrine and cardiovascular activity.

Isolation has a determinative effect upon the position
in the social hierarchy that a mouse will assume when he is
paired with another mouse. Not only do pre-isolated mice
tend to become dominant, but five weeks of isolation for
subordinate mice and five weeks of grouping for dominant
mice will result in a high percentage of reversals of
original hierarchial relations when the pairs are reconstituted.

The effects that fighting has upon the brain biogenic
amines norepinephrine, dopamine, and serotonin are complex.
The intense nervous activity of engaging in fighting accel-
erates the release and utilization of these amines in
neurotransmission and compensatory mechanisms, probably
of several kinds, are immediately called into play. Hence,
although prolonged or more intense stress may cause them to
be lowered, the initial effect of fighting is to simultaneously elevate all three brain amines. We suggested that
the elevation is caused by a natural stimulus-induced
inhibition of mitochondrial monoamine oxidase. The lowering occurs first in subcortical areas of the brain where
the cell bodies of amine-containing neurons reside, and

may occasionally be paralleled by amine elevations in the
telencephalon. We have suggested that this patterned
effect may reflect an accelerated rate of transport of
amines from their site of synthesis in cell bodies
towards nerve terminals.

Fighting once each day for only five minutes may
result in elevations of both brain norepinephrine and
dopamine, but the mechanism of these apparently adaptive
changes is not yet understood.

Such periodic fighting also results in marked elevations in the level of adrenal epinephrine and norepinephrine. Inasmuch as a single one-hour session of fighting
may lower adrenal epinephrine by 47%, these elevations
clearly reflect adaptive changes, probably increases in
the rate of amine biosynthesis.

Short episodes of daily fighting result in a distinct
cardiac hypertrophy. Short intermittent periods of intense
social stress, such as fighting, have profound long-lasting
effects that have broad implications for physical and
mental health.

ACKNOWLEDGMENTS

Supported by grants from the Air Force Office of
Scientific Research, The U. S. Army Medical Research and
Development Command, and the National Institute of Mental
Health. Mr. Robert Eskay performed the behavioral obser-
vations in the dominance-subordinance experiments. Addi-
tional assistance was provided in the various experiments
by Miss Anne Kennon, Mr. John Adams, Mr. Charles E. Goolsby,
Jr., Mrs. Peggie Adams, and Mrs. Gladys Senter.

REFERENCES

ACHESON, G. H. (Ed). Second Symposium on Catecholamines.
    Baltimore: Williams and Wilkins Co., 1966. Reprinted
    from Pharmacological Reviews, 1966, 18, 1-803.

AEBI, H. Mitochondrial structure as a controlling factor
   of monoamine oxidase activity and the action of
   amino-oxidase inhibitors. Biochem. Pharmacol., 1962,
   9, 135-140.

AGHAJANIAN, G. K., ROSECRANS, J. A., & SHEARD, M. H.
   Serotonin: release in the forebrain by stimulation
   of midbrain raphe. Science, 1967, 156, 402-403.

AGRAWAL, H. C., FOX, M. W., & HIMWICH, W. A. Neurochemical
   and behavioral effects of isolation-rearing in the
   dog. Life Sci., 1967, 6, 71-78.

ALLEE, W. C. Group organization among vertebrates.
   Science, 1942, 95, 289-293.

ANDEN, N. E., DAHLSTROM, A., FUXE, K., LARSSON, K.,
   OLSON, L., & UNGERSTEDT, U. Ascending monoamine
   neurons to the telencephalon and diencephalon. Acta
   Physiol. Scand., 1966a, 67, 313-326.

ANDEN, NE., FUXE, K., & HOKFELT, T. The importance of the
   nervous impulse flow for the depletion of the monoamines from central neurons by some drugs. J. Pharm.
   Pharmacol., 1966b, 18, 630-632.

BALDESSARINI, R. J., & KOPIN, I. J. Tritiated norepinephrine: release from brain slices by electrical stimulation. Science, 1966, 152, 1630-1631.

BARNETT, S. A. Social Stress. In J. D. Carthy and C. L.
   Duddington (Eds.) Viewpoints in Biology. London:
   Butterworths, 1964, v. 3, Pp. 170-218.

BARRETT, A. M., & STOCKHAM, M. A. The effect of housing
   conditions and simple experimental procedures upon
   the corticosterone level in the plasma of rats.
   J. Endocrin., 1963, 26, 97-105.

134   A. S. WELCH AND B. L. WELCH

BENNETT, E. L., DIAMOND, M. C., KRECH, D., & ROSENZWEIG,
M. R. Chemical and anatomical plasticity of brain.
Science, 1964, 146, 610-619.

BLISS, E. L., & ZWANZIGER, J. Brain amines and emotional
stress. J. Psychiat. Res., 1966, 4, 189-198.

BOURGAULT, P. C., KARCZMAR, A. G., & SCUDDER, C. L.
Contrasting behavioral, pharmacological, neurophysiological, and biochemical profiles of C57BL/6
and SC-I strains of mice. Life Sci., 1963, 8,
533-553.

BRONSON, F. H. Effects of social stimulation on adrenal
and reproductive physiology of rodents. In M. L.
Conalty (Ed.) Husbandry of Laboratory Animals.
New York: Academic Press, 1967, 1967, Pp. 513-544.

BROWN, B. B. CNS drug actions and interaction in mice.
Arch. Internat. Pharmacodynie, 1960, 128, 391-414.

BUTTERWORTH, K. R., & MANN, M. The adrenaline and
noradrenaline content of the adrenal gland of the
cat following depletion by acetylcholine. Brit. J.
Pharmacol., 1957, 12, 415-421.

CHANCE, M. R. A. Factors influencing the toxicity of
sympathomimetic amines to solitary mice. J. Pharmacol.
Exptl. Therap., 1947, 89, 289-296.

CHASE, T. M., BREESE, G. R., & KOPIN, I. J. Serotonin
release from brain slices by electrical stimulation:
regional differences and effect of LSD. Science,
1967, 157, 1461-1463.

CHRISTIAN, J. J., LLOYD, J. A., & DAVIS, D. E. The role of
endocrines in the self-regulation of mammalian populations. Rec. Prog. Horm. Res., 1965, 21, 501-570.

CLARKE, J. R. The effect of fighting on the adrenals,
thymus and spleen of the vole (Microtus agrestis).
J. Endocrin., 1953, 9, 114-126.

CONSOLO, S., GARATTINI, S., & VALZELLI, L. Amphetamine
toxicity in aggressive mice. J. Pharm. Pharmacol.,
1965a, 17, 53-54.

CONSOLO, S., GARATTINI, S., & VALZELLI, L. Sensitivity of
    aggressive mice to centrally acting drugs. J. Pharm.
    Pharmacol., 1965b, 17, 594-595.

CORRODI, H., FUXE, K., & HOKFELT, T. Refillment of the
    catecholamine stores with 3, 4-dihydroxyphenylalanine
    after depletion induced by inhibition of tyrosine
    hydroxylase. Life Sci., 1966, 5, 605-611.

DAHLSTROM, A., & FUXE, K. Demonstration of monoamines in
    the cell bodies of brain stem neurons. Acta Physiol.
    Scand., 1965a, 62 (Suppl. 232), 5-55.

DAHLSTROM, A., FUXE, K., KERNALL, D., & SEDVALL, G.
    Reduction of monoamine stores in the terminals of
    bulbospinal neurons following stimulation in the
    medulla oblongata. Life Sci., 1965b, 4, 1207-1212.

DAHLSTROM, A., & HAGGENDAL, J. Studies on the transport
    and life-span of amine storage granules in peripheral
    adrenergic neuron system. Acta Physiol. Scand., 1966,
    67, 278-288.

DAVIES, P. W., & BRONK, D. W. Oxygen tension in mammalian
    brain. Fed. Proc., 1957, 16, 689-692.

DAVIES, W. M. Day-night periodicity in pentobarbital
    response of mice and the influence of socio-psycho-
    logical conditions. Experientia, 1962, 18, 235-237.

ELEFTHERIOU, B. E., & CHURCH, R. L. Brain levels of
    serotonin and norepinephrine in mice after exposure
    to aggression and defeat. Physiol. Behav., 1968,
    3, 977-980.

FRIEDMAN, A. H., & WALKER, C. A. Circadian rhythms in rat
    mid-brain and caudate nucleus liogenic amine levels.
    J. Physiol. (Lond.), 1968, 197, 77-85.

FUXE, K. Distribution of monoamine nerve terminals in the
    central nervous system. Acta Physiol. Scand., 1965,
    64 (Suppl. 247), 37-85.

FUXE, K., & HANSON, L. C. F. Central catecholamine neurons
    and conditioned avoidance behavior. Psychopharmaco-
    logia (Berl.), 1967, 11, 439-447.

GARATTINI, S., GIACALONE, E., & VALZELLI, L.   Isolation,
    aggressiveness and brain 5-hydroxytryptamine turnover.
    J. Pharm. Pharmacol., 1967, 19, 338-339.

GARATTINI, S., & SHORE, P. A.(Eds.).   The Biological Role
    of Indole-alkylamine Derivatives.   Advances in
    Pharmacology, Vol. 6A and 6B.   New York: Academic
    Press, 1968.

GIACALONE, E., TANSELLA, M., VALZELLI, L., & GARATTINI, S.
    Brain serotonin metabolism in isolated aggressive
    mice.   Biochem. Pharmacol., 1968, 17, 1315-1327.

GINSBURG, B., & ALLEE, W. C.   Some effects of conditioning
    on social dominance and subordination in inbred
    strains of mice.   Physiol. Zool., 1942, 15, 485-506.

GREENBLATT, E. M., & OSTERBERG, A. C.   Correlations of
    activating and lethal effects of excitatory drugs in
    grouped and isolated mice.   J. Pharmacol. Exptl.
    Therap., 1961, 131, 115-119.

GUNN, J. A., & GURD, M. R.   The action of some amines
    related to adrenaline, cyclohexylalkylamines.   J.
    Physiol. (Lond.), 1940, 97, 453-470.

GUHL, A. M.   Gonadal Hormones and Social Behavior in Infra-
    human Vertebrates.   In W. C. Young and G. W. Corner
    (Eds.) Sex and Internal Secretions.   Baltimore:
    Williams and Wilkins, 1961, v. 2, Pp. 1240-1267.

HALBERG, F., JACOBSON, E., WADSWORTH, G., & BITTNER, J. J.
    Audiogenic abnormality spectra, twenty-four hour
    periodicity, and lighting.   Science, 1958, 128,
    657-658.

HENRY, J. P., MEEHAN, J. P., & STEPHENS, P. M.   The use of
    psychosocial stimuli to induce prolonged systolic
    hypertension in mice.   Psychosom. Med., 1967, 29,
    408-432.

HILLARP, N.-A., FUXE, K., & DAHLSTROM, A.   Demonstration and
    mapping of central neurons containing dopamine, nor-
    adrenaline, and 5-hydroxytryptamine and their reactions
    to psychopharmaca.   Pharmacol. Rev., 1966, 18,
    727-742.

HIMWICH, H. E., KETY, S. S., & SMYTHIES, J. R. (Eds.)
Amines and Schizophrenia. New York: Pergamon Press,
1967.

IVERSEN, L. L. The Uptake and Storage of Noradrenaline in
Sympathetic Nerves. Cambridge: Cambridge University
Press, 1967.

KAPELLER, K., & MAYOR, D. The accumulation of noradrenaline in constructed sympathetic nerves as studied by
fluorescence and electron microscopy. Proc. Royal
Soc., 1967, 167, 282-292.

KARCZMAR, A. G., & SCUDDER, C. L. Behavioral responses to
drugs and brain catecholamine levels in mice of
different strains and genera. Fed. Proc., 1967, 26,
1186-1191.

KARLI, P. Rat-mouse interspecific aggressive behavior and
its manipulation by brain ablations and by brain
stimulation. In S. Garattini and E. B. Sigg (Eds.)
Biology of Aggressive Behavior. Amsterdam: Excerpta
Medica Foundation, 1969.

KERKUT, G. A. Transport of glutamate to nerve terminals.
Neurosci. Res. Prog. Bull., 1967, 5, 322-325.

KETY, S. S., JAVOY, F., THIERRY, A.-M., & GLOWINSKI, J.
A sustained effect of electroconvulsive shock on the
turnover of norepinephrine in the central nervous
system of the rat. Proc. Nat. Acad. Sci., 1967,
58, 1249-1254.

KIMBRELL, G. M. A preliminary analysis of the agonistic
behavior patterns shown by three strains of mice, Mus
musculus, in the footshock situation. Ph.D. Disserta-
tion, Department of Psychology, University of
Tennessee, Knoxville, 1968.

KING, J. T., CHIUNG PUH LEE, Y., & VISSCHER, M. B. Single
versus multiple cage occupance and convulsive frequency in C3H mice. Proc. Soc. Exp. Biol. Med., 1955,
88, 661-663.

KRECH, D., ROSENZWEIG, M. R., & BENNETT, E. L. Environmental impoverishment, social isolation and changes in brain chemistry and anatomy. Physiol. Behav., 1966, 1, 99-104.

LADURON, P., & BELPAIRE, F. Transport of noradrenaline and dopamine-beta-hydroxylase in sympathetic nerves. Life Sci., 1968, 7, 1-7.

LAGERSPETZ, K. Y. H., TIRRI, R., & LAGERSPETZ, K. M. J. Neurochemical and endocrinological studies of mice selectively bred for aggressiveness. Rep. Inst. Psychol. (Turku), 1967, 29, 1-5.

LEAF, R. C., LERNER, L., & HOROVITZ, Z. P. The role of the amygdala in the pharmacological and endocrinological manipulation of aggression. In S. Garattini and E. B. Sigg (Eds.) The Biology of Aggressive Behavior. Amsterdam: Excerpta Medica Foundation, 1969.

LEHNINGER, A. L. Cell organelles: the mitochondrion. In G. C. Quarton, T. Melnechuk, and F. O. Schmitt (Eds.) The Neurosciences. New York: Rockefeller University Press, 1967, Pp. 91-100.

MAAS, J. W. Neurochemical differences between two strains of mice. Science, 1962, 137, 621-622.

MAGOUN, H. W. The Waking Brain. Springfield: Charles C. Thomas, 1963.

MARCUCCI, R., MUSSINI, E., VALZELLI, L., & GARATTINI, S. Decrease in N-acetyl-L-aspartic acid in brain of mice. J. Neurochem., 1968, 15, 53-54.

MAYNERT, E. W., & LEVI, R. Stress-induced release of brain norepinephrine and its inhibition by drugs. J. Pharmacol. Exptl. Therap., 1964, 143, 90-95.

MOORE, K. E., & RECH, R. H. Antagonism by monoamine oxidase inhibitors of alpha-methyltyrosine-induced catecholamine depletion and behavioral depression. J. Pharmacol. Exptl. Therap., 1967, 156, 70-75.

NIELSON, H. C., & FLEMING, R. M.   Effects of electrocon-
    vulsive shock and prior stress on brain amine levels.
    Exptl. Neurol., 1968, 20, 21-30.

NOVICK, W. J.   Effect of oxygen tension on monoamine
    oxidase activity.   Biochem. Pharmacol., 1966, 15,
    1009-1012.

PIRCH, J. H., & RECH, R. H.   Effect of alpha-methyltyrosine
    on the elactrocorticogram of unrestrained rats.
    Internat. J. Neuropharmacol., 1968a, 4, 315-324.

PIRCH, J. H., & RECH, R. H.   Effect of isolation on alpha-
    methyltyrosine-induced behavioral depression.   Life
    Sci., 1968b, 7, 173-182.

RAPP, J. P., & CHRISTIAN, J. J.   Splenic extramedullary
    hematopoiesis in grouped male mice.   Proc. Soc. Exp.
    Biol. Med., 1963, 114, 26-28.

REIS, D. J., & GUNNE, L.-M.   Brain catecholamines: rela-
    tion to the defense reaction evoked by amygdaloid
    stimulation in cat.   Science, 1965, 149, 450 451.

REIS, D. J., MIURA, M., WEINBREN, M., & GUNNE, L.-M.   Brain
    catecholamines: relation to defense reaction evoked
    by acute brainstem transection in cat.   Science, 1967,
    156, 1768-1770.

SCHEVING, L. E., HARRISON, W. H., GORDON, P., & PAULY, J. E.
    Daily fluctuation (circadian and ultradian) in biogenic
    amines of the rat brain.   Am. J. Physiol., 1968a,
    214, 166-173.

SCHEVING, L. E., HARRISON, W. H., & PAULY, J. E.   Daily
    fluctuation (circadian) in levels of epinephrine in
    the rat suprarenal gland.   Am. J. Physiol., 1968b,
    215, 799-802.

SCHILDKRAUT, J. J., & KETY, S. S.   Biogenic amines and
    emotion.   Science, 1967, 156, 21-30.

SCUDDER, C. L., KARCZMAR, A. G., EVERETT, G. M., GIBSON,
J. E., & RIFKIN, M. Brain catecholamines and
serotonin levels in various strains and genera of
mice and a possible interpretation for the correlations of amine levels with electroshock latency and
behavior. Internat. J. Neuropharmacol., 1966, 5,
343-351.

SHEARD, M. H. The effects of amphetamine on behavior in
the cat. Brain Res., 1967, 5, 330-338.

SPECTOR, S., GORDON, R., SJOERDSMA, A., & UDENFRIEND, S.
End-product inhibition of tyrosine hydroxylase as a
possible mechanism for regulation of norepinephrine
synthesis. Mol. Pharmacol., 1967, 3, 549-555.

SUDAK, H. W., & MAAS, J. W. Behavioral-neurochemical
correlation in reactive and nonreactive strains of
rats. Science, 1964, 146, 418-420.

VALZELLI, L. Drugs and aggressiveness. In S. Garattini
and P. A. Shore (Eds.) Advances in Pharmacology.
New York: Academic Press, 1967, v. 5, Pp. 79-108.

VALZELLI, L. Aggressive behavior induced by isolation.
In S. Garattini and E. B. Sigg (Eds.) Biology of
Aggressive Behavior. Amsterdam: Excerpta Medica
Foundation, 1969.

VALZELLI, L., & GARATTINI, S. Behavioral changes and 5-HT
turnover in animals. In S. Garattini and P. A. Shore
(Eds.) Advances in Pharmacology. New York: Academic
Press, 1968, v. 6/B, Pp. 249-260.

VOGT, M. The concentration of sympathin in different parts
of the central nervous system under normal conditions
and after the administration of drugs. J. Physiol.
(Lond.), 1954, 123, 451-481.

WEISSMAN, A., KOE, K. B., & TENEN, S. S. Anti-amphetamine
effects following inhibition of tyrosine hydroxylase.
J. Pharmacol. Exptl. Therap., 1966, 151, 339-352.

WELCH, B. L. Psychophysiological response to the mean
    level of environmental stimulation: a theory of en-
    vironmental integration. In D. McK. Rioch (Ed.)
    Symposium on the Medical Aspects of Stress in the
    Military Climate. Washington: U. S. Gov. Printing
    Office, 1965, Pp. 39-96.

WELCH, B. L. Aggression and Defense: Neural Mechanisms
    and Social Patterns. In C. D. Clemente and D. B.
    Lindsley (Eds.) Brain Function. Los Angeles:
    University of California Press, 1967, v. 5, Pp. 150-
    170.

WELCH, B. L., & WELCH, A. S. Graded effect of social
    stimulation upon d-amphetamine toxicity, aggressive-
    ness and heart and adrenal weight. J. Pharmacol.
    Exptl. Therap., 1966, 151, 331-338.

WELCH, B. L., & WELCH, A. S. Differential activation by
    restraint stress of a mechanism to conserve brain
    catecholamines and serotonin in mice differing in
    excitability. Nature, 1968a, 218, 575-577.

WELCH, B. L., & WELCH, A. S. Evidence and a model for the
    rapid control of biogenic amine neurotransmitters by
    stimulus modulation of monamine oxidase. Fed. Proc.
    (abs), 1968b, 27, 711.

WELCH, B. L., & WELCH, A. S. Greater lowering of brain and
    adrenal catecholamines in group-housed than in indi-
    vidually-housed mice administered DL-alpha-methyltyro-
    sine. J. Pharm. Pharmacol., 1968c, 20, 244-246.

WELCH, B. L., & WELCH, A. S. Rapid modification of isola-
    tion-induced aggressive behavior and elevation of brain
    catecholamines and serotonin by the quick-acting mon-
    amine oxidase inhibitor pargyline. Comm. Behav. Biol.,
    1968d, 1, 347-351.

WELCH, A. S., & WELCH, B. L. Effect of stress and para-
    chlorophenylalanine upon brain serotonin, 5-hydroxy-
    indoleacetic acid and catecholamines in grouped and
    isolated mice. Biochem. Pharmacol., 1968e, 17, 699-708.

WELCH, A. S., & WELCH, B. L. Failure of natural stimuli to accelerate brain catecholamine depletion after biosynthesis inhibition with alpha-methyltyrosine. Brain Res., 1968f, 9, 402-405.

WELCH, A. S., & WELCH, B. L. Reduction of norepinephrine in the lower brainstem by psychological stimulus. Proc. Nat. Acad. Sci., 1968g, 60, 478-481.

WELCH, B. L., & WELCH, A. S. Aggression and the biogenic amines. In S. Garattini and E. B. Sigg (Eds.) Biology of Aggressive Behavior. Amsterdam: Excerpta Medica Foundation, 1969.

WELCH, B. L., AND WELCH, A. S. Brain NE and DA: rapid elevation and subsequent stimulus-facilitated depletion by d-amphetamine. Fed. Proc. (abs), 1969, 28, 796.

WERDINIUS, B. Effect of probenecid on the levels of monoamine metabolites in the rat brain. Acta Pharmacol. Toxicol., 1967, 25, 18-23.

WISE, D. C., & STEIN, L. Facilitation of brain stimulation by central administration of norepinephrine. Science, 1969, 163, 299-301.

WOOLLEY, W. D. The Biochemical Basis of Psychosis. New York: John Wiley and Sons, 1962a.

WOOLLEY, D. E., & TIMIRAS, P. S. Estrous and circadian periodicity and electroshock convulsions in rats. Am. J. Physiol., 1962b, 202, 379-382.

YEN, C. Y., STAGNER, R. L., & MILLMAN, N. Ataractic suppression of isolation-induced aggressive behavior. Arch. Internat. Pharmacodyn., 1959, 123, 179-185.

AGGRESSION, NOXIOUSNESS, AND BRAIN STIMULATION IN UNRESTRAINED RHESUS MONKEYS

R. Plotnik, D. Mir, and J. M. R. Delgado

Department of Psychology, San Diego State College, San Diego, California and Department of Psychiatry, Yale University School of Medicine, New Haven, Connecticut

Although there are numerous reports of intra- and inter-species aggression elicited by electrical brain stimulation (Adams, 1968; Akerman, 1966; Delgado, 1955, 1966, 1968; Delgado et al., 1968; Heath, Monroe, & Mickle, 1960; Hess, 1957; Holst & Paul, 1962; Phillips, 1964; Roberts, Steinberg, & Means; Wassman & Flynn, 1962), there has been little research (Adams &Flynn, 1966) on the relationship between evoked aggression and reinforcing properties of the electrical brain stimulation (EBS). By determining the reinforcing properties of EBS, it is possible to differentiate between, what we have called, primary and secondary aggression. Primary aggression could be elicited by EBS through cerebral mechanisms which are independent of aversive sensations. Secondary aggression could be elicited by EBS or peripheral stimuli which first produce noxious sensations which subsequently cause aggression. This distinction is important because secondary aggression has been elicited by peripheral shock in hamsters and several strains of rats (Ulrich, 1966; Ulrich & Azrin, 1962), cats (Ulrich, Wolff, & Azrin, 1964) pigeons (Reynolds, Catania, & Skinner, 1963), and monkeys (Azrin, Hutchison, & Hake, 1963). Although foot shock produced aggression, this does not indicate the existence of an aggressive center in the animal's feet since it is inferred that shock elicited aversive sensations which resulted in aggression. Similarly, before various neural centers or circuits are postulated for aggression, it is necessary to know whether the aggression elicited by EBS

was primary or secondary. As shown in Figure 1, primary
aggression evoked by EBS and secondary aggression produced
by skin shock would be independent, not mediated by a
common aversive mechanism, but would overlap in the expression of the aggressive response. However, if the aggression
elicited by EBS is secondary, then brain stimulation and
shock could activate a similar mediating mechanism, i.e.,
arousal of internal aversive stimuli.

Although an animal cannot verbalize the sensations
produced by EBS, the rewarding or punishing properties of
the stimulation can be defined by the animal's operant
performance in obtaining or avoiding such a stimulus. The
adjectives "aversive, noxious, and negative" will be used
synonymously to refer to stimuli the animal will work to
avoid. Since stimuli may be noxious (fearful stimuli)
without being described as painful, and since painful and
fearful stimuli might be indistinguishable on the basis of
the animal's operant performance, we can only operationally define noxiousness.

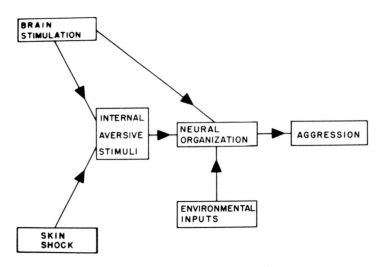

Figure 1. Model of two mechanisms by which brain stimulation could elicit aggression. Aggression is referred to as
primary if it is elicited independent of internal aversive
stimuli and called secondary if it is dependent upon
arousal of such stimuli.

Previous reports on intra-species aggression elicited by brain stimulation in opossums (Roberts et al., 1967), pigeons (Akerman, 1966), chickens (Holst et al., 1962), ducks (Phillips, 1964), cats (Adams, 1968; Delgado, 1955; Wassman et al., 1962), monkeys (Delgado, 1966, 1968), and man (Delgado et al., 1968; Heath et al., 1955), did not define the reinforcing properties of brain stimulation and thus did not distinguish between primary and secondary aggression. Robinson's paper (Robinson, 1968) was the first to demonstrate primary intra-species aggression elicited by non-aversive brain stimulation. There is also evidence that in the cat, rage (Nakao, 1958) and prey-catching elicited by hypothalamic stimulation (Roberts & Kiess, 1964) and tail shock involve independent but over-lapping systems (Adams & Flynn, 1966). Results from prey-catching should perhaps not be generalized to other forms of aggression, since some animals show little predatory activity and the behavioral patterns of prey-catching are not considered analogous to other forms of aggression (Carthy & Ebling, 1964; Davis, 1964; Eibl-Eibesfeldt, 1967). For these reasons, we have restricted the term aggression to intra- or inter-species attack and defensive behaviors which are independent of predation. For a more detailed definition and discussion of aggression see papers by Moyer (1968) and Scott (1968).

It might be thought that the distinction between primary and secondary aggression could be clarified by self-report in humans following brain stimulation. To our knowledge, there are only two published cases of aggression or rage elicited by brain stimulation in humans (Delgado et al., 1968; Heath et al., 1948). In one study (Heath et al., 1958), brain stimulation elicited rage and the patient reported the stimulation was not painful. However, in subsequent testing, either rage or fear were evoked. In the second study (Delgado et al., 1968), there is no patient report of sensations elicited by brain stimulation which resulted in aggression. Thus, there is insufficient data from human research to clarify the role of centrally elicited aversive sensations in mediating aggression.

Since there are no studies of intra-species aggression elicited by aversive brain stimulation and only a few studies on inter-species aggression (Adams et al., 1966; Brown & Cohen, 1959; Cohen & Brown, 1957; Delgado, Roberts, & Miller, 1954; Roberts, 1958), all on cats, we began a series of experiments on secondary aggression. The present study first defined the reinforcing properties of brain stimulation and then investigated the possible role of aversive properties of the stimulation in mediating aggression. Rhesus monkeys were used as subjects since they have a considerable repertoire of aggressive and social responses and are not usually predatory. Since studies on aggression in the wild (Eibl-Eibesfeldt, 1967), following brain stimulation (Holst & Paul, 1962; Levison & Flynn, 1965) and brain lesions (Plotnik, 1968; Rosvold, Mirsky, & Pribran, 1954) have shown that an animal's aggressive response may be completely different when tested in isolation, with similar or different species, and with humans or inanimate objects, the animals were studies under multiple environmental conditions. We asked the following questions: (a) Does all aversive brain stimulation elicit aggression? (b) Do peripheral shock and aversive brain stimulation elicit similar aggressive responses? (c) Under what environmental conditions does brain stimulation and peripheral shock elicit aggression and nocioceptive pathways?

METHOD

Subjects. The subjects, four male and three female, adult (4.2-7.3 Kg) rhesus monkeys (macaca mulatta) were purchased from a local dealer and housed in quarantine for six weeks before testing was initiated. These seven monkeys (A0, A2, A6, A7, A8, 67, 71) were implanted with intracerebral electrodes. In addition, four monkeys (A3, A5, 19, 22) were used as controls. Monkeys A7, female, and A6, male, and their control test partners, A3 and A22, females; A5 and A19, males, were caged separately and were placed together only during test sessions. Monkeys A2, A8, 67 (males) and A0, 71 (females) were caged separately before testing, but during the experiment they were caged together as a colony. Throughout the experiment, all monkeys were maintained at 95% of normal body weight.

Apparatus. Monkeys were tested restrained in Foringer chairs or free in cages located in sound attenuated and RF shielded rooms. They were observed through closed circuit television and never saw investigators during test periods unless reactions to humans were being explored. Three cages

were used: cage #1 (3-1/2 × 5 × 8 ft long) to study colony
of five monkeys; cage #2 (2-1/2 × 3-1/2 × 5 ft long) to test
monkeys in pairs; and cage #3 (2-1/2 × 2-1/2 × 3 ft long)
to explore the raction to foot shock in paired monkeys.
All cages were built of formica and plexiglass with glass
fronts. The floor of cage #3 was constructed of parallel
brass grids wired together in alternate sequence for shock
delivery. Cages #1 and #2 provided ample space for monkeys
to move freely about. Cage #3 had minimal space requiring
close proximity of the two animals.

The shock source for the Foringer chair was a 60 cps
variac transformer with an isolated output. Electrodes
were taped across one leg of the monkey. Current was monitored on an oscilloscope across a 1000 ohms resistor in
series with the animal, and intensity ranged from 100-150
mA peak depending on the animal's skin resistance. Shock
duration was 0.5 seconds.

The shock source for cage #3 was a commercially available high voltage vibrator (6,000 v), with a frequency of
140 Hz and spike pulse width of 1 msec. The intensity was
adjusted until the monkeys began to fight and shock duration
was 0.2 sec.

The radio controlled stimulator was a 3 channel unit,
32 × 32 × 14 mm, which weighed 25 gms and was fixed to a
collar placed around the monkey's neck. The unit was
connected to three pins of the permanently implanted
electrode socket. Pulse width, frequency, and amplitude
were adjusted by radio control. The characteristics of
electrical stimulation were constant current, monopolar,
cathodal square pulses, 0.5 msec pulse duration, and 100 Hz.

The radio controlled skin shocker was an FM receiver
(Delgado, 1963) which triggered a high voltage vibrator
with an output of 0.6 mA at 6,000 v. The radio shocker
measured 17 × 17 × 4 cm, weighed 400 gm plus 360 gm for
batteries and was mounted on the monkey's back. Its output
terminated in a belt formed of two pieces of 1/2 inch copper
tubing around monkey's waist. The high voltage vibrator
used in the shock source of cage #3 was identical to that
used in the radio shocker. In both cases shock duration was
0.3 sec delivered every 30 sec during the 30 min session
with a total of 60 shocks per session.

Procedure for testing monkeys restrained in chairs.
After the monkeys were adapted to the chairs, they were
trained to lever press for food pellets on a continuous
reinforcement schedule (CRF). When this response reached
a stable rate during ten minute periods, monkeys were
trained to avoid foot shock on a Sidman Avoidance (SA)
schedule in which a 0.5 sec shock occurred every 5 sec unless the monkey pressed the lever postponing shock for 15
sec. Monkey could avoid all shocks by pressing the lever
every 14 sec.

When the monkey was receiving 30 or less shocks per
1 hour Sidman session, it began training on a multiple
schedule (Figure 2) which consisted of 2 five-minute
periods lasting 30 minutes. A monkey had to discriminate
between the two components in order to continuously avoid
shock or obtain food. There was no cue for alternation,
so a monkey had to sample the reinforcement contingency to
determine which component was operative. For example, with
foot shock as reinforcement, the first 5 min component of
the multiple schedule was SA and a rapid press rate would
result in maximum shock avoidance. After 5 min the program
changed to the second component in which each lever press
now produced a foot shock and maximum shock avoidance could
be achieved by inhibition of lever pressing. After 5 min
the program changed back to SA and the best strategy for
shock avoidance was now rapid lever pressing and so on
through the schedule. With food as reinforcement, the
multiple schedule began with a 5 min component during
which free food (FF) was given to the monkey every 5 sec
and each lever press postponed food delivery for 15 sec
with maximum food occurring if monkey inhibited lever pressing. After 5 min of FF the program changed to 5 min of CRF
and rapid lever pressing resulted in maximum reinforcement.
Thus, either with foot shock or food reinforcement, the
monkey could avoid or obtain maximum reinforcement only by
alternating between rapid lever pressing and complete inhibition of lever pressing. The monkey's baseline bar
press rate was determined by testing the monkey on the
multiple schedule without reinforcement.

Training continued on the multiple schedule until the
following criterion were reached on two successive days:
(a) for positive reinforcement (food), a CRF bar press rate
at least twice as rapid as rate for the FF components; (b)
for negative reinforcement (shock), avoidance of all but

MULTIPLE SCHEDULE

POSITIVE REINFORCEMENT

FREE FOOD PELLET EVERY
5 SEC. -- LEVER PRESS   CRF
POSTPONES PELLET 15 SEC.

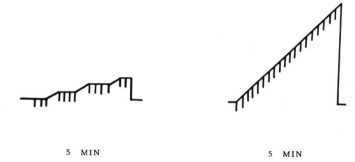

5   MIN   5   MIN

NEGATIVE REINFORCEMENT

SIDMAN AVOIDANCE   EACH PRESS PRODUCES AN
                                     AVERSIVE REINFORCEMENT

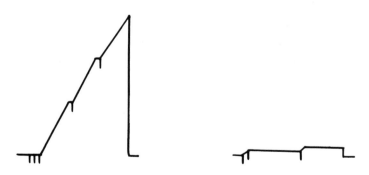

Figure 2. A diagram of the multiple schedule and an
illustration of the best strategy to obtain or avoid
reinforcements on alternating components. Slope of
line indicates lever press rate and each downward blip
indicates a reinforcement.

30 shocks in the SA components. When the monkey reached
both criterions intracerebral electrodes were permanently
implanted.

Operative procedure. Under sterile conditions, four
electrode assemblies were stereotaxically implanted in each
monkey, A7, A6, A2, A0, 67, 71, A8, according to the technique already described (Delgado, 1955). Each electrode
assembly had a diameter of 1 mm and was constructed of
seven #36 teflon-coated stainless steel wires bonded together with plexiglass. One millimeter of each wire's tip
was bared and speced 3 mm apart on a vertical axis. Following a two week recovery period, the monkeys were restrained
in chairs, and testing resumed.

Postoperative testing in chair. Radio controlled
electrical stimulation was applied to each electrode point
for 5 sec at increasing intensities (0.05-1.5 mA) to study
elicited responses. Each monkey was then retested on the
multiple schedule with food and shock reinforcement until
criterion was reached. To evaluate reinforcing properties
of brain stimulation, the same multiple schedule was used
but brain stimulation was substituted for food and foot
shock. Four to six half-hour brain stimulation sessions
were given daily with at least 15 min between periods and
the motor reaction to brain stimulation was recorded. The
duration of brain stimulation was from 0.1 to 5 sec and the
intensity, ranging from 0.2 - 1.5 mA, was monitored on an
oscilloscope across a 1000 ohms resistor in series with the
monkey. The DC electrode resistance was 20-40,000 ohms and
the resistance to pulsed stimulation was 3-5000 ohms. Performance on the multiple schedule with food, foot shock,
and no reinforcement was also tested 2-3 times weekly to
maintain the monkey's discriminative performance.

Definition of positive, negative, and neutral brain
stimulation. After each monkey had reached criterion,
10 samples of its performance on the multiple schedule with
each reinforcement (food, foot shock, and no reinforcement)
were randomly chosen. These 30 records were divided into
three performance groups on the basis of the three different
reinforcers; food-positive reinforcement; foot shock-negative; foot shock-negative reinforcement; control or neutral -
no reinforcement. Data from these three groups were then
subjected to discriminative analysis (Seal, 1964) by computer, and weights for each reinforcement group were deter-

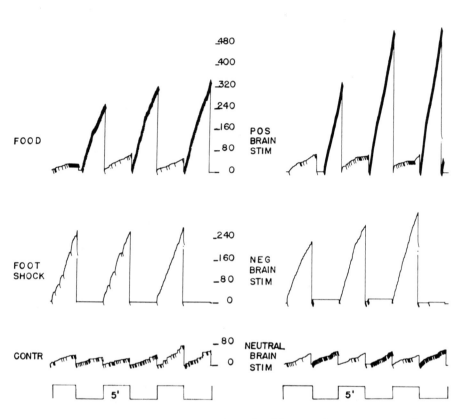

Figure 3. Cumulative records of A6's performance on the
multiple schedule with no reinforcement (control), food,
foot shock, and brain stimulation as reinforcement.
Brain stimulation was defined as positive (pos), negative (neg), and neutral because it closely resembled
performance on food, foot shock, and control.

mined. Results showed that there was no overlap in the
monkey's bar press performance on the three different reinforcements. Each 30 min brain stimulation record was
then computer analyzed and classified, with a certain
probability, as positive, negative, or neutral on the basis
of weights determined from food, foot shock, and control
data. Figure 3 shows the cumulative records of A6's
discriminative performance on control, food, and shock
compared with brain stimulation as reinforcement. The
slope of the line indicates the bar press rate and each
downward blip indicates a reinforcement. When reinforcements occur in close succession, the downward blips fuse
into a solid black line as shown in the food and positive
brain stimulation records. Brain stimulation was defined
as positive if it resembled the monkey's performance on
food (positive reinforcement), as negative (aversive,
noxious) if it resembled the monkey's performance on foot
shock (negative reinforcement), and as neutral if it resembled the monkey's baseline or control performance (no
reinforcement). Therefore, the reinforcing effects of
brain stimulation were defined on the basis of how closely
the monkey's performance on brain stimulation matched the
monkey's performance to known neutral (no reinforcement),
positive (food), and negative (foot shock) reinforcements.
We could determine how reinforcing the brain stimulation
was by the probability level with which a brain stimulation
performance was classified. As lever pressing performance
during brain stimulation approached performance levels in
food, shock or control testing, the motivational properties
of these stimuli were evaluated as similar. Thus, the
higher the probability level for classification of brain
stimulation as positive, negative, or control (1.0 was
highest probability), the more rewarding or punishing was
the brain stimulation. Probability levels were divided
into high (H), .8-1.0; medium (M), .6-.79; and low (L),
.2-.59, which were considered to represent degrees of reinforcement. Notations used for positive, negative, and
neutral reinforcement are P, N, and T respectively. The
degree of reinforcement is indicated by the probability
level, i.e., H-N indicates a brain stimulation record
classified with a high probability as negatively reinforcing.

Brain stimulation defined as negative or positive was
usually tested at several different stimulus intensities
and durations. After all electrode points were tested for

reinforcement properties, monkeys were studied unrestrained.

   Procedure for testing monkey unrestrained. Monkeys
were adapted to cage and individually trained to lever
press for food pellets. Control observations were then
made to establish baseline frequencies of aggressive responses in the colony and aggressive, grooming interactions, sexual, and instrumental responses in paired
monkeys. Monkey A6 was paired and tested on alternate
days with a dominant (A5) and a submissive partner (A19).
Similarly, monkey A7 was tested on alternate days with a
dominant (A3) and a submissive partner (A22). Dominance
pattern was determined by aggressive interactions and food
lever priority tests during which a light signaled and remained on when the food lever was operative (5-10 min).

   When a monkey was stimulated in the colony a submissive
monkey was always present for attack (a monkey submissive to
A8 was present when A8 was stimulated). By pairing A6 or A7
with either a dominant or submissive partner, we tested
whether a submissive monkey would attack its dominant partner if that were the only monkey present.

   Environmental conditions and aggression. The frequency
and direction of aggression elicited by negative brain stimulation was studied under the following conditions. Monkeys
A6 and A7 were each tested restrained in a chair, five feet
away from the following stimuli presented singly: a familiar and unfamiliar human; their dominant or submissive
monkey partner also in a chair; a toy tiger on a chair or
a mirror with no other stimulus present. A familiar human
was defined as the male technician that daily handled,
tested, and fed the monkeys. An unfamiliar human was a
male that the monkeys had never seen before and a different
unfamiliar human was present during testing under restrained
and unrestrained conditions. The instructions to the humans
were to sit quietly in front of the monkey and to try to
maintain eye contact with it.

   This above procedure was repeated with both A6 and A7
unrestrained in cage #2. The toy tiger, which was about
3/4 the size of the monkey, was placed inside the cage
while the human sat five feet in front of the cage and the
mirror was the reflective window in the side of the compartment. Sixty stimulations were given under each restrained and unrestrained condition.

Table 1

Behavioral responses studied in monkeys A6 and A7
with their respective dominant and submissive
partners. Frequency or duration (sec) of
responses were recorded. Abbreviations
will be used in subsequent tables and figures

AGGRESSIVE RESPONSES   ABBREVIATION

attack	A
threaten window	TW
threaten monkey	TM
grimace	G
attacked or threatened	AT
displaced	D

GROOMING INTERACTIONS

present for grooming	PG
groom partner (sec)	GP
initiate grooming	IG
groomed by partner (sec)	BG
number of times groomed	TG

SEXUAL RESPONSES

present for mounting	PM
mount partner	M

INSTRUMENTAL RESPONSE

time pressing lever (sec)	F

SELF-DIRECTED RESPONSE

self-grooming (sec)	SG

Scoring procedure. From another room an observer scored the monkeys' responses via the TV monitor and any interaction could be played back since responses were also recorded on video tape. The observer used a 40 item keyboard to record the frequencies of sexual and aggressive behaviors and seconds of grooming and lever pressing. Only the presence or absence of aggressive responses elicited by brain stimulation were studied in the colony. In paired monkeys, effects of brain stimulation on aggressive, grooming, sexual, and instrumental responses were analyzed, as shown in Table 1.

Aggressive behavior was defined as (a) threat response which is a stereotyped motor pattern of the dominant monkey consisting of mouth opening, staring at the submissive monkey with head bobbing and occasional vocalization; (b) attack, which began with a chase and ended with the dominant monkey grabbing or biting the submissive monkey which responded by fleeing, grimacing, and infrequently fighting back; (c) grimace, which is a submissive gesture consisting of lip retraction to expose the teeth and is made in response to a threat or attack; and (d) displacement, in which the dominant monkey's approach resulted in the submissive monkey abandoning an area that the dominant monkey then occupies. No threat or grimace responses are observed in displacement. A more detailed description of aggressive responses has been published (Hinde & Rowell, 1962).

Each monkey received two daily 30 min brain stimulation sessions--50-60 stimulations per session--with one hour and a half between sessions. The responses for the two sessions were combined and percentage of aggression elicited by brain stimulation calculated on the basis of 110-120 stimulations. If a single brain stimulation elicited multiple threat or attack, it was counted as one aggressive response.

Aggressive responses were scored as occurring DURING or FOLLOWING brain stimulation. If the aggressive responses occurred within a 10 sec period following termination of brain stimulation, that response was defined as occurring POSTSTIMULATION.

Testing procedure for brain stimulation. Table 2 shows the experimental design for testing colony and paired

Table 2

Experimental design for control and brain stimulation
sessions with monkeys tested in colony and paired conditions

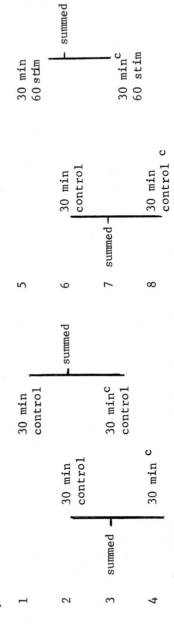

COLONY

Sequence	Control session [a]	Brain stimulation session [a]
Morning	30 min	30 min--60 stim
Afternoon	30 min	30 min--60 stim

PAIRED MONKEYS

Sequence [b]	Control session [a]	Brain stimulation session [a]
1	30 min control	
2	30 min control	
3	30 min[c] control	
4	30 min [c]	
5		30 min 60 stim
6	30 min control	
7		
8	30 min control [c]	30 min[c] 60 stim

[a] 1-1/2 hour between each 30 min session
[b] Begun at 9:00 AM
[c] Lever operative during first 10 min of session

monkeys. In the colony, two control sessions (half-hour each) per day were given for 15 days before brain stimulation began. In the paired monkeys, four control sessions (half-hour each) were given daily for six days for each pair before brain stimulation. At the beginning and throughout the 5-8 months of brain stimulation testing in paired monkeys, four control periods per day were recorded on the average of four to five days a month. There was a total of 60 half-hour control sessions for A6 and A7 when each was the dominant and submissive partner of its pair. Control sessions 1 and 3 and sessions 2 and 4 were combined to form two one-hour control periods which provided a more complete sample of the monkeys' behavior and controlled for possible differences in activity level throughout the day. Means, standard deviations, and standard deviation ranges were computed for each kind of response observed in the 30 control periods.

As shown in Table 2, when brain stimulation began in the paired monkeys, sessions 5 and 7 were brain stimulation sessions and sessions 6 and 8 were control sessions without brain stimulation. Responses influenced by brain stimulation were evaluated in two ways. First, in order to evaluate the immediate effects of brain stimulation on behavior, a comparison was made between the frequency of responses elicited by brain stimulation for combined periods 5 and 7 with frequency of response computed from the 30 combined control sessions 1 and 3. Second, a comparison was made between frequency of responses for combined control sessions (no brain stimulation) 6 and 8 with frequency of responses computed from the 30 control sessions 2 and 4. This comparison evaluated the long term effects of brain stimulation, since the control session (no brain stimulation) occurred at least one hour and a half after the brain stimulation session. Only responses which fell outside the plus and minus two standard deviation range of control responses were considered significantly changed by brain stimulation. An increase or decrease of grooming interactions and sexual activity was calculated from stimulus bound responses and similar responses occurring throughout the test session due to possible cumulative effects of stimulation.

The effect of brain stimulation on an instrumental response was evaluated by recording the time a monkey spent lever pressing for food pellets. It received one food pellet for every 10 presses (FR 10) during first 10 min of

sessions 2, 4, 5, and 7, and a light near the lever
signaled when the lever was operative.

Histology. After completion of the study, monkeys
were sacrificed under anesthesia, the brain was perfused
with formalin and cut stereotaxically into 10 mm blocks,
after which high contrast serial photography was taken
while the block was being cut. Frozen sections 50μ thick
were then prepared and selected slides were stained with
the method of Kluver and Berrera (1953). The atlas of
Snider and Lee (1961) was used for stereotaxic orienta-
tions and for selection of coordinates.

RESULTS

Measurement of social interactions. Social dominance
hierarchy in the colony of five monkeys was determined from
15 control sessions (one hour each) and results are shown
in Figure 4. The hierarchy, as defined by direction of
aggression, was linear with A0 dominant followed by A2, 67,
71, and A8 in descending order. There was a direct relationship between dominance defined by direction of aggression
and by food priority tests. With all five monkeys present,
A0, boss, monopolized the lever and as each successive
dominant monkey was removed, the monkey next in hierarchial
order controlled the lever. Only aggressive interactions
were recorded in the colony, and brain stimulation sessions
began at the termination of control observations.

In two monkeys, each paired with a dominant and submissive monkey, grooming interactions, sexual, instrumental,
and aggressive responses were scored. Aggressive interactions, determined from 6 control sessions (one hour each)
are shown in Figure 4. The dominance structure for each
pair was linear and did not change throughout testing (5-8
months). Dominance patterns were identical whether defined
by aggressive interactions or food priority tests. When A6
and A7 were dominant, they monopolized the lever; when submissive, their dominant partners controlled the food lever.
Thus, the dominance structure in colony and paired monkeys
was clearly established before brain stimulation began.

Throughout brain stimulation sessions, 30 control
periods (1 and 3, 2 and 4) sampled grooming interactions,
sexual, aggressive, and instrumental responses in each

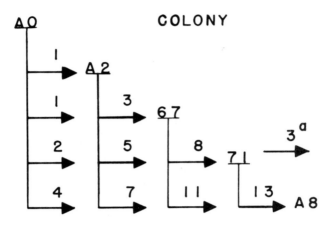

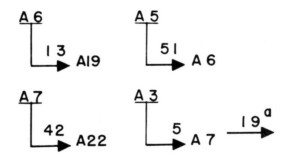

Figure 4. Social dominance hierarchy, determined from aggressive interactions, for colony and paired monkeys. The letter indicates the monkey, the arrow indicates the direction of aggression, and the number indicates the frequency of threats and attacks.

[a] Threatening outside of the cage.

pair, and from these control periods the mean and standard
deviation of each response were calculated (Table 3).
Standard deviation range (± 2) for each response was computed to indicate the limits within which the frequency of
a response would normally occur 95 times out of 100 (0.05
probability). A change in response frequency was attributed to effects of brain stimulation if the frequency was
outside this range.

Results from 30 hours of control observations in
paired monkeys indicate that: 1) aggressive interactions
were linear, infrequent, and usually occurred during the
10 min period that the food lever was operative; 2) after
being attacked or threatened by its dominant partner, A7
never grimaced but usually threatened toward window in the
side of the test compartment (TV camera behind window) in
which its reflection was visible; its dominant partner
made no response to A7's threats in window; 3) after being
attacked or threatened by its dominant partner, A6 usually
grimaced and never threatened toward the window; 4) sexual
responses were unstable and infrequent, A6, male, never
mounted. A7, female, mounted its dominant and submissive
partners; 5) instrumental response (lever pressing for
food) was the most stable response; when dominant A6 and
A7 controlled the lever and when submissive, they infrequently spent a few seconds at the lever when their
dominant partner left it to drink; 6) in contrast to
aggressive and sexual responses, grooming interactions
were more stable and frequent; monkeys engaged in grooming
or being groomed during most of test session (14-47% of
time); and 7) the inhibiting effects of brain stimulation
could be evaluated by frequency decreases in grooming interactions and instrumental responses; for all other responses,
only an increased frequency of responding could be evaluated.

Brain stimulation and aggression. This experiment
had two parts: 1) the stimulation of 174 electrode points
in seven unrestrained monkeys (5 in colony and 2 in pairs)
in order to locate brain areas from which aggression could
be elicited; and, 2) once aggression had been elicited by
brain stimulation, the study of paired monkeys in order to
thoroughly analyze this as well as other responses (grooming, sexual, and instrumental) influenced by brain stimulation. Table 4 shows the relationship between electrode

Table 3. Means and standard deviations for aggressive, grooming, sexual, and instrumental responses from A6 and A7 tested with their respective dominant and submissive partners. Data for each condition from 30 one hour control sessions and scores indicate A6 or A7 responding or being responded to by its partner

RESPONSES	A6 DOMINANT		A6 SUBMISSIVE		A7 DOMINANT		A7 SUBMISSIVE	
	M	SD	M	SD	M	SD	M	SD
Attack	1	2	0	0	3	2	0	0
Threaten Window	0	0	0	0	0	0	3	5
Threaten Monkey	0	0	0	0	1	1	0	0
Attacked or Threatened	0	0	3	3	0	0	3	3
Aggression, 10 min Food Period	1	1	0	0	2	3	2	4
Grimace	0	0	4	3	0	0	0	0
Displaced	0	0	0	0	0	0	0	0
Present for Grooming	19	8*	14	6*	15	7*	12	5*
Groom Partner	86	99	271	255	688	316*	1180	514*
Initiate Grooming	5	5	4	3	9	4*	9	4*
Groomed by Partner	860	404*	483	234*	506	234*	637	356
Number of Times Groomed	9	4*	11	5*	7	3*	7	4
Self-grooming	7	15	10	15	54	103	8	31
Present for Mounting	0	0	2	2	2	2	3	4
Mount Partner	0	0	0	0	3	3	2	8
Time pressing Food Lever	600	2*	0	0	600	2*	3	11

* Responses used to evaluate inhibitory effects of brain stimulation.

sites, reinforcing properties of brain stimulation, and
intra-species aggression elicited in paired and colony
monkeys.

In three monkeys, stimulation of 14 of the 174 electrode points (8.0%) elicited aggression and, in each case,
aggression followed stimulation which was always defined
as noxious. No aggression was elicited by brain stimulation in four monkeys, which had 21 points defined as
aversive. Thus, only aversive brain stimulation elicited
aggression but not all aversive brain stimulation produced
aggression. The remaining 117 electrode points (67.2%)
were neutral or positive and did not elicit aggression
either during or following stimulation which was presented
for five seconds and usually at several different intensities. The five second stimulus duration maximized the
probability of eliciting aggression since we had found that
very brief aversive stimulations (0.1-0.5 sec) elicited
aggression. To eliminate motor reactions which could

Table 4

The relationship between reinforcing effects of brain
stimulation and elicitation of aggression in
unrestrained monkeys. Stimulation parameters
were 100 Hz, 0.02-1.5 mA and 0.1-5.0 seconds duration

Monkeys	Number of electrodes	Percentage of electrodes	Reinforcing effect	Aggression elicited
A2, A6, A7	14	8.0	Aversive	YES
A0, A2, A6 A8, 67, 71	21	12.0	Aversive	NO
A0, A2, A6,A7 A8, 67, 71	22	12.6	Positive	NO
A0, A2, A6,A7 A8, 67, 71	117	67.2	Neutral	NO
	174	99.8		

interfere with an aggressive response during stimulation, we used a low intensity stimulus that produced little or no motor movement. To test whether five seconds of motor movement would elicit poststimulation aggression, we used a higher intensity stimulus which elicited a mild-strong motor reaction. In spite of these testing procedures, aggression was never observed during or after neutral or positive brain stimulation, in paired or colony conditions.

The reinforcing properties of brain stimulation were usually defined with 0.5 sec stimulus duration in restrained monkeys. In unrestrained monkeys, longer stimulus durations were often used for testing neutral and positive brain stimulation. We did not test whether brain stimulation at longer stimulus durations had the same positive or neutral reinforcing effects as at short durations, for we found that reinforcing effects tested at 1.0 and 1.5 mA, 0.5 sec duration usually defined maximum reinforcing properties of that stimulation. The duration and intensity of aversive brain stimulation was the same for restrained and unrestrained monkeys.

Reversal of reinforcement effects. Table 5 shows the relationship between changes in reinforcing effects of stimulation and elicitation of aggression from the same electrode site. In monkey A2, brain stimulation defined as positive at 0.3 mA elicited no aggression while at higher intensities, 0.8 and 1.3 mA, the same stimulation became negative and elicited 78% and 100% aggression respectively. In monkey A7, brain stimulation defined as neutral at 0.5 mA elicited no aggression while at a higher intensity, 1.0 mA, it was negative and elicited 55% and 77% aggression when A7 was dominant and submissive. Thus, brain stimulation of the same electrode defines as positive or neutral did not elicit aggression, until by increased stimulus intensity or duration, stimulation became noxious to the monkey.

Aggression elicited by noxious brain stimulation could only occur after stimulation, since the motor response produced during stimulation interfered with all other responses. Brain stimulation elicited a variety of motor responses such as turning of body and/or head, retraction of lips, opening mouth, closing eyes, running, and jumping. To eliminate competing motor responses and maximize the

Table 5. Brain structures from which stimulation elicited aggression. Stimulus parameters were identical for restrained and free testing conditions with 120 stimulations at each intensity. In the same structure, a change in stimulus intensity and/or duration resulted in different reinforcing effects and percentages of aggression.

Paired Monkeys

Monkey	Structure	mA	Dur sec	Reinforcing effect[a]	% Aggression[b] Dom	Sub[c]
A7	Nucl tractus spinalis nervi trigemini (ventral border)	0.05[d]	5.0	H-Neutral	0	0
		0.05[d]	0.5	H-Neutral	0	0
		0.1[c]	0.5	H-Neutral	0	0
		0.5	0.1	H-Neutral	0	0
		0.5	0.5	H-NEGATIVE	20	11
		1.0	0.1	H-NEGATIVE	55	77
		1.0	0.2	H-NEGATIVE	56	79
		1.5	0.1	H-NEGATIVE	39	38
	Nucl tractus spinalis nervi trigemini (dorsal border)	1.0	0.5	H-NEGATIVE	21	37
		1.5	0.5	H-NEGATIVE	17	17
	Nucl tractus spinalis nervi trigemini bordering pedunculus cerebellaris superior	1.5	0.5	H-NEGATIVE	35	19
	Colliculus inferior (deep placement)	1.5	0.5	H-NEGATIVE	88	99

Table 5. Continued, page 2

Tractus spinalis nervi trigemini					
	0.05^d	5.0	H-Neutral	0	0
	0.05^d	0.5	H-Neutral	0	0
	0.5	0.5	L-NEGATIVE	19	21
	1.0	0.1	H-Neutral	0	0
	1.5	0.1	H-NEGATIVE	0	0
Area tegmentalis (fasciculi thalamicus and lenticularis)					
	1.0	0.5	H-NEGATIVE	32	28
	1.5	0.5	H-NEGATIVE	9	4
A6 Nucl corporis geniculati medialis					
	0.08^d	5.0	H-Neutral	0	0
	0.5	0.1	H-Neutral	0	0
	0.5	0.5	H-NEGATIVE	60	0
	1.0	0.1	H-NEGATIVE	34	0
	1.5	0.1	H-NEGATIVE	13	0
Nucl reticularis magnocellularis					
	0.05^d	5.0	H-Neutral	0	0
	0.5	0.1	H-Neutral	0	0
	1.0	0.1	L-NEGATIVE	13	0
	1.5	0.1	H-NEGATIVE	34	0
Nucl ventralis posterior medialis					
	1.5	0.5	H-NEGATIVE	8	0

Table 5. Continued, page 3.

Colony

Monkey's social rank	Structure	mA	Dur sec	Reinforcing effect[a]	% Aggression[f] Monkey	Window	Social rank of monkey attacked
A2 was 2nd of four monkeys	Substantia nigra (pars compacta)	0.6	0.5	H-NEGATIVE	82	18	3rd and 4th monkeys
	Substantia nigra (pars compacta)	0.3	0.5	H-Positive	0	0	
		0.8	0.5	H-NEGATIVE	78	0	3rd monkey
		1.3	0.5	H-NEGATIVE	100	0	3rd monkey
	Nucl ventralis lateralis (pars medialis)	0.7	0.5	H-Neutral	0	0	
		1.0	0.5	H-NEGATIVE	27	13	3rd monkey
		1.3	0.5	H-NEGATIVE	33	20	3rd monkey
	Area tegmentalis limiting substantia grisea centralis	0.3	0.5	H-Neutral	0	0	
		0.6	0.5	L-NEGATIVE	28	0	3rd monkey
		0.9	0.5	H-Negative	63	0	3rd and 4th monkeys
	Cortex pyriformis bordering meninges (40 stimulations in each condition)	1.4	0.5	H-NEGATIVE	23	53	3rd monkey
A2 was tested alone	"			"	--	15	Threats to window

Table 5. Continued, page 4

Cortex pyriformis
bordering meninges
(40 stimulations in
each condition)

H-NEGATIVE

			2nd monkey
A2 was 1st of two monkeys	3	5	2nd monkey
	5	20	2nd monkey
	3	78	2nd monkey
	1	75	2nd monkey
A2 was 2nd of two monkeys	0	53	

a H, M, and L refer to high, medium, and low probability respectively
b % aggressive responses when monkey was dominant (Dom) and submissive (Sub)
c Threats to outside window
d Below motor threshold
e Motor threshold
f % aggressive responses against another monkey or window

probability of aggression occurring during stimulation, we
decreased the intensity of stimulation so that either no
(0.05 mA) or slight (0.1 mA) motor response was produced.
In addition, stimulus duration was increased so that
stimulation occurred almost continuously for a 30 min
session (5 sec on / 2 sec off). As shown in Table 5, this
stimulation was defined as neutral in the restrained
monkey, and elicited no aggression during or after stimulation.

Aggression dependent on social rank. The occurrence,
direction, and expression of the aggressive response elicited by brain stimulation depended on the social dominance
rank of the monkey. When submissive, A6 always showed the
motor reaction during aversive stimulation; never threatened or attacked its dominant partner after stimulation;
sometimes grimaced (submissive gesture) after stimulation
although not threatened by its dominant partner; (Figure 5)
and was sometimes threatened or attacked by the dominant
partner, apparently because A6's motor reaction to stimulation caused it to enter the dominant monkey's area or
startled the dominant monkey. In contrast, when dominant,
A6 showed the motor reaction to negative stimulation;
never grimaced following stimulation; and threatened or
attacked its submissive partner (Figure 6). Thus, A6
showed dominant and submissive aggressive responses following the SAME aversive stimulation, and the response depended on monkey's social rank.

A7 showed a slightly different pattern of poststimulation aggression. When submissive, A7 never grimaced but
threatened the window following aversive stimulation. Its
dominant partner showed no reaction to A7 threatening the
window. On a few occasions, A7 threatened its dominant
partner, which was looking in another direction. A7 never
made eye contact when threatening the dominant partner, and
if caught threatening, A7 was immediately attacked. When
A7 and its dominant partner were tested in a compartment
without reflective surfaces, A7 never made threats toward
the outside. When dominant, A7 switched between threats or
attacks to monkey and threats to window. If A7 and its
submissive partner (A22) were tested in cage #3 (no reflective surface), A7 threatened or attacked A22 about the same
percentage of stimulations (47%) as combined attacks and
threats to A22 and window (55%) in cage #2.

Figure 5.   In the presence of and without being threatened
by its dominant partner, monkey A6 (submissive) grimaces
following aversive brain stimulation (nucl. corporis
geniculati medialis, 1.0 mA, 0.1 sec).

Figure 6. Monkey A6 (dominant) attacks its submissive partner following stimulation of the same area with the same parameters that elicited the grimace shown in Figure 5.

Results from paired monkeys were identical to results from the colony of five monkeys. Table 5 shows that following aversive brain stimulation, A2, second in dominance, threatened or attacked submissive monkeys in colony; less frequently threatened outside window; never attacked boss of colony; and aggression was always poststimulation. Of the five monkeys, A2 was the only monkey that showed aggression following aversive brain stimulation.

Effects of brain stimulation on non-aggressive responses. Table 6 shows the effects of brain stimulation on grooming interactions, sexual, aggressive, and instrumental responses in paired monkeys. Aversive brain stimulation which elicited poststimulation aggression (9 of 50 sites) significantly suppressed social interactions of A6 and A7, when dominant and submissive, and frequently suppressed instrumental response of A7. Neutral and positive brain stimulation decreased (11/50 sites) and increased (7/50 sites) social and sexual interactions during brain stimulation sessions. Stimulation of some negative, neutral and positive points produced an increase (8/50 sites) or decrease (3/50 sites) in grooming and sexual interactions during control sessions, which means the effects of stimulation were present one hour and a half after the stimulation session itself (long-term effects). Stimulation of one half of the electrode sites (23/50 sites) had no effect on aggressive, grooming, sexual, or instrumental responses. The most reliable and predictable effect of brain stimulation on grooming behavior was the suppression of grooming responses by aggression-producing noxious brain stimulation. Aversive brain stimulation which did not elicit aggression usually did not disrupt grooming interactions.

If the stimulation intensity of an aversive point was decreased to below motor threshold and duration was increased to five seconds, the stimulation was defined as neutral, and there was neither disruption nor increase of grooming, sexual, aggressive, or instrumental responses.

Sexual responses scored were presenting for mounting and mounting, which have both sexual and social components (Hinde & Rowell, 1962). Because of the instability of these responses, only an increased frequency could be evaluated. Monkey A6, male, never showed increased mounting, while monkey A7, female, showed increased mounting of dominant and submissive partner during and following several brain stimu-

Table 6

A representative sample of effects of brain stimulation on aggressive, grooming, sexual, and instrumental responses in paired monkeys. Scores are for stimulated monkey responding or being responded to with 120 stimulations at each intensity and when monkey was dominant and submissive. EBS refers to electrical brain stimulation.

Brain structure	Rf[a]	mA	sec	mA	sec	CHAIR Brain Stimulation[b] 5&7 Inc*	5&7 Dec*	Control[c] 6&8 Inc*	UNRESTRAINED Brain Stimulation[b] 5&7 Inc*	5&7 Dec*	Control[c] 6&8 Inc*	Brain Stimulation[d] 5&7 Dec*	Control[c] 6&8 Inc*
EBS[e]	H-P	1.0	0.5	.5-1	5.0	G			G				
EBS[f]	H-N	0.5	0.5	0.5	0.5	TM 60%	BG		AT,G	BG			
	H-N	1.0	0.1	1.0	0.1	TM 34%	PG,BG TG		AT,G				
	H-N	1.5	0.1	1.5	0.1	TM 13%	PG,BG TG,F				PG,BG	PG,BG	
EBS[g]	H-N	0.5	5.0	.5-.8	5.0			PG					PG
EBS[h]	H-N	1.0	0.5	1.0	0.5	NONE							
EBS[i]	H-N	0.5	0.5	0.5	0.5	TW 20%	F,PG		TW 11%	G,IG			
						TM 0%	GP,IG			PG			
							TG,BG						

Table 6. Continued, page 2.

	H-N	1.0	0.1	1.0	0.1	TW 22% / TM 33%	F,PG GP,IG PG,GP IG	TW 77%	PG,GP IG	
	H-N	1.5	0.1	1.5	0.1	TW 18% / TM 21%	PG,GP IG	TW 38%	PG,GP IG	G
EBS^j	H-T	0.5	.4-.6	5.0			F,PG GP,IG TG,BG		M,PG BG,TG	G M,PG TG
EBS^k	H-T	1.0	.5-1	5.0			BG,IG TG		G	
EBS^l	L-N	0.5	0.5	0.5		TW 15% / TM 4%	F,PG GP,IG BG,TG	TW 21%	GP,PG IG	

SUMMARY (A6 and A7)

EFFECT OF BRAIN STIMULATION

	Number of electrodes	Percentage of electrodes
Increased aggression and decreased social responses	9	18
No aggression and decreased social responses	11	22
No aggression and increased social responses	7	14
No effect on aggressive or social responses	23	46
	50	100

Table 6. Continued, page 3.

a H, M, and L refer to High, Medium, and Low probability respectively;
   N, P, and T refer to negative, positive, and neutral respectively.

b Increase or decrease in responses due to brain stimulation when monkey was dominant.

c Increase or decrease in responses during control sessions following brain stimulation
   sessions.

d Increase or decrease in responses due to brain stimulation when monkey was submissive.

e A6; nucl. ventralis posterior lateralis limiting nucl. pulvinaris oralis; motor
   response--none.

f A6; nucl. corporis geniculati medialis; motor response--lip retraction on right side
   of face, closure of right eye, usually jumped to upper cage and poststimulation barking.

g A6; fornix, corpus; motor response--head and body turned 45° to right.

h A6; nucl. corporis geniculati medialis magnocellularis; motor response--head jerked to
   the right.

i A7; nucl. tractus spinalis nervi trigemini; motor response--mouth opened and teeth
   slightly exposed, head turned 90° to left, left hand moved up and left eye closed.

j A7; colliculus inferior, deep placement; motor response--retraction of right upper lip,
   right arm raised and head tilted left.

k A7; midline and at base of brain in anterior limit of pedunculus cerebri; motor response--
   head tilted back, eyes closed.

l A7; tractus spinalis nervi trigemini; motor response--head and body tilted 45° to left.

Table 7

Relationship between the probability with which brain
stimulation was classified as aversive and the
occurrence of poststimulation aggression. Data
represent all stimulations (each electrode
was stimulated at several different
intensities) defined as aversive

	Number of stimulations eliciting aggression	Range of aggression (%) elicited	Number of stimulations without aggression
Low-Negative (.2-.59)[a]	3	13-28	3
Medium-Negative (.6-.79)	0		1
High-Negative (.8-1.0)	22	8-100	22

[a] Probability with which brain stimulation was classified
aversive.

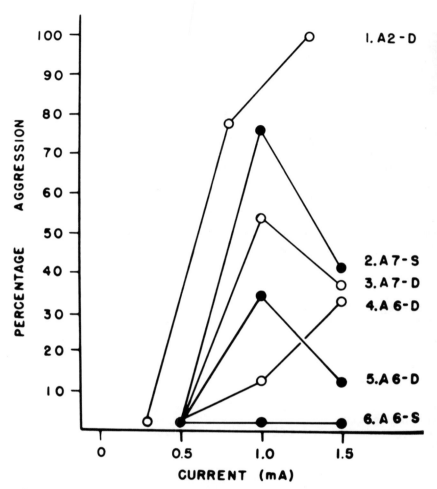

Figure 7. Relationship between stimulus intensity and
percentage of poststimulation aggression. Stimulus
duration held constant: 0.1 sec for A6 & A7; 0.5 sec
for A2. D and S indicate dominant and submissive.
Electrode points stimulated: (1) substantia nigra, pars
compacta; (2 & 3) nucl. tractus spinalis nervi trigemini;
(4) nucl. reticularis magnocellularis; (5) nucl. corporis
geniculati medialis; and (6) same area as in 4 and 5.

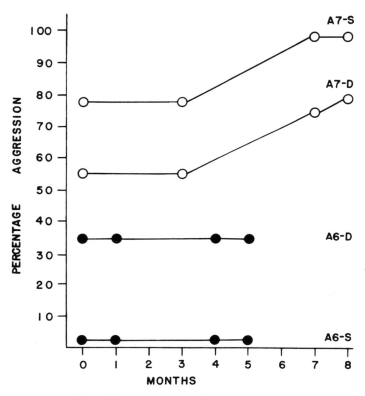

Figure 8. Reliability across time of poststimulation
aggression elicited by aversive brain stimulation of same
area with same parameters. D and S indicate dominant and
submissive. A7 stimulated in nucl. tractus spinalis
nervi trigemini (1.0 mA, 0.2 sec) and A6 stimulated in
nucl. corporis geniculati medialis (1.0 mA, 0.1 sec) with
120 stimulations in each condition.

lation sessions. Normally, A7 did not mount its dominant partner.

    Noxious brain stimulation and aggression. Table 7 shows that some brain stimulations classified as aversive with a low probability or a high probability elicited aggression while other did not. There was no way to predict from bar press performance which of the 44 high probability aversive brain stimulations would elicit aggression. Low probability aversive brain stimulation did not elicit aggression more than 28% of the time (120 stimulations) while, in some cases, high probability aversive brain stimulations elicited aggression 70-100% of the time. Although boss of the colony and normally aggressive, A0 never made aggressive responses following aversive brain stimulation.

    Figure 7 shows the relationship between intensity of noxious brain stimulation and percentage aggression elicited. With duration constant, as intensity of stimulation was increased, aggressive interactions were observed to increase or decrease. It was difficult to test effects of different stimulus durations on elicitation of aggression, since the motor movement at stimulus durations longer than 0.5 or 1.0 seconds was very pronounced.

    Throughout testing, stimulation (aversive) of the same electrode reliably elicited aggression (Figure 8). During the five month test period, noxious stimulation elicited a constant percentage of aggression (34%) when A6 was dominant, and no aggression when it was submissive. At the end of the eight month test period, whether dominant or submissive, A7 made more aggressive responses following aversive stimulation than when initially tested. Thus, poststimulation aggression did not habituate, but either remained constant or increased.

    Drugs and evoked aggression. Since aversive stimulation reliably elicited aggression, we explored methods to inhibit poststimulation aggression. Morphine, chlorpromazine, positive and neutral brain stimulation were paired with aversive brain stimulation, as shown in Table 8. In monkey A6, aversive stimulation was followed by one second of positive or neutral brain stimulation which inhibited poststimulation aggression but not the instrumental response. Morphine (3 mg/kg) or chlorpromazine (.75 mg/kg)

Table 8

Inhibiting effects of positive or neutral brain stimulation (EBS) and drugs on poststimulation aggression elicited by aversive EBS. Data from 120 stimulations for each condition in which monkey was dominant (Dom) and submissive (Sub).

Drug or EBS preceding Aversive EBS	Aversive EBS	Positive or Neutral EBS following Aversive EBS	% Aggression Dom	% Aggression Sub	Decreased Social Responses Dom*	Decreased Social Responses Sub*	Decreased Lever Pressing Dom*
				Monkey A7			
	EBS[b]		63[a]	84[a]	PG,GP IG	PG,GP IG	Yes
	EBS[b]	EBS[c] POSITIVE	4**	29**	PG,GP IG,BG	PG,GP IG	Yes
	EBS[b]	EBS[d] NEUTRAL	10**	25**	PG,GP IG,BG TG	PG	Yes
EBS[c]	EBS[b]		16**	70	PG,GP IG,BG TG	PG,GP IG	Yes
1 mg/Kg 30 min	EBS[b]		34*	67	PG,GP IG,BG TG	GP,PG TG	Yes

Table 8. Continued, page 2

3 mg/Kg MORPHINE	30 min	EBS[b]	0**	0** PG,GP IG,BG TG	PG,GP TG	Yes
.75 mg/Kg CHLORPRO-MAZINE	30 min	EBS[b]	4**	---	PG,GP IG,BG TG	Yes

Monkey A6

EBS[e]	35[a]	0[a] BG,TG PG	None	No
EBS[f] POSITIVE ... EBS[e]	0**	0 BG,TG PG	PG,BG TG	No
EBS[g] NEUTRAL ... EBS[e]	0**	0 BG	None	No
3 mg/Kg MORPHINE	30 min	EBS[e]	0**	-- None	----	No
.75 mg/Kg CHLORPRO-MAZINE	30 min	EBS[e]	0**	-- BG,TG	----	No

[a]Mean of 360 stimulations; [b]Nucl tractus spinalis nervi trigemini, 0.2 sec duration, 1.0 mA; [c]Nucl centrum medianum, 5.0 sec duration, 0.5 mA; [d]Nucl ventralis lateralis, 5.0 sec duration, 0.3 mA; [e]Nucl corporis geniculati medialis, 0.1 sec duration, 1.0 mA; [f]Lobus anterior cerebelli, 1.0 sec duration, 0.5 mA; [g]Pedunculus cerebri, 1.0 sec duration, 0.5 mA; *Significant at 0.05; **Significant at 0.01.

given IP 30 min before testing, suppressed poststimulation
aggression but did not inhibit the motor response to stimulation or the instrumental response. Morphine along had no
effect on grooming, sexual, instrumental, or aggressive
responses while chlorpromazine suppressed grooming interactions. In monkey A7, aversive brain stimulation followed
by five seconds of positive or neutral stimulation inhibited
poststimulation aggression. Aversive stimulation preceded
by five seconds of positive stimulation inhibited aggression
but not motor reaction to stimulation. Morphine, in the
absence of brain stimulation, had no behavioral effects,
while chlorpromazine suppressed social and instrumental
responses. The smaller dosage of morphine (1 mg/Kg) did
not significantly inhibit aggression when A7 was submissive.

    <u>Aversive stimulation and passive avoidance</u>. To test
whether aversive brain stimulation would motivate new learning, each time A7 touched the food lever, mounted, groomed,
or was groomed by its partner, it received 0.2 sec of aversive brain stimulation every two seconds until contact behavior ceased. As shown in Table 9, if A7 was dominant, 13
aversive stimulations significantly suppressed lever pressing and all social contact; if A7 was submissive, 8 reinforcements inhibited all social contact. Thus, A7 was conditioned to avoid social contact with its dominant and submissive partner and to avoid lever pressing for food. During control periods following aversive stimulation, A7,
whether dominant or submissive, showed a significant increase in grooming interactions.

    <u>Aggression and conditioning</u>. To determine whether
poststimulation aggression could be conditioned, a five-
second tone (Scientific Prototype Audio Stimulator set at
maximum frequency and intensity) preceded the 0.2 sec
aversive brain stimulation and terminated at onset of
stimulation. This occurred once every 24 seconds for 30
min or 60 pairings. Then, the tone was presented alone for
60 trials, once every 25 sec. This one hour session was
repeated twice daily and with A7 dominant and submissive.
Previous testing had indicated that the tone alone had no
effect on behavior. As shown in Figure 9, poststimulation
aggression was not conditioned and A7 made no conditioned
motor responses. A conditioned response was defined as a
response which resembled the stereotypic motor reaction
produced by brain stimulation.

Table 9

Conditioning monkey A7 to avoid social contact and lever pressing with aversive brain stimulation as punishment. Stimulation of Nucl tractus spinalis nervi trigemini (0.2 sec duration, 1.0 mA) continued every 2 sec until social contact or lever pressing for food pellets ceased. Data from two 30 min sessions when A7 was dominant and submissive.

DOMINANT

RESPONSE	CONDITIONING[a]	CONTROL[b]
Initiates grooming	0*	22**
Grooms partner (sec)	0*	642
Number of times groomed	5	28**
Groomed by partner (sec)	0*	601
Mounts partner	1	0
Pressing lever (sec)	7**	600
Total stimulations	13	

SUBMISSIVE

	CONDITIONING[a]	CONTROL[b]
Initiates grooming	5	50**
Grooms partner (sec)	0*	2133
Number of times groomed	3	19*
Groomed by partner (sec)	0	805
Pressing lever (sec)	0	0
Total stimulations	8	

a Scores summed for two 30 min sessions
b Scores summed for two 30 min control sessions which
   followed the two conditioning sessions
* Significant at 0.05
** Significant at 0.01

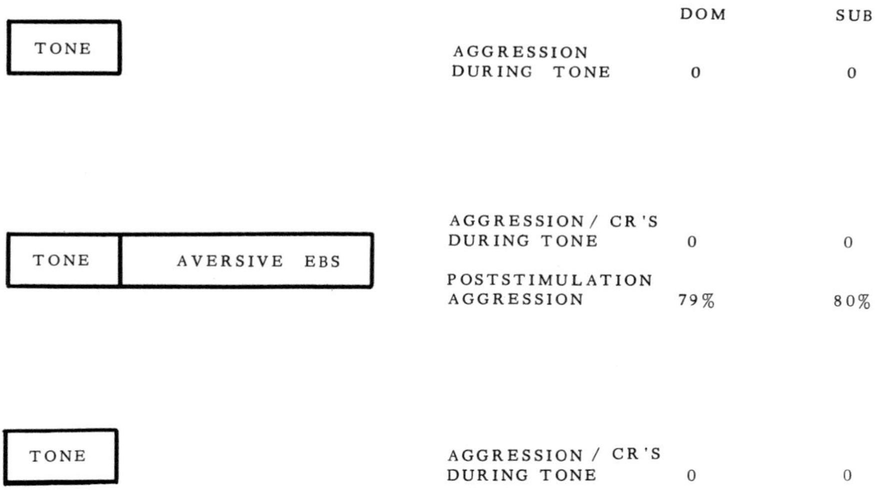

	DOM	SUB
TONE		
AGGRESSION DURING TONE	0	0

	DOM	SUB
TONE | AVERSIVE EBS		
AGGRESSION / CR'S DURING TONE	0	0
POSTSTIMULATION AGGRESSION	79%	80%

	DOM	SUB
TONE		
AGGRESSION / CR'S DURING TONE	0	0

Figure 9. An attempt to condition either the poststimulation aggressive response or the motor response produced by
aversive electrical brain stimulation (EBS). Monkey A7 was
stimulated in nucl. tractus spinalis nervi trigemini (1.0
mA, 0.2 sec) with 120 stimulations in each condition. CR
refers to conditioned response.

% POSTSTIMULATION AGGRESSION

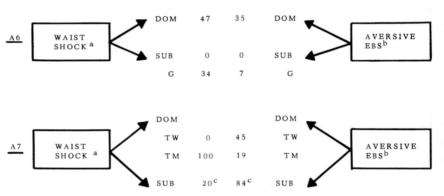

Figure 10.   Comparison of poststimulation aggression
elicited by aversive electrical brain stimulation (EBS)
and waist shock.

a Data from 60 trials
b Mean percentage of 360 trials.   A7 stimulated in nucl.
  tractus spinalis nervi trigemini (1.0 mA, 0.2 sec) and
  A6 stimulated in nucl. corporis geniculati medialis
  (1.0 mA, 0.1 sec).
c Threatening toward outside window.

Aggression elicited by aversive brain stimulation and peripheral shock. The frequency and kind of aggressive response elicited by skin shock was compared with that produced by aversive brain stimulation. A radio controlled skin shock source was strapped on the monkey's back and shock was applied across two electrodes that formed a belt. Sixty shocks were given (one every 25 sec.) to A6 and A7 when they were dominant and submissive. As seen in Figure 10, both skin shock and aversive brain stimulation elicited poststimulation aggression, but with somewhat different frequencies. In A6, the frequency of attack was similar following shock and aversive brain stimulation, but skin shock elicited a much higher percentage of grimaces. Following skin shock, A7 always attacked or threatened its submissive partner and never threatened the window. Following aversive brain stimulation A7 threatened its partner less frequently and the window more frequently. When submissive, A7 threatened window more frequently following aversive brain stimulation than after skin shock. Thus, skin shock elicited more frequent intra-monkey aggressive interactions than did aversive brain stimulation. The same kind of attacking and threatening response followed skin shock and noxious brain stimulation. In A0, boss of the colony, aggression was never elicited by aversive brain stimulation, but was produced following radio controlled skin shock.

Similar to aversive brain stimulation, the direction, occurrence and expression of the aggressive response following skin shock was determined by social rank. Following skin shock, A6, dominant, attacked or threatened the submissive monkey and when submissive, A6 grimaced without being attacked. Neither A6 nor A7 showed postshock aggression against its dominant partner. Thus, social rank determined whether skin shock produced a dominant, submissive or no aggressive response. Similar to aversive brain stimulation, skin shock inhibited all grooming responses during the shock session, and in addition, suppressed all grooming interactions during control observations one and a half hour later.

In the above experiment, only one monkey in a pair was shocked or stimulated. Would the aggressive pattern remain stable if both monkeys were shocked: To answer this question, A6 and A7 were tested with their partners on a shock grid in cage #3. Figure 11 shows that although both

% POSTSTIMULATION AGGRESSION

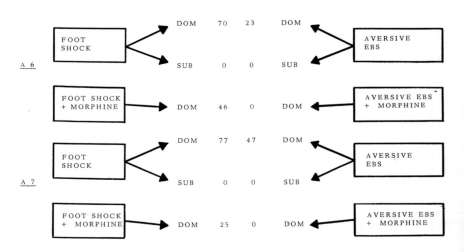

Figure 11.   Percentage of and effects of morphine on poststimulation aggression elicited by aversive electrical
brain stimulation (EBS) and foot shock.   Monkeys tested
in cage #3 with 120 stimulations in each condition.   Brain
areas and parameters of stimulation same as in Figure 10.

monkeys were shocked, postshock aggression was always
initiated by the dominant partner, and percentage of aggression was higher than after noxious brain stimulation.
Since morphine had completely inhibited aggression following aversive brain stimulation, we tested its effect on
postshock aggression. Morphine, administered IP 30 min
before testing suppressed but did not completely inhibit
postshock aggression. Although drugged, A6 and A7 were
never attacked by their submissive partners.

From the above comparison of noxious stimuli, it can
be concluded that: (1) skin shock, foot shock, and some
noxious brain stimulation were effective stimuli for
eliciting aggression; (2) the direction, occurrence, and
kind of aggressive response elicited by these noxious
stimuli were determined by social rank; (3) skin and foot
shock elicited a higher percentage of aggressive responses
than did aversive brain stimulation; (4) in one monkey
(AO) waist shock elicited aggression, although aversive
brain stimulation of three different areas did not; (5)
similar patterns of aggressive responses were observed
following skin shock, foot shock and aversive brain
stimulation; and (6) in addition to elicitation of aggression, noxious stimuli significantly suppressed grooming
interactions.

Targets for aggression. Since we found that social
rank determined occurrence, frequency and kind of intra-
species aggression elicited by stimulation, we explored
effects of different stimuli on poststimulation aggression
and results are shown in Table 10. Following aversive
brain stimulation A6, restrained, threatened a toy tiger
(Figure 12) most frequently and a dominant partner and
mirror least frequently; A6, unrestrained, threatened a
toy tiger most frequently and dominant partner and mirror
least frequently. A7, restrained, threatened mirror most
frequently and never threatened human or dominant partner;
A7, unrestrained, threatened mirror and toy tiger most
frequently and dominant partner and human least. When A6
and A7 were restrained and shocked with a familiar human
present, A6 threatened more frequently (99%) following
shock than aversive brain stimulation (14%) while A7 never
threatened a human. Following shock or aversive brain
stimulation, AO restrained or unrestrained never threatened
a familiar or unfamiliar human. Thus, after either noxious
brain stimulation or foot shock, two monkeys never threaten-

Table 10

Percentage of poststimulation aggression elicited by aversive electrical brain stimulation (AEBS) and peripheral shock to different stimuli when monkey was restrained and unrestrained. A6 was stimulated in Nucl corporis geniculati medialis (0.1 sec duration, 1.0 mA) and A7 was stimulated in Nucl tractus spinalis nervi trigemini (0.2 sec duration, 1.0 mA) with 60 stimulations in each condition.

Monkey	Stimulus	% Poststimulation Aggression		
		Restrained		Unrestrained
		AEBS	Shock	AEBS
A6	Mirror	0		0
	Toy Tiger	100		83
	Familiar Human	14	99	32
	Unfamiliar Human	73		77
	Dominant Monkey	0		0
	Submissive Monkey	28		34
A7	Mirror	88		91
	Toy Tiger	60		90
	Familiar Human	0	0	0
	Unfamiliar Human	0		0
	Dominant Monkey	0		0
	Submissive Monkey	57		47

Figure 12. Monkey A6 threatens toy tiger following
aversive brain stimulation (nucl. corporis geniculati
medialis, 1.0 mA, 0.1 sec).

ed a human. After aversive brain stimulation, the object
most frequently threatened differed for A6 and A7, but was
always a non-monkey stimulus.

    Electrode placement. Table 11 shows that stimula-
tion of 35 points in 19 different cerebral areas was aversive and that stimulation of 7 of these areas was neutral
or positive. In some cases, the different reinforcing
effects from the same area could be attributed to different
placements within the structure. For example, of eight
electrodes in cortex pyriformis, only stimulation of two
electrodes bordering the meninges were noxious. Within the
amygdala, stimulation of nucleus lateralis was aversive
while that of nuclei centralis and basalis were not.
Stimulation of corpus mamillare was aversive while two
electrodes in lateral and preoptic hypothalamus were positive and neutral respectively. Points in the commissura
supramamillaris and fasciculus mamillo thalamicus were
neutral. In other cases the different reinforming effects
from the same structure could not be explained anatomically.

    There were 49 electrodes in the thalamus of which
seven were aversive (basal portions of nuclei ventralis
lateralis, ventralis posterior medialis andlateralis and
corporis geniculati proper and its pars magnocellularis and
three elicited aggression. No aversive areas were found in
24 placements in nuclei medialis, centrum medianum, parafascicularis and other midline and intralaminar nuclei,
which have been thought to participate in the central
mediation of pain.

    Aggression was elicited from four of five placements
in the dorsolateral region of the mesencephalic tegmentum
(anterior coordinate 7.5-8.5). The dorsal limit of this
area was formed by nuclei ventralis posterior lateralis and
medialis; the medial limit was the substantia grisea centralis; and the lateral limit was formed by an area extending from the fasciculus thalamicus and lenticularis to the
ventral lateral medial part of the nucleus subthalamicus,
substantia nigra (pars compacta) and pedunculus cerebri
lateral to fossa interpeduncularis. Placements which were
partially enclosed by the above area and extending caudally
were positive reinforcing and included the nucleus and
decussatio tegmenti ventralis (limiting substantia nigra,
pars diffusa) the fasciculus longitudinalis medialis,
tractus tegmenti centralis and nucleus reticularis mesen-

Table 11

Relationship between brain areas, reinforcing properties
of stimulation and elicitation of aggression

Aversive brain stimulation AND aggression	Positive brain stimulation NO aggression
Cortex pyriformis, bordering meninges (1)a	Hippocampus (1)
Nucl. ventralis lateralis, pars medialis (1)	Fornix, corpus (1)
Nucl. ventralis posterior medialis (1)	Area hypothalamica lateralis (1)
Nucl. corporis geniculati medialis (1)	Nucl. anterior ventralis (2)
Area tegmentalis, fasciculi thalamicus	Nucl. ventralis posterior lateralis limiting
and lenticularis; and, limiting	nucl. pulvinaris oralis (1)
substantia grisea centralis (2)	Nucl. centrum medianum (2)
Substantia nigra, pars compacta (2)	Nucl. medialis dorsalis (3)
Colliculus inferior, deep placement (1)	Nucl. and decussatio tegmenti ventralis
Tractus spinalis nervi trigemini (2)	limiting substantia nigra (3)
Nucl. tractus spinalis nervi	Area tegmentalis, ventromedial (4)
trigemini (2)	Fasciculus longitudinalis medialis and tractus
Nucl. reticularis magnocellularis (1)	tegmentalis centralis (2)
	Nucl. reticularis mesencephali (2)
	Lobus anterior cerebelli (1)

Aversive brain stimulation NO aggression	Neutral brain stimulation NO aggression
Cortex pyriformis, bordering meninges (1)	Cortex pyriformis (6)
Nucl. amygdalae lateralis (1)	Gyrus uncinatus (5)
Nucl. ventralis posterior lateralis (1)	Gyrus hippocampi (2)
Substantia grisea centralis (5)	Gyrus hippocampi (2)
Lemniscus lateralis (1)	

Table 11.   Continued, Page 2

Nucl. caudatus (1)
Tractus opticus (1)
Area preoptica (1)
Commissura supramamillaris (1)
Fasciculus mamillothalamicus (1)
Nucl. ventralis anterior (1)
Nucl. anterior ventralis (2)
Nucl. ventralis lateralis (2)
Nucl. ventralis posterior lateralis (1)
Nucl. lateralis dorsalis (2)
Nucl. corporis geniculati lateralis (2)
Nucl. pulvinaris (4)
Stria medullaris (1)
Nucl. medialis dorsalis (11)
Nucl. centrum medianum (2)
Nucl. parafascicularis (1)
Nucl. paracentralis (2)
Nucl. centralis inferior (1)
Nucl. reuniens (2)
Area tegmentalis (5)
Nucl. ruber, pars parvocellularis (3)
Nervus oculomotorius (2)
Pedunculus cerebri (6)
Commissura posterior (2)
Colliculus superior, superficial
   placement (1)

Colliculus inferior, superficial placements (2)
Nucl. ventralis posterior medialis (1)
Nucl. corporis geniculati medialis
   magnocellularis (2)
Nucl. subthalamicus (1)
Pedunculus cerebri, lateral to fossa
   interpeduncularis (1)
Colliculus superior, deep placements (4)
Colliculus inferior, deep placements (2)
Gyrus dentatus (2)
Nucl. amygdalae centralis (1)
Nucl. amygdalae basalis (1)
Stria terminalis (2)
Fimbria hippocampi (1)
Cyrus cinguli (7)
Corpus callosum (7)
Capsula interna (4)
Globus pallidus (1)
Nucl. tractus mesencephalicus nervi
   trigemini (2)
Nucl. nervi abducentis (1)
Genu nervi facialis (1)
Nucl. reticularis parvocellularis (1)
Nucl. olivaris inferior (1)
Peduculus cerebellaris superior (4)
Lobus anterior cerebelli (5)
Crus I cerebelli (1)
Meninges, cerebellum (2)

a Refers to number of placements
  within the structure.

cephali.

In both colliculi, stimulation of deeper areas was noxious while stimulation of superficial areas was neutral. Of eight aversive points, only one elicited aggression. All five placements in the substantia grisea centralis were noxious but aggression was not evoked. All four placements in the tractus spinalis nervi trigemini were aversive and elicited aggression. Points in the tractus mesencephalicus were neutral. Placements in the lemniscus lateralis and in the nucleus reticularis magnocellularis, dorsal to lemniscus medialis, were aversive but only the latter produced aggression.

DISCUSSION

Brain stimulation and aggression. In the present study, primary aggression was never observed during or following stimulation of 117 neutral or positive brain areas. In agreement with a previous study (Delgado, 1965), during pilot work we observed one restrained monkey that infrequently threatened the experimenters during neutral stimulation and two monkeys that threatened during aversive stimulation. When these animals were unrestrained and stimulated in the presence of a submissive monkey at the same parameters and in the same electrodes that elicited aggression when restrained in the chair, no aggression was observed during or following brain stimulation. Since aggression can be elicited normally by movement in front of or toward a restrained monkey, aggression evoked by brain stimulation in the above monkeys was confounded with uncontrolled environmental conditions.

Although we found no evidence for primary aggression during neutral or positive brain stimulation, Robinson (1968) has reported primary aggression during non-aversive brain stimulation. This discrepancy might be explained by a difference in electrode location.

There is some evidence from other experiments that primary aggression has been elicited during neutral or positive brain stimulation. Previous studies on brain stimulation and aggression can be divided into three categories: studies on inter- or intra-species aggression elicited by brain stimulation without defining reinforcing effects

e.g., Adams, 1968; Akerman, 1966; Chapman, 1958; Delgado,
1966; Delgado et al., 1968; Heath & Mickle, 1960; Skultety,
1963; Ursin, 1964; Ursin & Kaada, 1960); studies on reinforcing properties of brain stimulation without investi-
gating inter- and intra-species aggression (e.g., Brown &
Cohen, 1959; Cohen & Brown, 1957; Delgado, Roberts & Miller,
1954; Miller, 1961; Roberts, 1958); and studies on prey-
catching elicited by brain stimulation and reinforcing
properties of brain stimulation sometimes defined (Adams &
Flynn, 1966; Egger & Flynn, 1963; Levison & Flynn, 1965;
McDonnell & Flynn, 1964; Roberts & Kiess, 1964; Sheard &
Flynn, 1967).

It can be concluded that (a) investigators have studied
either reinforcing affect of brain stimulation or aggression
but seldom both; (b) most research on brain stimulation and
aggression has been performed on cats and dealt mainly with
inter-species aggression; (c) disagreements in the literature about brain areas from which aggression was elicited
may be due to the involvement of different central mechanisms; and, (d) there is only one other paper which has
(Adams & Flynn) compared the aggressive responses elicited
by both shock and brain stimulation, without studying, however, intra-species aggression.

In order to clarify the distinction between primary and
secondary aggression elicited by brain stimulation, it is
suggested that future studies first define the reinforcing
properties of brain stimulation and then study both intra-
and inter-species aggression.

The procedures and problems of defining reinforcing
properties of brain stimulation have been discussed elsewhere (Hawkins & Pliskoff, 1964; Hodos & Valenstein, 1962;
Olds, 1962, Valenstein, 1964). There is one problem
especially relevant to our discussion of aggression. Approach (rewarding) and avoidance or escape (punishing)
responses have both been reported following stimulation of
the same electrode (Bower & Miller, 1958; Olds, 1960; Olds
& Olds, 1963). How would we explain the possibility that
aggression could be elicited by brain stimulation that was
both rewarding and punishing?

The statement that either rewarding or punishing
effects can be produced by stimulation of the same electrode

point is somewhat misleading since one would assume that
stimulus parameters were identical for elicitation of opposite reinforcing effects. But in these studies, rewarding
effects were produced by short durations of brain stimulation, while punishing effects were elicited by longer
stimulus durations. Bower & Miller (1958) found that rats
which showed an aversive effect from prolonged brain stimulation preferred relatively short intervals of that stimulation. Roberts (1958) also found that brain stimulation can
initially elicit a positively reinforcing state, followed
by a transition to an aversive state as the train of stimulus continues. Similarly, we found that stimulus duration
determined motivational effects. Brain stimulation of the
same electrode point was defined as neutral at duration of
0.1 sec and negative at 0.5 sec, with intensity held constant. Therefore, rewarding or punishing effects can be
obtained from the same electrode but with different stimulus
durations. More important, we found that the behavioral
response of the animal was directly related to the reinforcing effect of the stimulus, which in turn was related to
stimulus duration. When brain stimulation was defined as
neutral or positive, there was no poststimulation aggression.
But when this same brain stimulation was aversive, poststimulation aggression was observed. Therefore, rewarding
and punishing effects were NOT produced by the same brain
stimulation parameters and the occurrence of poststimulation
was directly related to the negative reinforcing effect of
the brain stimulation.

Aversive brain stimulation and aggression. In the
present study, aggression was always associated with aversive
brain stimulation, but all aversive brain stimulation did not
elicit aggression. We could not predict which aversive
brain stimuli would elicit aggression from the monkey's
instrumental performance in the chair since brain stimulation
defined as aversive with a high probability sometimes did and
sometimes did not elicit aggression. There are two interpretations of why all aversive brain stimulation did not
elicit aggression. First, there may be a qualitative difference in the aversiveness of brain stimuli, i.e., a stimulus
which elicited fear or startled the monkey may have been less
aversive than a stimulus which elicited sensations like those
produced by peripheral shock. It may be that only the latter
stimuli elicited aggression. Data from electrical brain
stimulation in humans supports the idea of a qualitative
difference in aversiveness of sensations. Patients reported

that some sensations were uncomfortable or requested that
the stimulation be terminated but did not describe these
sensations as painful and at other times described painful
sensations (Ervin & Mark, 1964; Monnier, 1968; Obrador &
Dierssen, 1966; Orthner & Roeder, 1966; Riechert, 1960).
Thus, there is evidence for sensations which may be aversive or uncomfortable but not painful.

Secondly, aversive brain stimulation that produced
aggression could have simultaneously stimulated an aversive
area whereas aversive brain stimulation that did not elicit
aggression might have stimulated only an aversive area.
This interpretation has difficulty explaining why aggression
was not observed on each stimulation if an aggressive area
was stimulated simultaneously. In addition, why would
morphine, which raises the threshold for noxious stimulation, abolish the aggressive response elicited by aversive
brain stimulation if an aggressive area was being stimulated simultaneously.

Since only aversive brain stimulation elicited aggression, and aggression always occurred after stimulation, and
morphine abolished the elicited aggression, we favor the
interpretation that brain stimulation defined as noxious,
produced aversive sensations which resulted in secondary
aggression. The mediating mechanism (aversive sensations)
is probably similar for aggression elicited by brain stimulation and peripheral shock, since both aversive stimuli
produced similar kinds of aggression.

It is possible that the aggressive response itself,
either through its execution, consequences, or autonomic
effects, is noxious to the animal. If this were true, any
stimuli associated with an aggressive response would be
avoided by the animal and therefore defined as noxious.
It would then be necessary to differentiate between brain
stimulation which was aversive and thus resulted in aggression from brain stimulation which was noxious because it
was associated with aggression which was aversive. It could
be shown that the aggressive response itself was non-aversive if an animal (a) worked to obtain a stimulus which
elicited an aggressive response, (b) was conditioned without
without punishment to perform aggressive responses, (c) did
not avoid or escape a stimulus that elicited aggression.
There is no evidence for condition (a), controversial
evidence for condition (b), and convincing evidence for

condition (c).

With regard to condition (b), animals have been conditioned to perform aggressive response with and without
punishment. Rats were classically conditioned to fight by
pairing a tone and foot shock (Vernon & Ulrich, 1966;
Cree, Hitzing & Schaeffer, 1966), and instrumentally conditioned with water (Ulrich et al., 1963) and intracranial
stimulation (Stachnik, Ulrich & Mabry, 1966) as reinforcements. These experiments would seem to indicate that the
aggressive response was not aversive, since it would be
difficult to condition an animal to perform a response
that was noxious. But it has been shown that under certain
conditions, animals will perform a response which is aversive. Rats crossed a shock grid to obtain water or intracranial stimulation (Olds & Sinclair, 1957). The response
of an animal crossing a shock grid (aversive) to obtain
water or brain stimulation may be similar to an animal
making an aggressive response (aversive) to obtain water or
brain stimulation. Therefore, conditioning aggressive behav-
ion without aversive reinforcement does not necessarily establish the reinforcing properties of that response.

There is evidence that brain stimulation was aversive
without the occurrence of aggression. In the present study,
monkeys restrained and tested in isolation worked to avoid
brain stimulation that produced no aggression. When the
monkey was stimulated with its submissive partner, aversive
brain stimulation often elicited aggression. Thus, the
occurrence of poststimulation aggression did not determine
the aversive properties of brain stimulation, since the
monkey previously worked to avoid this brain stimulation in
the absence of aggression.

Evidence that the aggressive response itself was non-
aversive was convincingly demonstrated by Robinson (1968).
Intra-species aggression was elicited by brain stimulation
which the monkeys neither worked to obtain or avoid. If
aggression itself was aversive, stimuli associated with the
aggressive response should be aversive. Since in the above
experiment (Robinson, 1968) brain stimulation which elicited
aggression was not aversive, we can conclude that the aggressive response itself was non-aversive. For this reason,
we believe that in our experiment brain stimulation was
aversive for reasons other than being associated with
aggression.

Other authors have discussed the possibility that
brain stimulation produced aggression by arousal of painful
or aversive sensations and concluded that (a) it seems unlikely that pain sensations contributed significantly to
elicitation of aggression (Nakao, 1958); (b) it is possible
that defense and escape response elicited by midbrain stimulation may be secondary to feeling pain (Kaada, 1967); (c)
there is some evidence that brain stimulation elicited
aggression secondary to arousal of unpleasant sensations
but cerebral mechanisms for perception of pain and aggression probably have different anatomical and physiological
organization (Delgado, 1966); and (d) even though cats
which were stimulated at placements yielding attack with
several forms of vocalization reacted to the hypothalamic
stimulation as they did to tail shock, it should not be
assumed that the two forms of stimulation elicit identical
responses (Adams & Flynn, 1966). Only additional research
can clarify the relationship between primary and secondary
aggression.

In most cases aggression elicited by noxious brain
stimulation could only occur after stimulation because of
competing motor effects produced by stimulation. If the
intensity of aversive stimulation was reduced so that no
motor reaction occurred during stimulation, the stimulation
became non-aversive and there was no aggression during or
after five seconds of stimulation. A strong motor reaction,
elicited by brain stimulation, never elicited aggression
unless the monkey also avoided that stimulation. Neutral
or positive brain stimulations, which were aversive at
different parameters, did not elicit aggression at the
neutral or positive parameters.

Poststimulation aggression elicited by noxious brain
stimulation was similar in expression to that observed during
normal aggressive interactions. Aggression was directed
either against another monkey, window, human, or toy tiger
and, if none of these stimuli were present, no aggression
was observed.

In agreement with previous work (Delgado, 1967; Delgado
& Mir, 1969), social dominance rank of the stimulated monkey
determined not only the occurrence and direction but also
the kind of aggressive response. In the colony, a stimulated
monkey attacked a submissive monkey, and never attacked a

dominant monkey. In paired testing, the stimulated monkey
attacked its submissive partner. When its dominant partner
was present, the stimulated monkey never attacked, but instead either displaced its aggression by threatening a
window, showed a submissive gesture (grimace), or made no
aggressive response. Thus, depending on the social dominance rank, the same brain stimulation elicited opposite
poststimulation aggressive response (threat or grimace),
no aggressive responses, or displaced aggressive responses.
Since social dominance rank may be equally important deter-
minant in other species, the rank of the stimulated animal
should be clearly established.

     Robinson (1968) has reported that during non-aversive
brain stimulation, a submissive monkey attacked a dominant
monkey. In our experiment, we never observed a reversal in
dominance during or after brain stimulation or shock. This
difference may be due to the fact that in our monkeys
social dominance roles were established during a three week
period, while in Robinson's experiment, the social roles
were established in a two hour session.

     Has aversive brain stimulation been shown to elicit
secondary aggression in other animals? There are no experiments in which reinforcing effects of brain stimulation were
determined and intra-species aggression was studied (except
for present experiment and Robinson's). Results from
studies on inter-species aggression and prey-catching indicate that cats avoided or escaped from brain stimulation
(aversive) which elicited the following aggressive responses: defense, rage or anger (Adams & Flynn, 1966;
Brown & Cohen, 1959; Cohen & Brown, 1957); flight, fear,
or alarm (Delgado et al., 1954; Roberts, 1958); and
affective attack (Adams & Flynn, 1966). Thus, in the cat
as in the monkey, there is evidence for secondary aggression
elicited by aversive brain stimulation. This indicates the
importance of future differentiation between primary and
secondary aggression.

     Effects of brain stimulation on non-aggressive re-
sponses. In addition to eliciting aggression, aversive
brain stimulation also suppressed social and instrumental
responses. The inhibition of these responses was not
specific to aversive brain stimulation, since some neutral
and positive brain stimulation, which did not elicit aggression, also significantly suppressed responses. Social re-

sponses were suppressed independently of instrumental responses, which indicates the importance of utilizing multiple test conditions. If only social responses were observed,
one might conclude that a monkey was incapacitated by brain
stimulation, but we found that although a monkey did not
interact socially during brain stimulation, it could press
a lever for food. Several combinations of changes in
grooming interactions and sexual responses during and after
stimulation were observed. Social responses suppressed
during brain stimulation sessions more often increased than
decreased during later control periods. Grooming and sexual
responses which increased during stimulation sessions were
observed to increase during control periods. The only predictable relationship was that aversive brain stimulation
which elicited poststimulation aggression always suppressed
grooming and usually instrumental responses. Aversive brain
stimulation which did not elicit aggression usually did not
disrupt grooming or instrumental behaviors.

Parameters and reliability of aversive brain stimulation. When the intensity of aversive brain stimulation was
increased, duration held constant, percentage of poststimulation aggression either increased or decreased. Similar
results have been reported for aggression elicited by foot
shock, in which an increase in shock intensity either resulted in increased fights (Dreyer & Church, 1968) or fewer
fights, due to increasing debilitating effect of shock
(Ulrich & Asrin, 1962). The reason for decreased percentage
of aggression following highest intensity of brain stimulation is difficult to explain. Since the stimulus duration
was so brief (0.1-0.5 sec), a monkey was not debilitated by
the motor reaction elicited by brain stimulation at higher
intensities. Perhaps spread of electrode current to adjacent areas at higher intensities inhibited poststimulation
aggression, or the higher stimulus intensities were so
aversive that the monkey was disoriented following stimulation.

The reinforcing properties of aversive brain stimulation were evaluated with several learning tasks. We found
that noxious brain stimulation: (1) motivated new behav-
ior--lever pressing to avoid stimulation; and (2) served as
punishment in two passive avoidance tasks--lever pressing
for food and social contact. When A7 was punished with
aversive brain stimulation for each social contact, the
number of social contacts significantly increased during

control periods an hour and a half after the stimulation
session (long-term effects). Thus, not only did aversive
brain stimulations inhibit social and instrumental responses for one hour, but these same social responses
significantly rebounded in later control periods.

Similar results on analogous learning tasks were reported in cats following noxious brain stimulation (Delgado
et al., 1954). Neither that study nor the present experiments found any motivational properties associated with
various motor reactions elicited by neutral brain stimulation. A difference in instrumental responding to noxious
brain stimulation was found between the present study and
previous reports on the dat (Delgado et al., 1954; Roberts,
1958). When a flight-like response elicited by hypothalamic
stimulation was used as the aversive stimulus, cats showed
no avoidance responding but learned to escape from this same
stimulus (Roberts, 1958). No avoidance-escape dichotomy was
found for monkeys in the present study. Similar to the
findings in cats (Miller, 1961) and monkeys (Delgado, 1966)
that centrally aroused rage could not be classically conditioned, we found that in monkeys poststimulation aggression elicited by noxious brain stimulation was not conditioned.

Various degrees of response fatigability or habituation
to brain stimulation have been reported (Delgado, 1966;
Delgado & Mir, 1966; Ursin, Wester, & Ursin, 1967). No
fatigability or habituation was found in the occurrence of
poststimulation aggression elicited by noxious brain stimulation either across daily sessions or across time (5-8
months).

A response elicited by brain stimulation of one area
can be facilitated or inhibited by a simultaneously-occur-
ring brain stimulation of a different area (Egger & Flynn,
1963; Holst & Paul, 1962,1963; McDonnell & Flynn, 1964). In
agreement with later studies, we found that either neutral
or positive brain stimulation as well as morphine or chlorpromazine would significantly inhibit the poststimulation
aggressive response. The inhibition produced by neutral or
positive brain stimulation cannot be attributed solely to
the elicitation of competing motor response, since other
social and instrumental responses were not inhibited when
neutral or positive stimulation were presented alone.
Morphine selectively inhibited poststimulation aggression

without affecting either the motor reaction to stimulation
or other social and instrumental responses. Chlorpromazine
inhibited poststimulation aggression, but also suppressed
social and instrumental responses. We had predicted that
morphine would have a greater inhibiting effect on poststimulation aggression than chlorpromazine. Morphine has
been shown to reduce sensitivity to aversive brain stimulation (Vernier et al., 1961) while chlorpromazine did not
block the rage reaction elicited by hypothalamic stimulation in cats (Funderburk, Foxwell, & Hakala, 1967). Our
prediction was not confirmed, since both morphine and
chlorpromazine had similar inhibiting effects on aggression.

There is one major difference between our study and
reports of aggression elicited by brain stimulation in ducks
(Phillips, 1964), pigeons (Akerman, 1966), chickens (Holst
& Paul, 1962), opossums (Roberts et al., 1967), cats (Adams,
1968; Delgado, 1955; Wasman & Flynn, 1962), and monkeys
(Penfield & Jasper, 1954). In the present study, aggression always occurred after stimulation, while in the above
studies aggression occurred during stimulation. Our study
is in agreement with a series of experiments on brain
stimulation in free monkeys (Delgado, 1955, 1959, 1962,
1963, 1964, 1965a, 1965b, 1966, 1967, 1968). In the latter
experiments aggression was elicited during brain stimulation in only two monkeys and after stimulation in eight
monkeys.

Similar to results on monkeys, aggression has rarely
been reported during brain stimulation in humans. There is
a report of rage elicited during stimulation which was described as not painful (Heath, Monroe, & Mickle, 1955) but
this response varied between rage and fear on subsequent
tests. One patient, in a fit of rage, threw herself against
a wall following seven sec of amygdaloid stimulation
(Delgado et al., 1968), but it is difficult to evaluate the
aggressive content of this response. There are reports of
brain stimulation in humans that elicited fear but not
aggression (Chapman, 1958; Jasper & Rasmussen, 1956;
Penfield et al., 1954) and neither fear nor aggression
(Kaada, 1967; Lesse, 1957).

Thus, it is difficult to elicit aggression during
brain stimulation in either humans or monkeys, probably
because the brain areas are difficult to localize, and the
occurrence of aggression may be significantly influenced by

environmental and learning factors.

Comparison of aggression elicited by skin shock and aversive brain stimulation. If aggression can be mediated by aversive sensations, one would predict that similar aggressive responses could be elicited by shock and noxious brain stimulation. The stimulus intensity of shock and brain stimulation should be equated if the behavioral responses they elicit are compared. A method has been described for determining the threshold of aversive brain stimulation (Nakao, 1958) and foot shock (Weiss & Laties, 1959), and could be used to equate intensities. Since the two studies which compared aggression elicited by noxious brain stimulation and shock did not equate stimulus intensity, a qualified answer must be given to the above question.

In the present study: (a) foot or waist shock elicited postshock aggression similar to that elicited by noxious brain stimulation; (b) the occurrence, direction, and kind of aggressive response elicited by either shock or noxious brain stimulation was dependent on the monkey's social rank; (c) the aggression elicited by shock occurred on a larger percentage of trials than that following noxious brain stimulation; (d) morphine and chlorpromazine had a similar inhibiting effect on poststimulation aggression, whether elicited by brain stimulation or shock; and (e) shock and noxious brain stimulation that elicited aggression significantly decreased grooming interactions. The higher percentage of aggression produced by shock with respect to brain stimulation-induced aggression may be due to a higher intensity of shock stimulus, rather than to a difference in reinforcing effects of shock and noxious brain stimulation.

In another study, Adams & Flynn (1966) compared the affective and quiet biting attack elicited by noxious brain stimulation with that elicited by tail shock. These authors concluded that the two forms of stimulation elicited different but overlapping responses. The halloween stance elicited by hypothalamic stimulation was never observed to tail shock and attack elicited by tail shock led to biting any part of the rat's body, while attack due to brain stimulation was commonly directed at the rat's neck. Before it is concluded that peripheral shock elicits a different kind of response than brain stimulation, it is necessary to equate stimulation and/or explore different parameters of shock to deter-

mine if responses similar to brain stimulation can be
elicited.

On the basis of these two experiments, we conclude
that shock and brain stimulation elicit similar aggressive
responses in monkeys and perhaps different aggressive and
prey-catching responses in cats.

Environmental conditions and brain stimulation. Aggressive responses elicited by noxious brain stimulation
were consistent for a monkey (A6 and A7), restrained or
unrestrained, when tested with its dominant and submissive
partner; familiar and unfamiliar human; mirror and toy
tiger. But, specific targets to which aggressive responses
were directed, were different between monkeys, i.e., after
noxious brain stimulation, one monkey (A7) never threatened
humans but threatened a mirror, while another monkey (A6)
threatened humans but never threatened a mirror. Both
monkeys, unrestrained, threatened or attacked a toy tiger
more than their submissive monkey partners. We tested
whether two monkeys (A7 and A0) which never threatened a
human (familiar or unfamiliar) following aversive brain
stimulation, would threaten a human following a different
noxious stimulus. We found that neither monkey threatened
a human (familiar or unfamiliar) following shock.

In agreement with previous studies (Holst & Paul, 1962,
1963; Levison & Flynn, 1965), our results demonstrate the
importance of carefully specifying the conditions under
which aggression is elicited and of testing an animal with
multiple stimuli. In addition to using a multiple-stimuli
test situation, the baseline aggressive response rate should
be determined since Ursin (1964) found that cats with varying backgrounds (wild, moderately wild, tame) differed
reliably in their aggressive responses to a standard series
of provocations supplied by experimenter. Thus, discrepan-
cies in previous results on aggression elicited by brain
stimulation may be due to the animals' background, differences in aggressive response rates, and/or to the animals'
preferences for different stimuli to attack and threaten.
This is especially true of experiments which studied aggression elicited by brain stimulation in restrained animals with
humans as the only stimuli.

Relationship between central pain areas and aversive
brain stimulation. There are two problems in discussing the

relationship between aversive brain stimulation and central
mediation of pain. First, although excellent work has been
done on the cerebral structures mediating pain (Bowsher,
1957, 1961; Mehler, 1966), our knowledge of these areas is
far from complete. Second, our electrode placements were
not extensive enough within a single structure to explain
in all cases the different reinforcing effects obtained
from stimulation of the same area.

Knowledge of the central mediation of pain has been
expanded by studies on brain stimulation and lesion data
from humans undergoing treatment for intractable pain and
extra-pyramidal motor disturbances. Although reports of
subjective sensations elicited by brain stimulation in the
course of above treatment are valuable, there are inter-
pretative problems because patients with intractable pain
have a strong tendency for reacting to central and peripheral stimuli with reports of pain (Ervin & Mark, 1960,
1964; Obrador & Dierssen, 1966; Olds, 1960, 1962, 1963;
Olds & Sinclair, 1957), while some patients with extra-
pyramidal motor disturbances may have diminished reactivity.

In interpreting the aversive effects elicited by brain
stimulation the possible involvement of pain mechanisms has
to be considered. Stimulation of the nucleus ventralis
posterior lateralis and medialis were aversive (only stimulation of the latter elicited aggression) and these areas
have been shown to participate in the mediation of pain
(Bowsher, 1957, 1961; Hassler, 1968; Kruger, 1966; Mehler,
1962). Stimulation of nucleus ventralis posterior lateralis
and medialis in human patients with illnesses other than
intractable pain, indicated that although pain was rarely
reported, unpleasant sensations, generally well localized
and described as numbness, electricity, tingling needles
were often described (Ervin & Mark, 1960, 1964; Gybels,
1968; Moyer, 1968; Olds, 1960, Penfield & Jasper, 1954)
indicating a differentiation between painful and unpleasant
sensations elicited by brain stimulation.

The basal and medial portion of the nuclei ventralis
lateralis may be related to aversive sensations because
spinothalamic fibers, which mediate pain, projects to and
overlaps with cerebellar projections to this area (Mehler,
1966).

Four electrodes in the nucleus corporis geniculati medialis (only one produced aggression) and its pars magnocellularis were aversive while two points in the nucleus geniculi lateralis were not. There is evidence that spinothalamic fibers project to the region of the corporis geniculati medialis and its pars magnocellularis although the extent of this projection has not yet been determined (Poirier et al., 1968; Mehler, 1966). This region is contiguous with the caudal part of the nuclei ventralis posterior medialis and aversive points were distributed throughout this area which has been called the "Po" region.

Twenty-four electrodes were located in a general area that may participate in the mediation of poorly localized pain. This area includes the nuclei centralis lateralis and parafascicularis which receives projection from the spinothalamic tract (Bowsher, 1957; Mehler, 1962; Miller, 1961), and the nucleus centrum medianum for which projections from the spinothalamic tract have been proposed (Bowsher, 1957, 1961, 1962) and denied (Mehler, 1962, 1966a, 1966b). This disagreement may be due to species and nuclei delimitation differences. Brain stimulation of this area in humans elicits sensations which are difficult to describe; requests that the stimulation be terminated and not repeated (Ervin & Mark, 1960, 1964); and an exacerbation of spontaneous pain or occurrence of poorly localized unpleasant sensations (Sano et al., 1966). In the present study, the 24 electrodes located throughout this area (nucleus medialis dorsalis, near the lamina medullaris interna, in the nuclei paracentralis, parafascicularis, centrum medianum, centralis inferior and reuniens) produced neutral or positive reinforcing effects. Our results agree with recent anatomical evidence stressing the importance of the region of the nucleus corporis geniculati medialis rather than the above structures in mediating poorly localized pain.

Stimulation of five electrodes in the mesencephalic tegmentum produced aversive effect and aggression was elicited from four of them. These aversive effects may be due to stimulation of spinothalamic fibers which pass through this area on their way to the thalamus (Bowsher, 1957; Miller, 1961). The mesencephalic tegmentum is important in the central mediation of pain since lesions of the nuclei ventralis posterior, and intralaminar and midline nuclei did not abolish intractable pain in humans

and only the addition of mesencephatomy and basal thalatomy
produced long term relief from pain (Riechert, 1960; Ross,
1966; Stachnic et al., 1966). It should be noted that
differences between species in the location of brain areas
from which avoidance responses can be elicited by brain
stimulation (Olds & Sinclair, 1957) may be due to the fact
that in primates pain transmitting fibers in this area
adopt a more dorsolateral tegmental course than in the rat
or cat (Mehler, 1966b).

Electrodes located in the deeper layer of the colliculi
were aversive while the superficial layers proved to be
neutral. Five placements in the substantia grisea centralis
were aversive and none elicited aggression. These aversive
effects may be due to the spinothalamic fibers which project
to the medullary, pontine and mesencephalic reticular formation, superior and inferior colliculi, and substantia grisea
centrealis (Bowsher, 1957; Mehler, 1962; Miller, 1961).
Stimulation of these structures in cats and monkeys (Delgado,
1955; Magon et al., 1937; Spiegel & Wycis, 1966) produce
pain-like reactions. Stimulation of the mesencephalic tegmentum and adjacent substantia grisea centralis reproduced
a severe paroxysm of facial pain that the human patient had
felt spontaneously (Obrador & Dierssen, 1966).

It is significant that the four electrodes in the
tractus spinalis of nervi trigemini produced aggression
while two electrodes in the tractus mesencephalicus did not.
Clinically, it is well known that the tractus spinalis is
mainly related to pain while the tractus mesencephalicus is
not.

The aversive effects from stimulation of the cortex
pyriformis could be due to stimulation of the meninges,
though two placements in the meninges of cerebellus did
not produce noxious effects. Although there is no clear
explanation of the noxious effects from stimulation of the
nucleus lateralis of the amygdala, Jelasić (1966) has reported that in 7 of 14 patients an ipsilateral pain deep in
the forehead behind the eyes was elicited only from stimulation of the lateral part of the amygdala.

In summary, it is possible to trace the distribution of
aversive points as extending from the basal part of the
thalamus, through the dorsolateral tegmentum to more caudal
tegmental and tectal structures. With some exceptions most

of the areas with noxious properties were located in brain
structures which are known to participate in the central
mediation of pain.

With our histological procedures, it was not possible
to explain anatomically why stimulation of the same
structure elicited aversive effects in some cases with,
and in other cases without, aggressive effects. Possible
functional explanations have been discussed earlier.

SUMMARY

Intra- and inter-species aggression elicited by electrical brain stimulation has been reported in many different
animals. This aggression could be mediated centrally in two
different ways. Aggression, which we have called primary,
could be elicited by brain stimulation through cerebral
mechanisms that are independent of aversive sensations.
While aggression, referred to as secondary, could be
elicited by brain or peripheral stimulation which first
produced noxious sensations which subsequently cause aggression. By determining the reinforcing properties of
brain stimulation, it is possible to differentiate between primary and secondary aggression.

A total of 174 intracerebral electrodes were implanted
in seven rhesus monkeys in order to study the properties of
secondary aggression. The reinforcing effects of brain
stimulation were defined by discriminative analysis which
compared the monkey's operant performance on brain stimulation to its performance on known neutral (no reinforcement),
positive (food pellets), and negative (foot shock) reinforcers.

Results were as follows:

(a) Of the 174 points stimulated, 35 were defined as
having negative reinforcing properties (aversive electrical
brain stimulation = AEBS). From these AEBS points, 14
evoked aggression while 21 did not. One hundred and seven-
teen points were neutral or positive and did not elicit aggression.

(b) All evoked aggression occurred after and not during
brain stimulation.

(c) The occurrence, direction, and expression of the aggressive response elicited by AEBS or by skin shock, depended on the social rank of the stimulated monkey which attacked submissive monkeys but showed no aggression, redirected aggression, or a submissive response in the presence of a dominant partner.

(d) Peripheral shock elicited a higher percentage of poststimulation aggressive responses than did AEBS.

(e) AEBS which elicited aggression usually disrupted grooming interactions and lever pressing for food, while AEBS which had not elicited aggression usually did not disrupt the above responses.

(f) The instrumental avoidance pattern in the restrained monkey did not predict which of the 35 AEBS points would elicit aggression.

(g) Poststimulation aggression elicited by AEBS was reliable over eight months of testing.

(h) Neutral or positive brain stimulation suppressed aggression elicited by AEBS.

(i) Morphine and chlorpromazine inhibited aggression evoked by AEBS and by peripheral shock but did not suppress motor responses elicited by AEBS. In the absence of AEBS, morphine had no behavioral effects while chlorpromazine suppressed grooming interactions and lever pressing for food.

(j) When AEBS immediately followed a social contact or lever press for food, the monkey learned to avoid these responses.

(k) Aggression elicited by AEBS was not classically conditioned.

(1) Whether restrained or free the percentage of aggressive responses elicited by AEBS was consistent for each monkey tested singly with a dominant or submissive monkey, familiar or unfamiliar human, mirror or toy tiger. Differences, however, were observed between monkeys with respect to which and how frequently the above targets were threatened or attacked.

(m) Since in our experiment AEBS elicited aggression which always occurred after stimulation, we interpret this as evidence for the central elicitation of secondary aggression.

(n) Most areas with noxious properties were located in brain structures which are known to participate in the central mediation of pain.

REFERENCES

ADAMS, D. B. Cells related to fighting behavior recorded from midbrain central gray neuropil of cat. Science, 1968, 159, 894-896.

ADAMS, D. B. & FLYNN, J. P. Transfer of an escape response from tail shock to brain-stimulated attack behavior. J. Exp. Anal. Behav., 1966, 9, 401-408.

AKERMAN, B. Behavioral effects of electrical stimulation in the forebrain of the pigeon II. Protective behavior. Behaviour, 1966, 26, 339-349.

AKERT, K. In D. E. Sheer (Ed.), Electrical Stimulation of the Brain. Austin: University of Texas Press, 1961, p. 288.

ANAND, B. K., & DUA, S. Electrical stimulation of the limbic system of brain ("visceral brain") in waking animals. Indian J. Med. Res., 1956, 44, 107-119.

AZRIN, N. H., HUTCHISON, R., & HAKE, D. Pain-induced fighting in the squirrel monkey. J. Exp. Anal. Behav., 1963, 6, 620-621.

BOREN, J. J., & MALIS, J. L. Determining thresholds of aversive brain stimulation. Am. J. Physiol., 1961, 201, 429-433.

BOWER, G. H., & MILLER, N. E. Rewarding and punishing effects from stimulating the same place in the rat's brain. J. Comp. Physiol. Psychol., 1958, 51, 669-674.

BOWSHER, D. Termination of the central pain pathway in
    man; the conscious appreciation of pain. Brain,
    1957, 80, 606-622.

BOWSHER, D. The termination of secondary somatosensory
    neurons within the thalamus of Macaca mulatta: An
    experimental degeneration study. J. Comp. Neurol.,
    1961, 117, 213.

BOWSHER, D. R., & ALBE-FESSARD, D. In C. A. Keele and
    R. Smith (Eds.), The Assessment of Pain in Man and
    Animals. London: The Universities Federation for
    Animal Welfare (UFAW), 1962, p. 107.

BROWN, G. W., & COHEN, B. D. Avoidance and approach learn-
    ing motivated by stimulation of identical hypothalamic
    loci. Am. J. Physiol., 1959, 197, 153-157.

CARTHY, J. D., & EBLING, F. J., (eds.). The Natural
    History of Aggression. London: Academic Press, 1964.

CHAPMAN, W. P. Studies on the periamygdaloid area in
    relation to human behavior. Res. Publ. Assn. Nerv.
    Dis., 1958, 36, 258-277.

COHEN, B. D., & BROWN, G. W. Avoidance learning motivated
    by hypothalamic stimulation. J. Exp. Psychol., 1957,
    53, 228-233.

CREER, T. L., HITZING, E. W., & SCHAEFFER, R. W. Classical
    conditioning of reflexive fighting. Psychon. Sci.,
    1966, 4, 89-90.

DAVIS, D. E. In W. Etkin (Ed.), Social Behavior and Organi-
    zation among Vertebrates. Chicago: University of
    Chicago Press, 1964, p. 53.

DELGADO, J. M. R. Cerebral structures involved in trans-
    mission and elaboration of noxious stimulation.
    J. Neurophysiol., 1955a, 18, 261-275.

DELGADO, J. M. R. Evaluation of permanent implantation of
    electrodes within the brain. EEG Clin. Neurophysiol.,
    1955b, 7, 637-644.

DELGADO, J. M. R. Prolonged stimulation of brain in awake
monkeys. J. Neurophysiol., 1959, 22, 458-475.

DELGADO, J. M. R. In W. D. M. Patton and P. Lindgren (Eds.),
Proceedings of the First International Pharmacological
Congress. Oxford: Pergamon Press, 1962, vol. VIII,
p. 265.

DELGADO, J. M. R. Cerebral heterostimulation in a monkey
colony. Science, 1963a, 141, 161-163.

DELGADO, J. M. R. Telemetry and telestimulation of the
brain. In L. Slater (Ed.), Biotelemetry. New York:
Pergamon Press, 1963b, p. 231.

DELGADO, J. M. R. In C. C. Pfeiffer and J. R. Smythies
(eds.), International Review of Neurobiology. New
York: Academic Press, 1964, vol. VI, p. 349.

DELGADO, J. M. R. Chronic radiostimulation of the brain in
monkey colonies. Proc. Internat. Union Physiol. Sci.,
1965a, 4, 365-371.

DELGADO, J. M. R. M. Ya. Mikhel'son and V. G. Longo (Eds.),
Proceedings of the Second International Pharmacological
Congress. Oxford: Pergamon Press, 1965b, vol. I,
p. 133.

DELGADO, J. M. R. Aggressive behavior evoked by radio stimulation in monkey colonies. Amer. Zool., 1966, 6,
669-681.

DELGADO, J. M. R. Social rank and radio-stimulated aggressiveness in monkeys. J. Nerv. Ment. Dis., 1967, 144,
383-390.

DELGADO, J. M. R. Electrical stimulation of the limbic
system. Proc. XXIV Internat. Congr. Physiol. Sci.,
1968, 6, 222-223.

DELGADO, J. M. R., MARK, V., SWEET, W., ERVIN, F., WEISS,
G., BACH-Y-RITA, G, & HAGIWARA, R. Intracerebral
radio stimulation and recording in completely free
patients. J. Nerv. Ment. Dis., 1968, 147, 329-340.

DELGADO, J. M. R., & MIR, D. Infatigability of pupillary constriction evoked by hypothalamic stimulation in monkeys. Neurology, 1966, 16, 939-950.

DELGADO, J. M. R., & MIR, D. Fragmental organization of emotional behavior in the monkey. Ann. N. Y. Acad. Sci., 159, 731-751.

DELGADO, J. M. R., ROBBERTS, W. W., & MILLER, N. E. Learning motivated by electrical stimulation of the brain. Am. J. Physiol., 1954, 179, 587-593.

DELGADO, J. M. R., ROSVOLD, H. E., & LOONEY, E. Evoking conditioned fear by electrical stimulation of subcortical structures in the monkey brain. J. Comp. Physiol. Psychol., 1956, 49, 373-380.

DREYER, P. I., & CHURCH, R. Shock-induced fighting as a function of the intensity and duration of the aversive stimulus. Psychon. Sci., 1968, 10, 271-272.

EGGER, M. D., & FLYNN, J. P. Effects of electrical stimulation of the amygdala on hypothalamically elicited attack behavior in cats. J. Neurophysiol., 1963, 26, 705-720.

EIBL-EIBESFELDT, I. In C. D. Clemente and D. B. Lindsley (Eds.) Aggression and Defense. Los Angeles: University of California Press, 1967, vol. V, p. 57.

ERVIN, F. R., & MARK, V. H. Stereotactic thalomotomy in in the human. Part II. Physiologic observations on the human thalamus. Arch. Neurol. (Chicago), 1960, 3, 368-380.

ERVIN, F. R., & MARK, V. H. Studies of the human thalamus: IV. Evoked responses. Ann. N. Y. Acad. Sci., 1964, 112, 81-92.

FERNANDEZ DE MOLINA, A., & HUNSPERGER, R. W. Central representation of affective reactions in forebrain and brain stem: electrical stimulation of amygdala, stria terminalis, and adjacent structures. J. Physiol., 1959, 145, 251-265.

FERNANDEZ DE MOLINA, A., & HUNSPERGER, R. W. Organization
of the subcortical system governing defense and flight
reactions in the cat. J. Physiol., 1962, 160, 200-213.

FONBERG, E. Emotional reactions evoked by cerebral stimulation in dogs. Bulletin de L'Academie Polonaise des
Sciences, 1963, 11, 47-49.

FUNDERBURK, W. H., FOXWELL, M., & HAKALA, M. W. Effect of
psychotherapeutic drugs on rage responses to hypothalamic stimulation. Fed. Proc. Fed. Am. Soc. Exp.
Biol., 1967, 26, 290.

GYBELS, J. Neurophysiological identification of thalamic
nuclei during stereotactic thalatomy for pain. EEG
Clin. Neurophysiol., 1968, 24, 96.

HASSLER, R. Interrelationship of cortical and subcortical
pain systems. Internat. Pharmacol. Mtg., 1968, 3,
219-229.

HAWKINS, D. T., & PLISKOFF, S. S. Brain-stimulation intensity, rate of self-stimulation, and reinforcement
strength: an analysis through chaining. J. Exp. Anal.
Behav., 1964, 7, 285-288.

HEATH, R. G., & MICKLE, W. A. In E. R. Ramey and D. S.
O'Doherty (Eds.) Electrical Studies on the Unanesthetized Brain. New York: Hoeber, 1960, p. 214.

HEATH, R. G., MONROE, R. R., & MICKLE, W. A. Stimulation
of the amygdaloid nucleus in a schizophrenic patient.
Am. J. Psychiat., 1955, 111, 862-863.

HESS, W. R. The Functional Organization of the Diencephalon.
New York: Grune and Stratton, 1957.

HESS, W. R., & AKERT, K. Experimental data on role of hype-
thalamus in mechanism of emotional behavior. Arch.
Neurol. Psychiat., 1955, 73, 127-129.

HINDE, R. A., & ROWELL, T. E. Communication by postures
and facial expressions in the rhesus monkey (Macaca
mulatta). Proc. Zool. Soc. Lond., 1962, 138, 1-21.

HODOS, W., & VALENSTEIN, E. S. An evaluation of response
    rate as a measure of rewarding intracranial stimula-
    tion. J. Comp. Physiol. Psychol., 1962, 55, 80-84.

HOLST, E. VON, & PAUL, U. VON ST. Electrically controlled
    behavior. Sci. America., 1962, 206, 50-59.

HOLST, E. VON, & PAUL, U. VON ST. On the functional organi-
    zation of drives. Anim. Behav., 1963, 11, 1-20.

HUNSPERGER, R. W., BROWN, J. L., & ROSVOLD, H. E. Combined
    stimulation in areas governing threat and flight be-
    haviour in the brain stem of the cat. Prog. Brain Res.,
    1964, 6, 191-197.

HUTCHINSON, R. R., & RENFREW, J. W. Stalking attack and
    eating behaviours elicited from the same sites in the
    hypothalamus. J. Comp. Physiol. Psychol., 1966, 61, 360.

INGRAM, W. R. Brainstem mechanisms in behavior. EEG Clin.
    Neurophysiol., 1952, 4, 397-406.

JASPER, H. H., & RASMUSSEN, T. Some studies of clinical
    and electrical responses to deep temporal stimulation
    in man with some considerations of functional anatomy.
    Res. Publ. Assn. Nerv. Ment. Dis., 1956, 36, 316-334.

JELASIC, F. Relation of the lateral part of the amygdala
    to pain. Confin. Neurol., 1966, 27, 53-55.

KAADA, B. R. In C. D. Clemente and D. B. Lindsley (Eds.)
    Aggression and Defense. Los Angeles: University of
    California Press, 1967, vol. V, p. 95.

KAADA, B. R., ANDERSEN, P., & JANSEN, J., JR. Stimulation
    of the amygdaloid nuclear complex in unanesthetized
    cats. Neurology, 1954, 4, 48-64.

KLUVER, H., & BARRERA, E. A method for the combined stain-
    ing of cells and fibers in the nervous system. J.
    Neuropathol. Exptl. Neurol., 1953, 12, 400-403.

KRUGER, L. In R. S. Knighton and P. R. Dumke (Eds.)
    Henry Ford Hospital International Symposium on Pain.
    Boston: Little Brown, 1966, p. 67.

LESSE, S. In P. H. Hoch and J. Zubin (Eds.) Experimental
    Psychopathology. New York: Grune and Stratton, 1957,
    p. 246.

LEVISON, P. K., & FLYNN, J. P. The objects attacked by
    cats during stimulation of the hypothalamus. Anim.
    Behav., 1965, 13, 217-220.

MACDONNELL, M. F., & FLYNN, J. P. Attack elicited by stimu-
    lation of the thalamus of cats. Science, 1964, 144,
    1249-1250.

MACLEAN, P. D., & DELGADO, J. M. R. Electrical and chemical
    stimulation of frontotemporal portion of limbic system
    in the waking animal. EEG Clin. Neurophysiol., 1953,
    5, 91-100.

MAGON, H. W., ATLAS, D., INGERSOLL, E. H., & RANSON, S. W.
    Associated facial, vocal and respiratory components
    of emotional expression: an experimental study. J.
    Neurol. Psychopath., 1937, 17, 241-255.

MASSERMAN, J. H. Is the hypothalamus a center of emotion?
    Psychosom. Med., 1941, 3, 3-25.

MEHLER, W. R. The anatomy of the so-called "pain tract" in
    man. In J. D. French and R. W. Porter (Eds.) Basic
    Research in Paraplegic. Springfield, Ill.: C. C.
    Thomas, 1962, p. 26.

MEHLER, W. R. The posterior thalamic region in man. Confin.
    Neurol. 1966a, 27, 18-29.

MEHLER, W. R. In R. S. Knighton and P. R. Dumke (Eds.)
    Henry Ford Hospital International Symposium on Pain.
    Boston: Little Brown, 1966b, p. 11.

MEHLER, W. R., FAFERMAN, M. E., & NAUTA, W. J. H. Ascending
    axon degeneration following antero-lateral cordotomy.
    Brain, 1960, 83, 718-850.

MILLER, N. E. In D. E. Sheer (Ed.) Electrical Stimulation
    of the Brain. Austin: University of Texas Press, 1961,
    p. 387.

MONNIER, M. In A. Soulairac, J. Cahn, and J. Charpentier
    (Eds.) Pain. London: Academic Press, 1968, p. 115.

MOYER, K. E. A preliminary physiological model of aggres-
    sive behavior. Paper presented at AAAS Symposium on
    the Physiology of Fighting and Defeat. Dallas, Texas,
    December, 1968.

NAKAO, H. Emotional behavior produced by hypothalamic
    stimulation. Am. J. Physiol., 1958, 194, 411-418.

NASHOLD, B. S., & WILSON, W. P. Central pain. Observa-
    tions in man with chronic implanted electrodes in the
    midbrain tegmentum. Confin. Neurol., 1966, 27, 30-44.

OBRADOR, S., & DIERSSEN, G. Sensory responses to sub-
    cortical stimulation and management of pain disorders
    by stereotaxic methods. Confin. Neurol., 1966, 27,
    45-51.

OLDS, J. Approach-avoidance dissociations in rat brain.
    Am. J. Physiol., 1960, 199, 965-968.

OLDS, J. Hypothalamic substrates of reward. Physiol. Rev.,
    1962, 42, 544-604.

OLDS, M. E., & OLDS, J. Approach-avoidance analysis of rat
    diencephalon. J. Comp. Neur., 1963, 120, 259-283.

OLDS, J., & SINCLAIR, J. C. Self-stimulation in the obstruc-
    tion box. Am. Psychol., 1957, 12, 464.

ORTHNER, H., & ROEDER, F. Further clinical and anatomical
    experiences with stereotactic operations for relief of
    pain. Confin. Neurol., 1966, 27, 418-430.

PENFIELD, W., & JASPER, H. H. Epilepsy and the Functional
    Anatomy of the Human Brain. Boston: Little Brown,
    1954.

PHILLIPS, R. E. "Wildness" in the mallard duck: effects
    of brain lesions and stimulation on "escape behavior"
    and reproduction. J. Comp. Neur., 1964, 122, 139-155.

PLOTNIK, R.   Changes in social behavior of squirrel
    monkeys after anterior temporal lobectomy. J. Comp.
    Physiol. Psychol., 1968, 66, 369-377.

PLUTCHIK, R., McFARLAND, W. L., & ROBINSON, B. W.   Relation-
    ships between current intensity, self-stimulation
    rates, escape latencies, and evoked behavior in rhesus
    monkeys. J. Comp. Physiol. Psychol., 1966, 61,
    181-188.

POGGIO, G. F., & MOUNTCASTLE, V. B.   A study of the func-
    tional contributions of the lemniscal and spino
    thalamic systems to somatic sensibility. Bull. Johns
    Hopkins Hosp., 1960, 106, 266-316.

POIRIER, L. J., BOUVIER, G., OLIVER, A., & BOUCHER, R.   In
    A. Soulairac, J. Cahn, and J. Charpentier (Eds.) Pain.
    London: Academic Press, 1968, p. 33.

RIECHERT, T.   Die chirurgische Behandlung der zentralen
    Schmerzzustände, einschliesslich der stereotaktischen
    Operation en im Thalamus und Mesencephalon. Acta
    Neurochir., 1960, 8, 136-152.

REYNOLDS, G. S., CATANIA, A. C., & SKINNER, B. F.   Con-
    ditioned and unconditioned aggression in pigeons.
    J. Exp. Anal. Behav., 1963, 6, 73-74.

ROBERTS, W. W.   Both rewarding and punishing effects from
    stimulation of posterior hypothalamus of cat with
    same electrode at same intensity. J. Comp. Physiol.
    Psychol., 1958, 51, 400-407.

ROBERTS, W. W.   Rapid escape learning without avoidance
    learning motivated by hypothalamic stimulation in cats.
    J. Comp. Physiol. Psychol., 1958, 51, 391-399.

ROBERTS, W. W.   Fear-like behavior elicited from dorso-
    medial thalamus of cat. J. Comp. Physiol. Psychol.,
    1962, 55, 191-197.

ROBERTS, W. W., & BERQUIST, E. H.   Attack elicited by
    hypothalamic stimulation in cats raised in social
    isolation. J. Comp. Physiol. Psychol., 1968,

ROBERTS, W. W., & KIESS, H. O. Motivational properties of
    hypothalamic aggression in cats. J. Comp. Physiol.
    Psychol., 1964, 58, 187-193.

ROBERTS, W. W., STEINBERG, M. L., & MEANS, L. W. Hypothala-
    mic mechanisms for sexual, aggressive, and other motiva-
    tional behaviors in the opossum, Didelphis Viriginiana.
    J. Comp. Physiol. Psychol., 1967, 64, 187-193.

ROBINSON, B. W. The physiology of fighting and defeat:
    Summary and overview. Paper presented at AAAS Symposium
    on the Physiology of Fighting and Defeat, Dallas, Texas,
    December, 1968.

ROSS, G. S. In R. S. Knighton and P. R. Dumke (Eds.) Henry
    Ford Hospital International Symposium on Pain. Boston:
    Little Brown, 1966, p. 91.

ROSVOLD, H. E., MIRSKY, A. F., & PRIBRAM, K. H. Influence
    of amygdalectomy on social interaction in a monkey
    group. J. Comp. Physiol. Psychol., 1954, 47, 173-178.

SANO, K., YOSHIOKA, M., OGASHIWA, M., ISHIJIMA, B., & OHYE, C.
    Thalamolamibotomy. Confin. Neurol., 1966, 63-66.

SCOTT, J. P. Theoretical issues concerning the origin and
    causes of fighting. Paper presented at AAAS Symposium
    on the Physiology of Fighting and Defeat, Dallas, Texas,
    December, 1968.

SEAL, H. L. Multivariate Statistical Analysis for Biolo-
    gists. New York: Wiley and Sons, 1964.

SHEALY, C. N., & PEELE, T. L. Studies on amygdaloid nucleus
    of cat. J. Neurophysiol., 1957, 20, 125-139.

SHEARD, M., & FLYNN, J. P. Facilitation of attack behavior
    by stimulation of the midbrain of cats. Brain Res.,
    1967, 4, 324.

SKULTETY, F. M. Stimulation of periaqueductal gray and
    hypothalamus. Arch. Neurol., 1963, 8, 608-620.

SNIDER, R. S., & LEE, J. C. A Stereotaxic Atlas of the
    Monkey Brain. (Macaca mulatta). Chicago: University
    of Chicago Press, 1961.

SPIEGEL, E. A., KLETZKIN, M., & SZEKELY, E. G. Pain
    reactions upon stimulation of the tectum mesencephali.
    J. Neuropath. Exp. Neurol., 1954, 13, 212-220.

SPIEGEL, E. A., & WYCIS, H. T. Present status of stereo-
    encephalotomics for pain relief. Confin. Neurol.,
    1966, 27, 7-17.

STACHNIK, T. J., ULRICH, R., & MABRY, J. H. Reinforcement
    of intra- and inter-species aggression with intra-
    cranial stimulation. Am. Zool., 1966, 6, 663-668.

TEDESCHI, R. E., TEDESCHI, D. H., MUCHA, A., COOK, L.,
    MATTIS, P. A., & FELLOWS, E. J. Effects of various
    centrally acting drugs on fighting behavior of mice.
    J. Pharmacol. Exptl. Ther., 1959, 125, 28-34.

ULRICH, R. E. Pain as a cause of aggression. Am. Zool.,
    1966, 6, 643-662.

ULRICH, R. E., & AZRIN, N. H. Reflexive fighting in
    response to aversive stimulation. J. Exp. Anal. Behav.,
    1962, 5, 511-521.

ULRICH, R. E., JOHNSTON, M., RICHARDSON, J., & WOLFF, P. C.
    The operant conditioning of fighting behaviors in rats.
    Psychol. Rec., 1963, 13, 465-470.

ULRICH, R. E., WOLFF, P. C., & AZRIN, N. A. Shock as an
    elicitor of intra- and inter-species fighting behavior.
    Anim. Behav., 1964, 12, 14-15.

URSIN, H. Flight and defense behavior in cats. J. Comp.
    Physiol. Psychol., 1964, 58, 180-196.

URSIN, H., & KAADA, B. R. Functional localization within
    the amygdaloid complex in the cat. EEG Clin. Neuro-
    physiol., 1960, 12, 1-20.

URSIN, H., WESTER, K., & URSIN, R. Habituation to electri-
    cal stimulation of the brain in unanesthetized cats.
    EEG Clin. Neurophysiol., 1967, 23, 41-49.

VALENSTEIN, E. S. Problems of measurement and interpreta-
    tion with reinforcing brain stimulation. Psychol. Rev.,
    1964, 71, 415-437.

VERNIER, V. H., BOREN, J. J., KNAPP, P. G., & MALIS, J. L.
    Effect of depressant drugs on thresholds for aversive
    brain stimulation. *Fed. Proc.*, 1961, 20, 323 (ab-
    stract).

VERNON, W., & ULRICH, R. E. Classical conditioning of pain-
    elicited aggression. *Science*, 1966, 152, 668-669.

WASMAN, M., & FLYNN, J. P. Directed attack elicited from
    hypothalamus. *Arch. Neurol.*, 1962, 6, 60-67.

WEISS, B., & LATIES, V. G. Titration behavior on various
    fractional escape programs. *J. Exp. Anal. Behav.*, 1959,
    2, 227-248.

WHITLOCK, D. G., & PERL, E. R. Thalamic projection of
    spinothalamic pathways in monkey. *Exp. Neurol.*, 1961,
    3, 240-255.

A PRELIMINARY PHYSIOLOGICAL MODEL OF AGGRESSIVE BEHAVIOR

K. E. Moyer

Department of Psychology
Carnegie-Mellon University
Pittsburgh, Pennsylvania

KINDS OF AGGRESSION

Several authors have indicated that aggression is not a unitary concept (Scott, 1958; Bevan, Daves, & Levy, 1960; Jacobsen, 1961; Valzelli, 1967). I have proposed recently a system for classifying the different kinds of aggressive behavior and have reviewed the literature to support the idea that each kind has a different physiological basis (Moyer, 1968a). Since that paper is now available in the literature, I shall present here only a summary of that position and some of the more recent evidence on the matter.

There are different kinds of aggressive behavior, just as there are different kinds of consummatory behavior, and it will be impossible to develop a physiological model of aggression until that is recognized. Eating and drinking both can be classified as consummatory behavior and there are, to be sure, certain similarities in the kinds of responses and in the physiological mechanisms involved. It is obvious, however, that the details of the neurological and blood chemistry substrates for these two kinds of consummatory behavior are very different. Any attempt to find a single physiological basis of consummatory behavior would, therefore, lead to confusion and a rash of contradictory and unreproducible experiments.

223

Progress in the understanding of aggressive behavior will be made only when the different kinds of aggression are carefully and operationally defined. In order to make any general statement about the determinants of aggressive behavior, experimental manipulations must be applied to the subjects when they are tested in a variety of situations which define the various classes of aggression. A given manipulation may facilitate one kind of aggression, suppress another, and have no effect on the third. The kinds of aggression may be differentiated on the basis of the stimulus situations which elicit them. There is also evidence that the topographies of the aggressive responses also differ.

There are some obvious differences in the response patterns that animals show in different aggression inducing situations. Several authors have pointed out (Hutchinson & Renfrew, 1966; Roberts & Kiess, 1964; Wasman & Flynn, 1962) that the topography of behavior in predatory attack by the cat is quite different from a type of aggression which has been called "affective." The former involves relatively little emotional display. The cat does not hiss or growl, but slinks close to the floor and makes a silent, deadly attack on the rat. In "affective" aggression, however, there is evidence of pronounced sympathetic arousal. The back arches, the tail fluffs out, the ears lie back against the head, the animal hisses and growls, and may attack in a flurry of scratching and biting. Tinbergen (1953) has said that deer use their antlers when engaged in conflict with other male deer (inter-male aggression), but use their front hooves in defense against predators. When more detailed ethological analyses have been done, response topography may become a useful method of differentiating among the various kinds of aggression. At this point, however, the observations are too limited to permit a general classification on this basis.

The types of stimulus situations which elicit destructive behavior also are different for the different kinds of aggression. Aggression is generally stimulus bound and, in many classes of aggression, the stimulus situation to which the $\underline{S}$ will react with hostility is highly specific. The male mouse, for example, will attack another male, but generally it will not attack a female (Scott & Fredericson, 1951). The rat will attack a strange rat, but seldom a member of its own group (Barnett, 1963; Eibl-Eibesfeldt,

1961). Certain rats will attack mice, but will not attack rat pups (Myer & White, 1968). Almost 100% of the male hooded rats in our laboratory will attack and kill a frog or turtle. Eighty percent will kill a young chicken, but only 10 to 20 percent are mouse killers (Bandler & Moyer, 1968, unpublished).

Aggression evoked by brain stimulation is also stimulus bound. Cats stimulated in the hypothalamus attack rats persistently and effectively. The attack on a dead rat, however, is less sustained, and only brief transient attacks are made on a stuffed rat or a block of wood about the size of a rat (Levison & Flynn, 1965; Wasman & Flynn, 1962). A nonpredatory rat induced to kill mice by Carbachol stimulation of the hippocampus will not attack the experimenter's finger, even though it is placed in the rat's mount (Grant & Moyer, 1968, unpublished). On the other hand, a cornered albino rat, which will bite repeatedly the hand of the experimenter who attempts to pick it up, may not attack another male rat or a mouse placed in its cage (Korn & Moyer, 1968).

The following kinds of aggression are proposed primarily on the basis of the stimulus situations which elicit them. Predatory aggression is evoked by the presence of a natural object of prey. Inter-male aggressive behavior is released in most species by the presence of strange adult male conspecific. Fear-induced aggression is preceded always by attempts to escape; thus, the stimulus situation evoking this kind of aggression must involve both a threatening agent and the blocking of an escape route. The stimulus situation which will elicit irritable aggression is extremely broad and may involve inanimate as well as animate objects. It is differentiated from the other kinds of aggression by its inclusiveness and the irrelevance of the particular environment in which it occurs. The tendency to irritable aggression is enhanced by frustration, pain, deprivation or any other stressor.

The stimuli involved in the evocation of territorial defense involve a territory in which the subject has become established, and an intruder. The stimulus complex which elicits maternal aggression and differentiates it from other kinds is the presence of the young of that particular female and some threatening agent. Instrumental aggression is not specific to any particular stimulus situation.

Aggressive responses of any of the above classes may result
in a change in the environment which constitutes a reinforcement for the animal with a consequent increase in the
probability that the aggressive behavior will occur in a
similar situation. Sex related aggression is, in certain
circumstances, elicited by the same stimuli which elicit
sex behavior. However, there is little experimental
evidence on the variables of which this kind of aggression
is a function. Although, according to this model, the
kinds of aggression can be differentiated physiologically,
in the real world undoubtedly they interact. Thus, for
example, irritable aggression may enhance inter-male or
predatory aggression.

DIFFERENT PHYSIOLOGICAL BASES

Since details concerning what is known about the
physiological basis of the different kinds of aggression
are available elsewhere (Moyer, 1968a), only a few examples
will be presented here. The neural substrates of predatory
aggression have been differentiated experimentally from
those of irritable aggression. The now classic studies of
Flynn and his colleagues have demonstrated that predatory
attack in the cat is elicited by stimulation of the lateral
hypothalamus, but irritable aggression without escape
tendencies results from stimulation of the medial hypothalamus (Wasman & Flynn, 1962; Egger & Flynn, 1963). The
animal stimulated in the predatory area will ignore the
experimenter and attack a rat, but the cat stimulated in
the irritable aggression area will ignore a rat in its cage
and attempt to attack the experimenter.

The endocrine basis of inter-male aggression clearly
is different from that of predatory aggression. Karli
(1958) has shown that castration has no effect on the tendency for killer rats to kill mice, and the administration
of testosterone to non-killers does not increase their
tendency to kill. There is good evidence, however, that
the androgens are of primary importance in inter-male
aggression. Inter-male aggression does not appear in
either mice (Fredericson, 1950) or rats (Seward, 1945)
until after sexual maturity. Testosterone administered to
castrated mice results in a dramatic increase in the fighting of males, but not females (Tolamn & King, 1956).

Testosterone injections given to immature mice increase
the aggressive behavior of males (Levy & King, 1953), but
not of females (Levy, 1954). Prepuberally castrated mice
do not develop inter-male aggression. When testosterone
pellets are implanted in the same mice, the aggressiveness
appears only to disappear again when the pellets are removed (Beeman, 1947). Testosterone appears to be important
in, but not critical to, the manifestation of irritable
aggression. Castration reduces, but does not eliminate,
irritable aggression produced in rats by foot shock
(Hutchinson, Ulrich, & Azrin, 1965). A number of studies
have shown that the hypothalamus is involved in both fear-
induced and irritable aggression (Kling & Hutt, 1958;
Wheatly, 1944; Yasukochi, 1960). Stimulation of the
ventral part of the medial hypothalamus produces aggressive
behavior in the cat whereas stimulation of the dorsal part
of the same structure produces escape (Romaniuk, 1965).
The amygdala exerts control over at least three different
kinds of aggressive behavior. Total bilateral amygdalectomy raises the threshold for irritable aggression
(Schreiner & Kling, 1953, eliminates predatory aggression
in the cat (Summers & Kaelber, 1962), and rat (Woods, 1956),
and reduces fear reactions (escape tendencies) in a variety
of animals, with a consequent reduction in fear-induced
aggressive behavior (Karli, 1956; Rosvold, Mirsky, &
Pribram, 1954; Schreiner & Kling, 1953, 1956; Shealy &
Peele, 1957; Woods, 1956). The evidence indicates that
each of these kinds of aggression is controlled by different amygdaloid nuclei (Moyer, 1968a).

There also seems to be some indication that the different kinds of aggression may be differentiated on a chemical
basis as Miller (1965) has indicated that other behaviors
are coded chemically in the brain. Various kinds of
aggression are affected differentially by different drugs
(Hoffmeister & Wuttke, 1968; Jacobson, 1961; Valzelli,
1967). Leaf, Lerner, and Horowitz (1968) have done a
series of experiments which indicate that the catecholamines function to inhibit the manifestation of predatory
aggression in the rat. Several other studies indicate
that an increase in brain catecholamines produces hyper-
irritability in rats and mice (Everett, 1968; Everett &
Wiegand, 1962; Wende & Spoerlein, 1962; Randrup & Munkvad,
1968). Welch (1967) has suggested that an increase in the
catecholamines (or an increase in the sensitivity of the
receptor cells to them) may explain the increase in the

inter-male aggression manifested by isolated mice, and
dominant mice in a small colony.

In the light of this evidence and much more cited
elsewhere (Moyer, 1968a, 1968b, 1969), we are led to the
inevitable conclusion that aggression is a multifaceted,
multidetermined series of behavior patterns. The particular classification system suggested above may not be,
and probably is not, the one which will ultimately by the
most useful. It is most likely that further research will
clarify these kinds of aggression and further define the
physiological distinctions among them. However, although
we may argue about the most efficacious classification
system, the fact that there are different kinds of aggression seems now to be indisputable. It is obvious that, if
each of these kinds of aggressive behavior has a different
physiological basis, it will not be possible to construct
a physiological model which will fit each of them in detail. It may, however, be possible to identify mechanisms
or types of mechanisms which, although differing in detail,
are similar for all aggression types. An attempt will now
be made to elucidate some of these mechanisms.

BRAIN CIRCUITS AND AGGRESSION

The first premise of this model indicates that there
are in the brains of animal and man innately organized
neural circuits,[1] which when active in the presence of
particular complexes of stimuli, result in a tendency for
the organism to behave destructively toward certain stimulus complexes in the environment. Also, as suggested
above, the different kinds of aggression result from the
activity of different, although undoubtedly sometimes
overlapping, circuits. The factors which determine whether
or not these tendencies will result in action will be discussed below. A corollary of this proposition is that a

---

[1] The term circuit, as used here, merely implies that underlying any aggressive behavior there are a large number of
interconnected neurones which are located in different parts
of the brain. The circuit is in no sense closed, nor is
there a "center" for aggression. As indicated below, these
patterns of neurones have facilitating and inhibiting in-
puts from other systems and also have outputs to other
systems, and also have outputs to other systems.

particular aggressive behavior will not occur if its
neural circuit is suppressed, interrupted, or in some way
deactivated. A second corollary of this premise is that,
since aggressive behavior is stimulus bound, the activation of a neural circuit for aggression in the absence of
the appropriate stimulus complex will not result in aggressive behavior.

There is now, I believe, a massive amount of data to
support this basic premise. It has been reviewed in some
detail elsewhere (Moyer, 1968a, 1968b, 1969). In evalu-
ating these data, however, it constantly must be kept in
mind, as Plotnik and Delgado (1968) have pointed out, that
any given stimulation of the brain may activate pain
fibers, and that any aggressive behavior observed may be
secondary to the production of pain. There is, of course,
ample evidence that peripheral pain, in any species,
results in aggression toward a variety of stimulus objects
(Ulrich, 1966). Although one can make inferences about the
experience of an animal on the basis of the similarity of
response topography to the presentation of external stimuli,
whether, in fact, the animal is experiencing pain is unknowable. Whether the aggressive behavior resulting from
brain stimulation is secondary to the production of pain
can only be tested on humans; and, even then, the assumption is made that the verbal behavior produced is representative of an experiential communality between the
observer and the subject. As indicated below, however,
what data there is on aggression resulting from the activation of brain circuits in man clearly does not support
the proposition that such behavior is dependent necessarily
on a preliminary experience of pain.

Dr. Flynn and his colleagues (1968) have conducted an
outstanding series of experiments which unequivocally
demonstrate that there is a neural circuit which when
activated results in predatory aggression in the cat, and
further that this aggressive behavior is stimulus bound
(Levison & Flynn, 1965). He has further demonstrated that
the predatory circuit is anatomically different from what
I would call the irritable aggression circuit (Wasman &
Flynn, 1966). Since Dr. Flynn is on this symposium and
will present his own experiments and interpretations, I
shall not attempt to anticipate his presentation further,
except to indicate that he will outline many of the neuroanatomical components of these circuits.

In addition to the work of Delgado and Flynn, a number of other investigators have shown that activation of brain circuits through electrical or chemical means produces aggressive behavior. King and Hoebel (1968) have recently shown that electrical stimulation of the anterior-lateral hypothalamus can produce mouse killing in a non-killer rat. Richard Bandler, in our own laboratory, has been able to facilitate predatory behavior in the rat by stimulating of the same general region with Carbachol through an implanted cannula. He also has been able to suppress natural killing in the rat by the application of Atropine to the same hypothalamic area without any apparent blocking of other activities.

It is frequently difficult to discriminate between fear-induced aggression and irritable aggression in the studies that have been done on brain stimulation induced aggression. Experimenters frequently have failed to define operationally the type of aggressive behavior which they were observing. However, Kaada (1967), in his extensive review of the literature on brain mechanisms related to aggressive behavior, cites numerous studies which differentiate between attack behavior (irritable aggression), defense behavior (fear-induced aggression), and flight. On the basis of both stimulation and lesion studies, he concludes that, "All three behavior patterns appear to have their separate although somewhat overlapping representations in the brain."

It should be emphasized that the aggressive behaviors, of whatever kind, produced by the activation of particular brain circuits are not similar to the sham rage of the decorticate animal. These behaviors are well-organized, well-directed, and directly related to the relevant environmental stimulus. Wasman and Flynn (1962), in their description of the cat's behavior during stimulation, state that, "The cat's responses were clearly directed. It would pursue and invariably catch a fleeing rat. If the rat leaped in the air the cat waited and caught the rat in mid air or when it landed. The effectiveness of the attack was attested to by the frequent deaths and injuries to rats. . .(p. 62)."

There also is now a large amount of experimental data which supports the first corollary of this initial premise.

Many studies have shown that lesions in particular portions of the various aggression circuits virtually eliminate the particular aggressive behavior involved. Thus, the animal with lesions in the proper place does not respond aggressively to stimuli which it would viciously attack just prior to the operation. This material is reviewed in some detail elsewhere (Kaada, 1967; Karli, Vergnes, & Didiergeorges, 1968; Moyer, 1968a).

The importance of the interaction between the activity of particular brain circuits and the external stimulus has also received experimental support. Although a few studies have indicated that a brain stimulated cat will attack the empty air (an "hallucination") (Brown & Hunsperger, 1963; Yasukochi, 1960), most of the evidence supports the view that the aggressive response is stimulus bound and that some stimuli are preferred to others. In general, the animal stimulated in an area involving an aggressive circuit in the absence of relevant external stimuli may show affective arousal and restlessness, but it does not show attack behavior either against the wall, or against inappropriate external stimuli such as foam rubber block about the size of the animals normal prey (Levison & Flynn, 1965; Wasman & Flynn, 1962).

BRAIN CIRCUITS, AGGRESSION, AND MAN

For obvious reasons, most of the experimental work on the neurological substrates of aggressive behavior has been done using subhuman species. It is therefore appropriate to ask whether it is possible to make cross species generalizations, particularly to man for which the evolutionary gap is the greatest. Although homologous brain areas are generally involved in the various kinds of aggressive behavior in different species (the amygdala, hypothalamus, and midbrain, for example) there are some obvious exceptions. For example, the cingulate gyrus appears to be involved in fear-induced aggression in monkey (Anand & Dua, 1956; Glees, Cole, Whitty, & Cairns, 1950; Kennard, 1955a; Ward, 1948), but in irritable aggression in the cat and dog (Anand & Dua, 1956; Brutkowski, Fonberg, & Mempel, 1961; Kennard, 1955a, 1955b).

The weight of the evidence available seems to indicate that man, for all of his encephalization, has not escaped

from biological determinants of aggressive behavior: that
he too has brain circuits which when activated result in
an increased tendency to destructive actions. Although
the direct elicitation of hostile verbalizations and
actions by direct brain stimulation in man are relatively
rare (Ursin, 1960; Gloor, 1967), several cases have now
been reported. Further, those cases that are reported
result from stimulation of areas similar to those involved
in brain stimulated aggression in animals. One of the most
dramatic is cited by King (1961) who describes a patient
with an electrode implanted in the amygdaloid region who,
when stimulated, became angry, verbally hostile, and
threatened to strike the experimenter. Other cases of
brain stimulation in humans resulting in aggressive tendencies have been reported by Sem-Jacobsen (1960, 1966),
Ervin, Mark, and Sweet (1968). Pain is not reported as
preliminary experience in these studies.

The literature contains numerous case studies which
show a change in personality with an increase in hostility
and irascibility as a result of tumor growth in a variety
of brain areas, particularly in the temporal and hypothalamic regions. Pain, again, is not necessarily involved
(Vonderake, 1944; Wheatly, 1944). This evidence seems to
indicate that either the stimulation of aggression circuits, or the deactivation of circuits which suppress the
aggression circuits, results in aggression in man.

There also is indirect evidence that spontaneous
activity of the neurones of the temporal lobe, as well as
other areas of the brain, results in aggressive behavior.
It is well-recognized that some temporal lobe epileptics
are subject to sudden, violent outbursts of anger and
uncontrollable, destructive, sometimes murderous, behavior
which can be triggered by the most trivial provocations
(Gloor, 1967). In some individuals, activity in the
temporal lobe and in the thalamus leads to subjective
feelings of rage and the execution of impetuous and
assaultive behavior (Treffert, 1964). A number of studies
have shown that aggressive behavior such as fire setting,
aggressive sex behavior, murder, and other acts of violence
are associated with 14/second and 6/second positive spikes
in the EEG record (Schwade & Geiger, 1956, 1960; Woods,
1961). This assaultive behavior may or may not be associated with epileptic motor seizures. Even when it is,
there is reason to believe that the neurohumoral substrate

underlying the two behaviors are different in that they are affected differentially by brain lesions and drugs (F. R. Ervin, 1968 personal communication).

The individuals with the impulsive aggressive dyscontrol syndrome are on a continuum in regard to the frequency of their violent outbursts and the amount of provocation required to elicit such outbursts. It seems most unlikely that these individuals are endowed with a particular primitive neural organization which involves an aggression circuit which is not included in the brains of the rest of us. It is much more reasonable to assume that circuits for angry and aggressive behavior are built into all men's brains and, in some men, they are more easily fired or more difficult to suppress than in others. (See Jones, 1965, for a further discussion of this point and an excellent review of the literature.)

Evidence is accumulating rapidly that chronic aggressive and assaultive behavior in man can be alleviated by the surgical interruption of particular brain circuits. Feelings of anger and hostility, as well as assaultive acts, are controlled frequently by selective brain lesions. Lesions in the posterior hypothalamus (Sano et al., 1966; Sano, 1962), the temporal lobe (Pool, 1965), dorsomedial thalamus (Spiegel et al., 1951), and the anterior cingulum (Tow & Whitty, 1953; Le Beau, 1952) have all been used successfully to reduce uncontrollable hostility in man. These lesion results, although not conclusive, certainly lend credence to the idea that in man, as in animals, the activation of certain brain circuits results in aggressive behavior and that, when these circuits are rendered nonfunctional through lesions the aggressive behavior is controlled or reduced.

As far as I know, there is no good evidence for a differential physiological basis for the different kinds of aggression in man. This may be due, in part, to the lack of attention to the concept of different kinds of aggression. It may also be due, in part, to man's rich symbolic behavior and the ability to substitute symbolically one stimulus complex for another so that any differentiation of the kinds of aggression on the basis of stimulus situations evoking them is bound to have severe limitations. Further, there is clearly no necessity for assuming that all of the kinds of aggression identifiable in the various

animal species are necessarily identifiable in man. Until
more work is done on this problem, however, further consideration of it will be highly speculative.

DETERMINANTS OF BRAIN CIRCUIT ACTIVITY

The initial premise of this model simply states that
when a given brain circuit is active in the presence of a
given stimulus complex, destructive behavior will occur.
It is obvious, however, that aggressive behavior in both
animals and men is a relatively rare occurrence compared
with the variety of other manifest behaviors. It is,
therefore, essential that consideration be given to the
mechanisms which provide for the activation and deactivation of the neurological circuits which result in hostile
behavior.

It is proposed here that there are three possible
states (which blend into a continuum) of any aggression
circuit. First, the circuit may be inactive and insensitive.
In this condition, it cannot be fired by the usual stimulation which will provoke attack. One example of this state
can be found, as indicated above, in the immature or
castrated male rat. This preparation will not respond
with aggression or threat postures to the stimulus complex
of a strange male conspecific although that stimulus complex is adequate to elicit inter-male aggressive behavior
in the normal adult animal.

If the immature or castrated rat is administered
testosterone, the adequate stimulus for inter-male aggression will, in fact, elicit fighting behavior (Beeman, 1947;
Levy & King, 1953). Thus, it appears that the testosterone
in some way sensitizes the brain circuit involved in inter-
male aggression so that it is fired by the adequate stimulus complex. This then is the second state: the circuit
is sensitized, but is inactive until it is activated by
the appropriate stimulus. If the sensitivity is slight,
fewer cells may be activated by the stimulus situation and
the resultant attack may be half hearted, elicited only by
a narrow range of the most appropriate stimuli. On the
other hand, if the sensitivity is high, the subject will
respond to a wider range of stimuli and the attack behavior
will be relatively more intense.

In the third state, the particular aggression circuit may be active spontaneously in the absence of the appropriate stimulus. In this case, the cells of the circuit are firing, and the organism is in a restless state, is aroused, and may engage in exploratory behavior. It does not, however, make aggressive motor movements. It will respond more readily to the appropriate stimuli because activity in that circuit sensitizes relevant sensory modalities so that the receptors are more easily fired. MacDonnel and Flynn (1966) in a pioneering study have shown that the sensitivity of the muzzle area of the cat is increased during the electrical activation of the hypothalamic area which produces predatory aggression. In humans, it seems likely that activity in certain of the aggression circuits is accompanied by subjective feelings of anger and hostility (Schwade & Geiger, 1956; Treffert, 1964; Woods, 1961). The individual may engage in extensive aggressive fantasies and a large number of stimuli will suffice to elicit aggressive thoughts. It is unknowable, of course, whether animals have any comparable subjective state.

Although the above paragraphs seem to be a reasonable extrapolation of the available experimental data, it must be recognized that it is an extrapolation. Experimental confirmation would require that particular aggression circuits be located by implanted electrodes, and that the activation of those electrodes result in aggressive behavior. It will then be necessary to record from those electrodes to determine the relationship between the activity of the circuit and the behavior of the organism in both the presence and absence of the appropriate external stimulation. This is a feasible technique for freely moving animals (Komisaruk & Olds, 1968) but little use has been made of it in the study of aggressive behavior as yet.

Adams (1968) has shown that there are certain cells in the midbrain of the cat which are active only when the cat is engaged in fighting behavior. He also indicated that stimulation at the sites of the cells related to fighting produced hissing behavior in the cats. Repeated electrical stimulation in the amygdala of the cat at 5 second intervals for an hour a day for 1-15 days results in long lasting EEG seizure patterns. Some of these animals showed considerable increases in aggressive behavior

(Alonso-Deflorida & Delgado, 1958).

Hereditary Influences

There are a variety of factors which contribute to the sensitization of the aggression circuits in the brain, and the evidence suggests that some of these factors may be inherited. There are clear-cut strain differences in predatory tendencies. Seventy percent of wild Norway rats kill mice, whereas 12 percent of the domesticated Norways kill mice (Karli, 1956). In our own laboratory, we have shown that a significantly higher percentage of Long Evans hooded rats kill frogs, chickens, and turtles than do Sprague Dawley albinos (Moyer & Bandler, unpublished).

Hereditary influences clearly have been demonstrated in inter-male aggression. Scott (1942) has shown that different inbred strains of mice differ consistently and widely in their tendencies to engage in inter-male fighting, and that these differences were genetic and could not have been learned. A number of experimenters have shown that it is possible through selective breeding to develop aggressive and nonaggressive strains of animals; again, the aggression dealt with was inter-male (Hall & Klein, 1942; Lagerspetz, 1961; Stone, 1932; Yerkes, 1913). Although I know of no studies which demonstrate the inheritance of aggressive tendencies in man, there is little reason to believe that such tendencies are not inherited. Certainly, there are vast inherited differences in the human nervous and endocrine systems (Williams & Teitelbaum, 1956). If, as suggested in this model, human aggressive behavior is, in part, determined by neuro-endocrine mechanisms, it is only reasonable to assume that aggressive tendencies in man are inherited, just as the tendency to epilepsy is inherited (Lennox, 1947). There are chromosomal abnormalities in man which appear to result in excessive aggressiveness with lack of impulse control. One is Klinefelter's syndrome (Burnard, Hunter, & Hoggart, 1967; Telfer et al., 1968) and the XYY abnormality (Price & Whatmore, 1967a, 1967b; Telfer et al., 1968).

Endocrine Influences on Neural Development

The sensitivity of the aggression circuits and the consequent tendency to behave aggressively is evidently permanently influenced by the endocrine, particularly gonadal, status of the organism shortly after birth. A recent study by Conner & Levine (1968) indicates that rats castrated as neonates fight less under conditions of shock (irritable aggression) than do either weaning age castrates or intact rats. Further, the fighting level of the weaning castrates can be brought up to normal by testosterone administered exogenously, but the fighting behavior of the rats castrated as neonates remains unaffected by testosterone, but the fighting behavior of the rats castrated as neonates remains unaffected by testosterone. Conner & Levine conclude from this that the neural substrates which are modulated by the androgens in later life are permanently changed by the early castration. Recent evidence also indicates that these same neural substrates can be altered by the administration of testosterone propionate to female mice on the day of birth. When female mice are so treated, and subsequently isolated, they respond to the administration of testosterone in the same manner as males castrated at weaning, that is, with increased fighting (inter-male aggression). However, females treated with oil within the first 24 hours after birth do not fight when isolated and given testosterone (Edwards, 1968). Edwards thus concludes, "One may presume that the stimulation by endogenous testosterone in the male (and exogenous testosterone in the female) can 'organize' or cause the differentiation of a neural substrate for fighting."

An extensive series of experiments supporting and extending the above preliminary findings will be reported later in this symposium (Bronson & Desjardins, 1968).

Increased Sensitivity from Neural Facilitation

Aggression circuits can also be sensitized, or made more susceptible to being fired by the appropriate external stimulation by the facilitating effect of the activity of other neurone systems. Stimulation of particular sites in the midbrain reticular formation at a particular intensity will produce only mildly alerting responses in the cat. The activation of those sites will, however, facilitate the attack of a cat or a rat when that attack is initiated by stimulation of the lateral hypothalamus (Sheard, 1967; Sheard & Flynn, 1967). Sheard has also shown that hypothalamically induced predatory attack is also enhanced by intraperitoneal injections of amphetamine and suggests that the amphetamine action is similar to direct electrical

stimulation of the reticular system (Sheard, 1967). There
are also other areas in the brain which have been shown to
have a sensitizing or facilitating effect on hypothalamically induced predatory behavior (Egger & Flynn, 1963;
McDonnell & Flynn, 1964; Wasman & Flynn, 1966).

The research showing the sensitizing effect of the
activity of other neurone circuits on those circuits concerned with aggression has been primarily confined to
predatory aggression. However, it seems likely that a
similar mechanism exists for all of the kinds of aggression and that these facilitating circuits are probably
associated with the neurological substrates of other behavior systems. Although the studies have not yet been done
to demonstrate specific increases in neural sensitivity in
the irritable aggression circuit, one can draw such an
inference from certain behavioral studies. Aversive stimulation (Ulrich, 1966), as well as a variety of deprivation
states, including food deprivation (Davis, 1933; Scott,
1949), sleep deprivation (Laties, 1961), morphine deprivation in addicted rats (Boshka, Weisman, & Thor, 1966), and
frustration produced by withdrawal of reinforcement (ex-
tinction-induced aggression) (Azrin et al., 1966;
Hutchinson, 1968; Thompson & Bloom, 1966) all increase the
tendency for the subject to manifest irritable aggression
in the presence of an appropriate stimulus. All of the
above conditions function as stressors and, if long continued, may produce endocrine changes which may influence
the sensitivity of aggression circuits (see below): however, the relatively rapid onset of aggression after some
of these stressors implies a neural facilitation.

Decreased Sensitivity from Neural Inhibition

The sensitivity of the aggressive circuits also
appears to be influenced by inhibitory input from other
systems, although the experimental evidence on this point
is, as yet, limited. It is a difficult problem to determine whether the aggressive circuit itself, or some particular group of motor responses is being inhibited by the
action of a given system. Flynn (1967) has elaborated on
the brain areas in the cat which tend to decrease the
sensitivity of the hypothalamic portions of the predatory
circuit (and to some extent the circuit for what is probably irritable aggression). These include the dorsal
hippocampus, the baso-medial-lateral amygdala, as well as

portions of the midbrain and the thalamus. Flynn (1967) refers to these inhibitory circuits, and to the facilitating circuits mentioned above as modulating structures. Delgado (1960) has shown that aggressiveness in the monkey can be specifically inhibited by stimulation of particular points in the head of the caudate nucleus. The normally hostile monkey loses its aggressiveness, and will not attempt to bite the experimenter if given an opportunity. However, this does not appear to be an arrest reaction. The animal's motility or motor responsiveness to sensory stimulation is not lost during the caudate stimulation.

Both aggressive behavior and the hostile verbal reports in human psychotics can be inhibited by stimulation of the septal region. According to Heath (1963), the patient's behavior changes almost instantly from disorganized rage to happiness and mild euphoria. Heath also reports that this phenomenon has been demonstrated in a large number of patients. Thus, it should not be considered as an isolated finding. Again, there is no indication in the Heath reports that there is an arrest reaction. In fact, the stimulation appears to activate an entirely different complex neural circuit. The septal stimulation results in an euphoric response complete with the appropriate effect verbally reported as well as the motor components including smiles and muscle tension reduction.

Stimulation and lesion studies indicate that circuits for irritable aggression and escape behavior probably are controlled by separate but overlapping anatomical areas within the amygdala (as well as other places in the brain) (Moyer, 1967b; Kaada, 1967). It also seems likely that a portion of the amygdaloid area which, when stimulated, induces escape behavior, also has inhibitory functions in relation to those areas of the amygdala associated with irritable and predatory aggression (Fonberg, 1965; Egger & Flynn, 1963; Wood, 1958). Stimulation of the central nucleus of the amygdala of the dog results in fear and escape responses (Fonberg, 1965). The same is true for the cat (Anand & Dua, 1956; Wood, 1958). Lesions in the same area, however, result in a reduced threshold for irritable aggression in both animals. The cat with lesions in the central nucleus will, according to Wood (1958), cross the room in order to find another cat to attack. The dog with the same lesion exhibits great irritability to normal restraints and once started in a rage response be-

comes more wild, exhibiting what Fonberg calls an
"avalanche syndrome" (Fonberg, 1965). Thus, it seems
likely, as suggested by both authors, that the central
nucleus, which appears to be a part of an escape circuit,
also functions to inhibit the activity of the aggression
circuit. Lesioning this nucleus results in release of
that inhibition with the resulting excessive irritability.

All of these studies which relate to the decrease in
sensitivity of the aggressive circuits by neural inhibition seem to lead to the conclusion that the inhibitory
neural influences may also be related to the activation of
other motivational or motor predisposition circuits. These
mechanisms may function in a manner similar to the recipro-
cal innervation mechanism in muscle control. Thus, the
intense activation of the neurological substrate for the
euphoric or fear response may be neurologically incompatible with the simultaneous activity of the irritable
aggression curcuit because the activation of one circuit
involves inhibition in the other.

The model proposed in this paper implies that the
modulating systems discussed above are a constant influence
on any naturally occurring aggressive behavior. Whether
aggression will occur, or continue in any given stimulus
situation, will depend on the interactions of a variety of
facilitating and inhibitory influences on the particular
aggression circuit involved. A particular stimulus situation may activate two incompatible neural circuits at the
same time. For example, the fear circuit and the irritable
aggression circuit may both be activated. The behavior of
the animal in that situation may vacillate between aggression and escape. As the stimulus situation changes,
either as a function of the animal's own behavior or because of changes in the stimulus objects themselves, the
new information may differentially influence the ultimate
behavior pattern. Significant changes in the stimulus
situation may at any time produce a shift in the predomi-
nantly active system with a resulting change in behavior.

Blood Chemistry Influences

There is a considerable body of evidence to indicate
that the tendency to various kinds of aggressive behavior
varies as a function of changes in the organism's blood
chemistry (Moyer, 1968). As indicated above, it is pro-

posed in this model that certain blood constituents act on
the aggression brain circuits to increase their sensitivity with the result that they are more easily fired by the
relevant stimuli. The importance of androgens for the
manifestation of inter-male and irritable aggression has
already been discussed. There is recent evidence that
these androgenic effects may be masked or inhibited by the
administration of estrogens (Suchowski, 1968). Irritable
aggression in the female in certain species is cyclical
(Pearson, 1944) and can be manipulated by hormone injections
(Kislak & Beach, 1955). Maternal aggression in the rat can
also be deactivated and reactivated by estrogen and hydro-
cortisone injections (Endroczi et al., 1958), although this
particular finding may be quite specific to the strain used
(Revlis & Moyer, unpublished).

There is clinical evidence to indicate that similar
mechanisms exist in man. Progesterone reduces the irritability manifested as a part of the premenstrual tension
syndrome (Dalton, 1964; Greene & Dalton, 1953), and the
administration of androgens has been reported to increase
aggressiveness in males (Straus et al., 1952; Sands, 1954;
Sands & Chamberlain, 1952). However, castration (Hawke,
1950; Le Maire, 1956) and the administration of stilboes-
trol (Dunn, 1941; Sands, 1954) in some cases reduce
aggressive tendencies.

It is generally recognized that frustration and stress,
particularly if prolonged, are likely to result in increased
irritability and aggressive behavior. It may well be that
the frustration induced irritability results from the
sensitization of irritable aggression brain circuits by
the particular hormone balance which characterizes the
stress syndrome. At this point there is no experimental
verification of this hypothesis but the experimental designs for the testing of the hypothesis are obvious.

It is not clear at the moment whether the endocrine
changes in the blood stream, implicated above, increase the
sensitivity of the aggression circuits directly, or whether
they do so indirectly by differentially influencing the
amounts of neurotransmitters in particular portions of the
brain with a resulting change in the sensitivity of particular circuits. There is good evidence, for example, that
the brain chemistry of aggressive animals (isolated mice)
is different from that of normals, including differences in

turnóver rates of serotonin (Giacalone et al., 1968) and
norepinephrine and dopamine (Welch & Welch, 1968). Sigg,
Day, and Colombo (1966), however, have shown that isolation-induced aggression does not develop in castrated mice.
The endocrine-brain chemistry interactions and the causal
relationship to the aggressive behaviors remain to be
worked out.

In the light of the experimental evidence, there can
be no doubt that different kinds of aggression are, in part,
a function of particular hormonal balances, and that the
levels of aggressiveness can be directly manipulated by
endocrine changes. It is inferred here that the endocrine
induced changes in aggression result from the direct or
indirect sensitization or activation of particular brain
circuits. That hypothesis is, however, readily testable
although the testing techniques require considerable
technical skill. Sheard (1967) has shown that the attack
latency and attack intensity resulting from brain stimulation can be manipulated by the peripheral administration
of amphetamine. A similar technique could be used to study
the sensitization of particular brain circuits by the
peripheral administration of endocrines suspected to be
important in the various kinds of aggression. This model
would predict that the various kinds of aggression as defined above would be differentially sensitized by different endocrine balances, although it is reasonable to
suspect some overlap, as in the influence of androgens
on both inter-male and irritable aggression.

Satiation as a Desensitizer

The aggression circuits may also be desensitized by
the expression of aggressive behavior, although the underlying physiological mechanism for this phenomenon remains
completely obscure.

Experiments currently in progress in my laboratory
clearly indicate that predatory aggression, at least, can
be satiated even though the consumption of the prey is
not permitted. Further, the predatory tendency reoccurs
after a period of predation deprivation. All of the data
on this experiment have not yet been analyzed, but it seems
safe to make the following general points. If a killer rat
is given a mouse once a day, the latency of the kill will
become progressively shorter until it stabilizes at less

than a minute; generally a few seconds. The rat will continue to kill a mouse a day for prolonged periods even
though it is never permitted to eat the prey. It kills
quickly, and efficiently, with little effort. However, if
the rat is presented with a mouse at one minute after each
kill, the kill latency gets progressively longer and after
5 or 10 mice, the rat no longer attacks the mice but will
even permit the exploring mouse to walk over it and nestle
with it. The killing response is also inhibited 24 hours
later. If the rat kills, it will kill only one mouse.
Perhaps even more interesting, the rat's tendency to kill
frogs also seems to be reduced after satiation of the
mouse killing response (Bandler & Moyer, unpublished).

Whether the concept of inhibition of aggression by
satiation applies to any kind of aggressive behavior other
than predatory is, at the moment, an open question because
the relevant experiments have not been done. There is,
however, some indication that the concept may be relevant
to inter-male aggression. Scott and Fredericson (1951)
suggest that trained fighter mice are less effective as
fighters if they fight more often than every other day.
Although these authors attributed the devrease in fighting
tendency 24 hours after an encounter to fatigue produced
by the initial fight, an equally plausible explanation
would be in terms of some kind of satiation phenomenon.
Welch (1967) reports that in the situation where mice live
together in uncrowded conditions with abundant food,
dominant animals will, over a period of weeks or months,
make periodic unchallenged attacks on the subordinates.
He says, "It is almost as though the aggressiveness of the
dominant is repeatedly, if temporarily, reduced by the
stimulus of attacking, but seldom for very long."

Learning and the Manifestation of Aggressive Behavior

Aggressive behavior, like all other basic behaviors,
is strongly influenced by experience. Just as an animal
can be taught to overeat (Williams & Teitelbaum, 1956) or
undereat (Licktenstein, 1950; Masserman, 1943) through the
use of reinforcement, regardless of the state of deprivation, animals can also be taught to exhibit or inhibit
aggressive behavior by similar means. It is not appropriate to survey here the vast literature on learning and
aggressive behavior. These studies, particularly those on
rats and mice, have been reviewed in some detail by Scott

(1951, 1966). However, some of the implications of the
role of learning in aggressive behavior as they relate to
this model should be explored.

It is possible to increase the probability of occurrence of any aggressive or destructive response, no matter
what its initial motivational source, if that response is
followed by a positive reinforcement. The law of effect
operates just as effectively in the facilitation of motor
responses which are labeled aggressive as in those which
are not. In the classification system outlined above,
aggressive behavior, so determined, is termed instrumental
aggression (See Feshbach, 1964). A particularly pure case
of instrumental aggression is demonstrated in the study of
Stachnik, Ulrich, and Mabry (1966a, 1966b). By reinforcing
successive approximations to aggressive behavior in rats
through positively reinforcing brain stimulation, these
investigators were able to induce rats to attack other
rats, monkeys, and even cats. They note, however, that the
occasional pain-elicited aggressive attacks resulting from
counterattack by a control rat presented a noticeable contrast to the topography of the conditioned attack. We have
used the same procedure to reinforce the attack on a mouse
by a nonpredatory rat. It is relatively easy to induce the
rat to chase, harass, and nip at the mouse. However, although we have tried repeatedly, we have been unable to
induce mouse killing by this procedure. The typical predatory response of the rat biting through the spinal cord of
the mouse just never occurs in the nonpredatory rat and thus
it is impossible to reinforce it.

Another experiment from our laboratory illustrates the
distinctiveness of instrumental aggression. Karli (1956)
has shown that nonpredatory rats will starve to death with
a live mouse in the cage. However, it is possible to induce
mouse killing in nonpredatory rats by gradually teaching the
rat that the mouse is a source of food (Moyer, 1968, unpublished). Most rats when food deprived will eat a dead
mouse with the skin of the back slit. After a series of
trials with that food object and subsequently with an intact
dead mouse, and a live but totally anesthetized mouse,
these rats will attack and kill a lightly anesthetized mouse
that is still mobile but sluggish in its behavior. Again,
however, it is easy to discriminate this instrumental behavior which results in the death of the mouse from the
typical predatory response either naturally or chemically

induced. These rats almost never kill by bites on the back of the neck. Their attack is directed at the tail, the feet, and the belly of the mouse. The approach is tentative, the latencies of attack and the time between attack and kill are much longer than in the natural predatory response. It would seem unlikely that any manipulation of the physiological basis for predatory aggression would have much effect on this instrumental response.

Various types of aggression have been both classically and instrumentally conditioned (See Ulrich, 1966) for review). There is also evidence that the opportunity to behave aggressively is, in itself, rewarding. Monkeys when shocked will learn a chain pulling response in order to obtain a tennis ball which they may bite (Azrin et al., 1965), and a pigeon during extinction (a situation which in itself produces aggressive behavior) will learn to peck a key which produces another bird which is then attacked (Azrin, 1964). Predatory rats will learn a maze to obtain a mouse whereas non-killer rats will not (Myer & White, 1965) and cats during stimulation of the lateral hypothalamus in the area which produces predatory aggression will learn a Y-maze if an attackable rat is used as reinforcement (Roberts & Kiess, 1964). Berkowitz has summarized an impressive amount of evidence to show that "...stimuli are capable of eliciting aggressive responses to the extent that they have been associated with aggression in the individual's past"(Berkowitz, 1967).

Just as aggressive behavior can be facilitated by reward, it can be inhibited by punishment. Predatory aggression can be readily suppressed by punishment of the attack response (Myer, 1968). In spite of the fact that noxious stimulation produces irritable aggressive behavior (Ulrich, 1966), it can also, if sufficiently intense, inhibit aggressive tendencies. Aggressive behavior is suppressed in monkeys if the punishing shock is more intense than the shock which elicited the fighting (Azrin, 1964). The negative reinforcement involved in defeat during inter-male aggression results in a decrease in aggressive tendencies (Kahn, 1951; Lagerspetz, 1961). Miller, Murphy, and Mirsky (1955) have clearly shown that it is possible to manipulate social hierarchies in monkeys by punishing a dominant animal in the presence of a subordinate, and Ulrich indicates that when a monkey is severely bitten by

an opponent, there is an obvious decrease in the aggressiveness of the bitten subject.

In an established colony where animals have a frequent
opportunity to interact, it is easy to see that the learning mechanisms indicated above could account for the
development of dominance hierarchies. A given animal
could easily learn to respond to the cue complex of one
animal in the colony with aggressive responses but to another with avoidance, submissive, or aggression inhibitory
responses. One would certainly expect these learned
responses to interact with the other internal states of
the organism such as the activity of particular aggression
circuits. If an animal is punished in the presence of
food, the eating responses of that animal in the presence
of the cues associated with punishment will be inhibited
regardless of the amount of deprivation (and presumed
activity in the hunger or consummatory circuits) (Lichtenstein, 1950). One would expect no less of an influence of
learning on the manifestations of aggression. As Plotnik
and Delgado (1968) and Delgado (1963, 1966) have shown,
the brain stimulation induced aggressive behavior of monkeys
is related to the animal's prior experience. The effects of
lesions involving the aggression circuits are also influenced by the prior learning of the animal (Rosvold et al.,
1954; Sodetz & Bunnell, 1967a, 1967b). It is rare for the
activity of the aggression circuits to be so intense that
they appear to override well-established habit patterns,
although this does appear to occur in humans (Schwade &
Geiger, 1956).

There is little experimental evidence on the neural
mechanisms involved in learned inhibition of aggressive
responding. It could, according to this model, occur at
any one of several levels. As indicated above, the inhibition may occur at the level of the integrating aggression
circuit itself. For example, the subjective feeling of
anger in the human (which would be indicative of activity
in the circuit for irritable aggression) could be replaced
by fear of sufficient intensity that the irritable aggression circuit is inhibited and the individual no longer has
the subjective experience of anger. The inhibition could
also occur at the muscular level producing the extreme
tension state of inhibited rage in which the muscles in
opposition to the ones used in attack are contracted to a
point at which they prevent attack behavior. In this sit-

uation, however, the central integrative aggression circuit would continue to fire, and the human would continue to experience the subjective state of anger.

Man, of course, learns better and faster than all other animals. It is, therefore, reasonable to expect that the internal impulses to aggressive behavior would be more subject to modification by experience in man than in any other animal. Also, because of man's additional ability to manipulate symbols, and to substitute one symbol for another, one would expect to find 'a considerable diversity in the stimuli which will elicit or inhibit activity in the aggression circuits. One would also expect that the modes of expression of aggression to be more varied, diverse, and less stereotyped in man than in other animals.

IMPLICATIONS FOR AGGRESSION CONTROL

I am convinced that if we, as students of aggression, confine ourselves to our ivory tower of theory and experiment while the world around us seethes with aggression, we may very well awaken to find the ivory tower burned down upon our heads. I, therefore, feel compelled to mention, at least briefly, the implications that this model of aggressive behavior has for aggression control.

First, one may reduce the tendencies to aggression by manipulating the environment to minimize those facets of it which increase the sensitivity of the aggression curcuits. Specifically, this would include minimizing pain, frustration, deprivation, and a variety of other stressors. This may require extensive changes in the culture to alleviate the chronic frustration and deprivation of large segments of the population.

Secondly, one may develop inhibitory tendencies through the positive reinforcement of nonaggressive responses in the presence of aggression eliciting stimuli, or through the negative reinforcement of expressed aggression. Since negative reinforcement constitutes a stressor, the total effect of that approach must be carefully evaluated.

Finally, one can directly manipulate the internal environment to deactivate or desensitize the hostility circuits and thus reduce or eliminate the tendency of the

individual to respond to the external stimuli with an aggressive response. This can be accomplished through the
use of drugs which selectively suppress aggressive tendencies (Kalina, 1962; Resnick, 1967; Turner, 1967);
through hormone therapy (Dunn, 1941; Greene & Dalton, 1953;
Sands, 1954); bu the stimulation of brain circuits which
inhibit aggressive tendencies (Heath, 1963); and, finally,
by the surgical lesioning of portions of the aggressive
circuit (Sano, 1966; Sano et al., 1966; Tow ± Whitty,
1953). All of the above methods of the physiological control of aggressive behavior have been successfully used on
man (See Moyer, 1969, for a further discussion of this
point).

SUMMARY

     Aggression is not a unitary concept. The following
classes of aggressive behavior are suggested: predatory,
inter-male, fear-induced, irritable, territorial, maternal,
instrumental, and sex related. These kinds of aggression
may be differentiated on the basis of the stimulus situations which elicit them.

     Although the physiological bases of the various kinds
of aggression may overlap, they are essentially different
and it is possible to discriminate among these physiological substrates experimentally.

     The experimental evidence is examined to support the
proposition that there are in the brain innately organized
neural circuits for the various kinds of aggression. When
these circuits are active in the presence of particular
stimuli, the organism behaves aggressively. Thus, aggressive behavior is stimulus bound and dependent on the
functional integrity of teh aggression circuits.

     In spite of man's encephalization, he has not escaped
from the biological determinants of aggressive behavior.
The activation of certain brain areas in man results in
aggression. This occurs whether the activation is the
result of direct electrical stimulation, stimulation by
tumor growth, or spontaneous activity as is found in
certain types of epilepsy. Chronic aggressive and assaultive behavior in man can be alleviated by the surgical

interruption of particular brain circuits.

A variety of factors contribute to whether or not particular aggression circuits will be inactive and insensitive, sensitive and thus easily fired, or spontaneously active. There is evidence that some of the determinants of the sensitivity of the aggression circuits are hereditary and that the development of these circuits can be influenced by neonatal endocrine changes.

A number of neural systems in the brain which when stimulated do not result in aggressive behavior do, when activated, facilitate ongoing aggressive behavior and thus seem to increase the sensitivity of the aggression circuits. It is suggested that these facilitating systems may be activated by environmental changes which result in such states as deprivation, pain, and frustration.

The sensitivity of the aggression circuits may also be reduced by the activation of other neural systems in the brain. These inhibitory effects may come from other behavior systems in the brain which are neurologically incompatible with the aggression systems. One example might be euphoria. The sensitivity and/or activity of the aggression circuits is constantly being modulated by the facilitating and inhibiting input from other systems.

Changes in the blood chemistry, primarily, but not exclusively hormonal, also have an effect on the sensitivity of the aggression circuits. The experimental evidence leaves little doubt that different kinds of aggression are, in part, a function of particular hormonal balances, and that the levels of aggressiveness can be directly manipulated by endocrine changes.

Aggressive behavior, like all basic behaviors, is strongly influenced by learning. Thus, the tendency to behave aggressively to any stimulus complex may be either enhanced or inhibited depending on the nature of the reinforcement which follows the behavior.

The implications of this model for the control of aggressive behavior are briefly discussed.

ACKNOWLEDGMENTS

This work was supported in part by Grant #GB6652 from
the National Science Foundation.

REFERENCES

ADAMS, D. B. Cells related to fighting behavior recorded
from midbrain central gray neuropil of cat. Science,
1968, 159, 894-896.

ALONSO-DEFLORIDA, F., & DELGADO, J. M. R. Lasting behavioral and EEG changes in cats induced by prolonged
stimulation of amygdala. Am. J. Physiol., 1958,
193, 223-229.

ANAND, B. K., & DUA, S. Electrical stimulation of the
limbic system of the brain ('visceral brain') in the
waking animals. Indiana J. Med. Res., 1956, 44,
107-119.

AZRIN, N. H. Aggression. Paper read at the American
Psychological Association, Los Angeles, 1964.

AZRIN, N. H., HUTCHINSON, R. R., & HAKE, D. F. Extinction
induced aggression. J. Exp. Anal. Behav., 1966,
9, 191-204.

AZRIN, N. H., HUTCHINSON, R. R., & MCLAUGHLIN, R. The
opportunity for aggression as an operant reinforcer
during aversive stimulation. J. Exp. Anal. Behav.,
1965, 8, 171-180.

BARNETT, S. A. A Study of Behaviour. London: Methuen
& Co., 1963.

BEEMAN, E. A. The effect of male hormone on aggressive
behavior in mice. Physiol. Zool., 1947, 20, 373-405.

BERKOWITZ, L. Experiments on automatism and intent in
human aggression. In C. D. Clemente and D. B. Lindsley
(Eds.) Aggression and Defense. Berkeley, Calif.:
University of California Press, 1967, pp. 243-266.

BEVAN, W., DAVES, W. F., & LEVY, G. W. The relation of
    castration, androgen therapy and pre-test fighting
    experience to competitive aggression in male C 57
    BL/10 mice. Anim. Behav., 1960, 8, 6-12.

BOSHKA, S. C., WEISMAN, H. M., & THOR, D. H. A technique
    for inducing aggression in rats utilizing morphine
    withdrawal. Psychol. Rec., 1966, 16, 541-543.

BRONSON, F. H., & DESJARDINS, C. Alterations in aggres-
    siveness of adult mice by neonatal steroid adminis-
    tration. Paper presented at AAAS Symposium on the
    Physiology of Fighting and Defeat, Dallas, Texas,
    December, 1968.

BROWN, J. L., & HUNSPERGER, R. W. Neuroethology and the
    motivation of agonistic behaviour. Anim. Behav.,
    1963, 11, 439-448.

BRUTKOWSKI, S., FONBERG, E., & MEMPEL, E. Angry behavior
    in dogs following bilateral lesions in the genual
    portion of the rostral cingulate gyrus. Acta Biol.
    Exp. Polish Acad. Sci., 1961, 21, 199-205.

BURNAND, G., HUNTER, H., & HOGGART, K., Some psychological
    test characteristics of Klinefelter's syndrome. Brit.
    J. Psychiat., 1967, 113, 1091-1096.

CONNER, R. L., & LEVINE, S. Hormonal influences on aggres-
    sive behaviour. Paper presented at the First Inter-
    national Symposium on Aggressive Behavior, Milan,
    Italy, May, 1968.

DALTON, K. The Premenstrual Syndrome. Springfield, Ill.:
    Charles C. Thomas, 1964.

DAVIS, F. C. The measurement of aggressive behavior in
    laboratory rats. J. Genet. Psychol., 1933, 43,
    213-217.

DELGADO, J. M. R. Emotional behavior in animals and
    humans. Psychiat. Res. Rep., 1960, 12, 259-271.

DELGADO, J. M. R. Pharmacology of spontaneous and conditioned behavior in the monkey. Pharmacology of conditioning, learning and retention. Proceedings of the
Second International Pharmacological Meeting, Prague,
20-23 August, 1963, pp. 133-156.

DELGADO, J. Aggressive behavior evoked by radio stimulation
in monkey colonies. Amer. Zool., 1966, 6, 669-681.

DUNN, G. W. Stilbestrol induced testicular degeneration in
hypersexual males. J. Clin. Endocrinol., 1941, 1,
643-648.

EDWARDS, D. A. Mice: Fighting by neonatally androgenized
females. Science, 1968, 161, 1027-1028.

EGGER, M. D., & FLYNN, J. P. Effect of electrical stimulation of the amygdala on hypothalamically elicited attack
behavior in cats. J. Neurophysiol., 1963, 26, 705-720.

EIBL-EIBESFELDT, I. The fighting behavior of animals. Sci.
Am., 1961, 205, 112-122.

ENDROCZI, E., LISSAK, K., & TELEGDY, G. Influence of sexual
and adrenocortical hormones on the maternal aggressivity.
Acta Physiol. Acad. Sci. Hung., 1958, 14, 353-357.

ERVIN, F., MARK, V., & SWEET, W. Focal brain disease and
assaultive behaviour. Paper presented at the First
International Symposium on Aggressive Behavior, Milan,
Italy, May, 1968.

EVERETT, G. M. Role of dopamine in irritable and aggressive
behavior. Paper presented at the First International
Symposium on Aggressive Behavior, Milan, Italy, May,
1968.

EVERETT, G. M., & WIEGAND, R. G. Central amines and behavioral states: A critique and new data. Proceedings of the
First International Pharmacological Meeting, August,
1962, pp. 85-92.

FESBACH, S. The function of aggression and the regulation
of aggressive drive. Psychol. Rev., 1964, 71, 257-272.

FLYNN, J. P. The neural basis of aggression. Mimeographed
Report, 1967.

FLYNN, J. P. Sites within the brain from which aggressive
    behavior can be evoked. Paper presented at AAAS
    Symposium on the Physiology of Fighting and Defeat,
    Dallas, Texas, December, 1968.

FONBERG, E. Effect of partial destruction of the
    amygdaloid complex on the emotional-defensive behav-
    ior of dogs. Bulletin de l'Academie Polonaise des
    Sciences Cl. II, 1965, 13, 429-431.

FREDERICSON, E. The effects of food deprivation upon
    competitive and spontaneous combat in C57 black mice.
    J. Psychol., 1960, 29, 89-100.

GIACALONE, E., TANSELIA, M., VALZELLI, L., & GARATTINI, S.
    Brain serotonin metabolism in isolated aggressive
    mice. Biochem. Pharmacol., 1968, 17, 1315-1327.

GLEES, P., COLE, J., WHITTY, C., & CAIRNS, H. The effects
    of lesions in the cingular gyrus and adjacent areas
    in monkeys. J. Neurol. Neurosurg. Psychiat., 1950,
    13, 178-190.

GLOOR, P. Discussion of brain mechanisms related aggres-
    sive behavior by B. Kaada. In C. D. Clemente and
    D. B. Lindsley (Eds.) Aggression and Defense.
    Berkeley, California: University of California
    Press, 1967.

GREENE, R., & DALTON, K. The premenstrual syndrome.
    Brit. Med. J., 1953, 1, 1007-1014.

HALL, C. S., & KLEIN, S. J. Individual differences in
    aggressiveness in rats. J. Comp. Psychol., 1942,
    33, 371-383.

HAWKE, C. C. Castration and sex crimes. Am. J. Ment.
    Def., 1950, 55, 220-226.

HEATH, R. G. Electrical self-stimulation of the brain in
    man. Am. J. Psychiat., 1963, 120, 571-577.

HOFFMEISTER, P., & WUTTKE, W. On the actions of psychotro-
    pic drugs or the attack and aggressive-defensive behav-
    ior of mice and cats. Paper presented at the First
    Internat. Symp. on Aggressive Behavior Milan, May, 1968.

HUTCHINSON, R. R., ULRICH, R. E., & AZRIN, N. H.   Effects
    of age and related factors on the pain aggression re-
    action.   J. Comp. Physiol. Psychol., 1965, 59, 365-369.

HUTCHINSON, R. R., & RENFREW, J. W.   Stalking attack and
    eating behavior elicited from the same sites in the
    hypothalamus.   J. Comp. Physiol. Psychol., 1966, 61,
    300-367.

HUTCHINSON, R. R.   Effects of reward and extinction on
    aggressive behavior.   Paper presented at the First
    International Symposium on Aggressive Behavior,
    Milan, Italy, May, 1968.

JACOBSEN, E.   The clinical effect of drugs and their influ-
    ence on animal behaviour.   Revue de Psychologie Appli-
    quee, 1961, 11, 421-432.

JONAS, A. D.   Ictal and Subictal Neurosis: Diagnosis and
    Treatment.   Springfield, Ill.:   Charles C. Thomas,
    1965.

KAADA, B.   Brain mechanisms related to aggressive behavior.
    In C. D. Clemente and D. B. Lindsley (Eds.) Aggression
    and Defense.   Berkeley, California: University of
    California Press, 1967, pp. 195-234.

KAHN, M. W.   The effect of severe defeat at various age
    levels on the aggressive behavior of mice.   J. Genet.
    Psychol., 1951, 79, 117-130.

KALINA, R. K.   Use of diazepam in the violent psychotic
    patient: A preliminary report.   Colorado GP, 1962,
    4, 11-14.

KARLI, P.   The Norway rat's killing response to the white
    mouse.   Behavior, 1956, 10, 81-103.

KARLI, P.   Hormones steroides et comportement d'agression
    inter-specifique rat-souris.   J. Physiol. Gen. Pathol.
    1958, 50, 346-347.

KARLI, P., VERGNES, M., & DIDIERGEORGES, F. Rat-mouse
    interspecific aggressive behaviour and its manipula-
    tion by brain ablation and by brain stimulation.
    Paper presented at the First International Symposium
    on Aggressive Behavior, Milan, Italy, May, 1968.

KENNARD, M. A. The cingulate gyrus in relation to con-
    sciousness. J. Nerv. Ment. Dis., 1955a, 121, 34-39.

KENNARD, M. A. Effect of bilateral ablation of cingulate
    area on behavior of cats. J. Neurophysiol., 1955b,
    18, 159-169.

KING, H. E. Psychological effects of excitation in the
    limbic system. In D. E. Sheer (Ed.) Electrical
    Stimulation of the Brain. Austin: University of
    Texas Press, 1961, pp. 477-486.

KING, M. B., & HOEBEL, B. G. Killing elicited by brain
    stimulation in rats. Communications in Behavioral
    Biology, 1968 (in press).

KISLAK, J. W., & BEACH, F. A. Inhibition of aggressiveness
    by ovarian hormones. Endocrinology, 1955, 56, 684-692.

KLING, A., & HUTT, P. J. Effect of hypothalamic lesions
    on the amygdala syndrome in the cat. A.M.A. Arch.
    Neurol. Psychiat., 1958, 79, 511-517.

KOMISARUK, B. R., & OLDS, J. Neuronal correlates of behav-
    ior in freely moving rats. Science, 1968, 161, 810-813.

KORN, J. H., & MOYER, K. E. Behavioral effects of isolation
    in the rat: The role of sex and time of isolation.
    J. Genet. Psychol., 1968, 113, 263-273.

LAGERSPETZ, K. Genetic and social causes of aggressive
    behavior in mice. Scand. J. Psychol., 1961, 2,
    167-173.

LATIES, V. G. Modification of affect, social behavior and
    performance by sleep deprivation and drugs. J.
    Psychiat. Res., 1961, 1, 12-25.

LEAF, R. C., LERNER, L., & HOROVITZ, Z. P. The role of
    the amygdala in the pharmacological and endocrino-
    logical manipulation of aggression. Paper presented
    at the First International Symposium on Aggressive
    Behavior, Milan, Italy, 1968.

LE BEAU, J. The cingular and precingular areas in psycho-
    surgery (agitated behaviour, obsessive compulsive
    states, epilepsy). Acta Psychiat. Neurol., 1952,
    27, 305-316.

LE MAIRE, L. Danish experiences regarding the castration
    of sexual offenders. J. Crim. Law Criminol., 1956,
    47, 294-310.

LENNOX, W. G. The genetics of epilepsy. Am. J. Psychiat.,
    1947, 103, 457-462.

LEVISON, P. K., & FLYNN, J. P. The objects attacked by
    cats during stimulation of the hypothalamus. Anim.
    Behav., 1965, 13, 217-220.

LEVY, J. V. The effects of testosterone propionate on
    fighting behaviour in C57BL/10 young female mice.
    Proc. W. Va. Acad. Sci., 1954, 26, 14.

LEVY, J. V., & KING, J. A. The effects of testosterone
    propionate on fighting behaviour in young male
    C57BL/10 mice. Anat. Rec., 1953, 117, 562-563.

LICHTENSTEIN, P. E. Studies of anxiety: II. The effects
    of lobotomy on a feeding inhibition in dogs. J. Comp.
    Physiol. Psychol., 1950, 43, 419-427.

MACDONNELL, M. F., & FLYNN, J. P. Attack elicited by
    stimulation of the thalamus of cats. Science, 1964,
    144, 1249-1250.

MACDONNELL, M. F., & FLYNN, J. P. Control of sensory
    fields by stimulation of hypothalamus. Science, 1966,
    152, 1406-1408.

MACLEAN, P. D., & DELGADO, J. M. R. Electrical and chemical
    stimulation of frontotemporal portion of limbic system
    in the waking animal. EEG Clin. Neurophysiol., 1953,
    5, 91-100.

MASSERMAN, J. H. Behavior and Neuroses. Chicago, Ill.: University of Chicago Press, 1943.

MILLER, N. E. Chemical coding of behavior in the brain. Science, 1965, 148, 328-338.

MILLER, R. E., MURPHY, J. V., & MIRSKY, I. A. The modification of social dominance in a group of monkeys by interanimal conditioning. J. Comp. Physiol. Psychol., 1955, 48, 392-396.

MOYER, K. E. Kinds of aggression and their physiological basis. Communications in Behavioral Biology, 1968a, 2, 65-87.

MOYER, K. E. Brain research must contribute to world peace. Journal of the Fiji Medical School, 1968b, 3, 2-5.

MOYER, K. E. Internal impulses to aggression. Trans. N. Y. Acad. Sci., 1969.

MYER, J. S., & WHITE, R. T. Aggressive motivation in the rat. Anim. Behav., 1965, 13, 430-433.

MYER, J. S. Associative and temporal determinants of facilitation and inhibition of attack by pain. J. Comp. Physiol. Psychol., 1968, 66, 17-21.

PEARSON, O. P. Reproduction in the shrew (Blarina Brevicauda Say). Am. J. Anat., 1944, 75, 39-93.

PLOTNIK, R., & DELGADO, J. M. R. Aggression and pain in unrestrained rhesus monkeys. Paper presented at AAAS Symposium on the Physiology of Fighting and Defeat, Dallas, Texas, December, 1968.

POOL, J. L. The visceral brain of man. J. Neurosurg., 1954, 11, 45-63.

PRICE, W. H., & WHATMORE, P. B. Behavior disorders and pattern of crime among XYY males identified at a maximum security hospital. Brit. Med. J., 1967a, 1, 533-536.

PRICE, W. H., & WHATMORE, P. B.   Criminal behaviour and
    the XYY male.   Nature, 1967b, 213, 815-816.

RANDRUP, A., & MUNKVAD, I.   Relation of brain catechol
    amines to aggressiveness and other forms of behavioral
    excitation.   Paper presented at the First Internation-
    al Symposium on Aggressive Behavior, Milan, Italy,
    May, 1968.

RESNICK, O.   The psychoactive properties of diphenylhydan-
    toin: Experiences with prisoners and juvenile
    delinquents.   Internat. J. Neuropsychiat., 1967,
    Suppl. 3(2), S30-S48.

ROBERTS, W. W., & KIESS, H. O.   Motivational properties of
    hypothalamic aggression in cats.   J. Comp. Physiol.,
    1964, 58, 187-193.

ROMANIUK, A.   Representation of aggression and flight re-
    actions in the hypothalamus of the cat.   Acta Biol.
    Exp. Polish Acad. Sci., 1965, 25, 177-186.

ROSVOLD, H. S., MIRSKY, A. F., & PRIBRAM, K. H.   Influences
    of amygdalectomy on social behavior in monkeys.   J.
    Comp. Physiol. Psychol., 1954, 47, 173-178.

SANDS, D. E.   Further studies on endocrine treatment in
    adolescence and early adult life.   J. Ment. Sci.,
    1954, 100, 211-219.

SANDS, D. E., & CHAMBERLAIN, G. H. A.   Treatment of in-
    adequate personality in juveniles by dehydroisoan-
    drosterone.   Brit. Med. J., 1952, 1, 66-68.

SANO, K., YOSHIOKA, M., OGASHIWA, M., ISHIJIMA, B., &
    OHYE, C.   Posteromedial hypothalamotomy in the treat-
    ment of aggressive behaviors.   Confin. Neurol., 1966,
    27, 164-167.

SANO, K.   Sedative neurosurgery: With special reference to
    postero-medial hypothalamotomy.   Neurologia Medico-
    chirurgica, 1962, 4, 112-142.

SCHREINER, L., & KLING, A.   Behavioral changes following
    rhinencephalic injury in cat.   J. Neurophysiol.,
    1953, 16, 643-658.

SCHREINER, L., & KLING, A. Rhinencephalon and behavior. Am. J. Physiol., 1956, 184, 486-490.

SCHWADE, E. D., & GEIGER, S. C. Abnormal EEG findings in severe behavior disorder. Diseases Nervous System, 1956, 17, 307-317.

SCHWADE, E. D., & GEIGER, S. C. Severe behavioral disorders with abnormal electroencephalograms. Diseases Nervous System, 1960, 21, 616-620.

SCOTT, J. P. Genetic differences in the social behavior of inbred strains of mice. J. Hered., 1942, 33, 11-15.

SCOTT, J. P. Dominance and the frustration-aggression hypothesis. Physiol. Zool., 1948, 21, 31-39.

SCOTT, J. P. Aggression. Chicago, Ill.: University of Chicago Press, 1958.

SCOTT, J. P., & FREDERICSON, E. The causes of fighting in mice and rats. Physiol. Zool., 1951, 24, 273-309.

SCOTT, J. P. Agonistic behavior of mice and rats: A review. Am. Zool., 1966, 6, 683-701.

SEM-JACOBSEN, C. W., & TORKILDESEN, A. Depth recording and electrical stimulation in the human brain. In E. R. Ramey and D. S. O'Doherty (Eds.) Electrical Studies on the Unanesthetized Brain. Scranton, Pa.: Hoeber, 1960, 275-290.

SEM-JACOBSEN, C. W. Depth-electrographic observations related to Parkinson's disease. J. Neurosurg., 1966, 24, 388-402.

SEWARD, J. P. Aggressive behavior in the rat: I. General characteristics; Age and sex differences. J. Comp. Psychol., 1945, 38, 175-197.

SHEALY, C., & PELLE, J. Studies on amygdaloid nucleus of cat. J. Neurophysiol., 1957, 20, 125-139.

SHEARD, M. H. The effects of amphetamine on attack behavior in the cat. Brain Res., 1967, 5, 331-338.

SHEARD, M. H., & FLYNN, J. P. Facilitation of attack
    behavior by stimulation of the midbrain of cats.
    Brain Res., 1967, 4, 324-333.

SIGG, E. B., DAY, C., & COLOMBO, C. Endocrine factors
    in isolation-induced aggressiveness in rodents.
    Endocrinology, 1966, 78, 679-684.

SODETZ, F. J., & BUNNELL, B. N. Interactive effects of
    septal lesions and social experience in the hamster.
    Paper presented at the meeting of the Eastern
    Psychological Association, 1967a.

SODETZ, F. J., & BUNNELL, B. N. Septal ablation and the
    social behavior of the golden hamster. Paper pre-
    sented at the meeting of the Midwestern Psycho-
    logical Association, Chicago, 1967b.

SPIEGEL, E. A., WYCIS, H. T., FREED, H., & ORCHINIK, C.
    The central mechanism of the emotions. Am. J.
    Psychiat., 1951, 108, 426-432.

STACHNIK, T. J., ULRICH, R., & MABRY, J. H. Reinforcement
    of intra- and inter-species aggression with intra-
    cranial stimulation. Amer. Zool. , 1966a, 6, 663-668.

STACHNIK, T. J., ULRICH, R. E., & MABRY, J. H. Reinforce-
    ment of aggression through intracranial stimulation.
    Psychon. Sci., 1966b, 5, 101-102.

STONE, C. P. Wildness and savageness in rats of different
    strains. In K. S. Lashley (Ed.) Studies in Dynamics
    of Behavior. Chicago., Ill.: University of Chicago
    Press, 1932.

STRAUSS, E. B., SANDS, D. E., ROBINSON, A. M., TINDALL, W. J.
    & STEVENSON, W. A. H. Use of dehydroisoandrosterone
    in psychiatric treatment. Brit. Med. J., 1952, 64-66.

SUCHOWSKI, G. K. Sexual hormones and aggressive behavior.
    Paper presented at the First International Symposium
    on Aggressive Behavior, Milan, Italy, May, 1968.

SUMMERS, T. B., & KAELBER, W. W. Amygdalectomy: Effects
    in cats and a survey of its present status. Am. J.
    Physiol., 1962, 203, 1117-1119.

TELFER, M. A., BAKER, D., CLARK, G. R., & RICHARDSON, C. E. Incidence of gross chromosomal errors among tall criminal American males. Science, 1968, 159, 1249-1250.

THOMPSON, T., & BLOOM, W. Aggressive behavior and extinction induced response-rate increase. Psychon. Sci., 1966, 5, 335.

TINBERGEN, N. Fighting and threat in animals. New Biol. 1953, 14, 9-24.

TOLMAN, J., & KING, J. A. The effects of testosterone propionate on aggression in male and female C57BL/10 mice. Brit. J. Anim. Behav., 1956, 4, 147-149.

TOW, P. M., & WHITTY, C. W. Personality changes after operations on the cingulate gyrus in man. J. Neurol. Neurosurg. Psychiat., 1953, 16, 186-193.

TREFFERT, D. A. The psychiatric patient with an EEG temporal lobe focus. Am. J. Psychiat., 1964, 120, 765-771.

TURNER, W. J. The usefulness of diphenylhydantoin in treatment of non-epileptic emotional disorders. Internat. J. Neuropsychiat., 1967, Suppl. 3(2), S8-S20.

ULRICH, R. Pain as a cause of aggression. Am. Zool., 1966, 6, 643-662.

URSIN, H. The temporal lobe substrate of fear and anger. Acta Psychiat. Neurol. Scand., 1960, 35, 278-396.

VALZELLI, L. Drugs and aggressiveness. Advances in Pharmacology, 1967, 5, 79-108.

VONDERAHE, A. R. The anatomic substratum of emotion. The New Scholasticism, 1944, 18, 76-95.

WARD, A. A. The cingular gyrus; area 24. J. Neurophysiol., 1948, 11, 13-23.

WASMAN, M., & FLYNN, J. P. Directed attack elicited from hypothalamus. Arch. Neurol., 1962, 6, 220-227.

WASMAN, M., & FLYNN, J. P. Directed attack behavior during hippocampal seizures. Arch. Neurol., 1966, 14, 408-414.

WELCH, B. L. Discussion of aggression, defense, and neurohumors by Rothballer, A. B. In C. D. Clemente and D. B. Lindsley (Eds.) Aggression and Defense. Berkeley, California: University of California Press, 1967.

WELCH, B. L., & WELCH, A. S. Aggression and the biogenic amine neurohumors. Paper presented at the First International Symposium on Aggressive Behavior, Milan, Italy, May, 1968.

WENDE, C. V., & SPOERLEIN, M. T. Psychotic symptoms induced in mice by the intravenous administration of solutions of 3,4-dehydroxyphenylanine (DOPA). Arch. Internat. Pharmacodyn., 1962, 137, 145-154.

WHEATLY, M. D. The hypothalamus and affective behavior in cats. Arch. Neurol. Psychiat., 1944, 52, 296-316.

WILLIAMS, D. R., & TEITELBAUM, P. Control of drinking behavior by means of an operant-conditioning technique. Science, 1956, 124, 1294-1296.

WILLIAMS, R. J. Biochemical Individuality. New York: John Wiley & Sons, 1956.

WOOD, C. D. Behavioral changes following discrete lesions of temporal lobe structures. Neurology, 1958, 8 (Suppl. 1), 215-220.

WOODS, J. W. "Taming" of the wild Norway rat by rhinencephalic lesions. Nature, 1956, 178, 869.

WOODS, S. M. Adolescent violence and homicide: Ego disruption and the 6 and 14 dysrhythmia. Arch. Genet. Psychiat., 1961, 5, 528-534.

YASUKOCHI, G. Emotional responses elicited by electrical stimulation of the hypothalamus in cat. Folia Psychiat. Neurol. Japon., 1960, 14, 260-267.

YERKES, R. M. The heredity of savageness and wildness in
    rats. _J_. _Anim_. _Behav_., 1913, 3, 286-296.

ALTERED ADRENAL FUNCTION IN TWO COMBAT SITUATIONS IN
VIET NAM

Peter G. Bourne, M. D.[1]

Director, South Central Community Mental
Health Center
Atlanta, Georgia

The concept of stress has been accepted widely as a
specific somatic response to damage or threat of damage by
a wide variety of environmental agents, including events
having a psychological rather than physical impact. This
concept first was suggested by the observation made in 1911
by Cannon and de la Paz that the adrenal medulla releases a
hormone in the cat during the emotional excitement associated with exposure to a barking dog (Cannon & de la Paz,
1911). In 1936, Hans Selye presented evidence of a second
endocrine system, the pituitary-adrenal cortical axis.
This system, responding often to more subtle aspects of
psychic and physical stress, induced even more global and
profound influences on metabolic function (Selye, 1936).
The work of Cannon and the proposal by Selye of a "General
Adaptation Syndrome" led to the expectation by some investigators that these hormones would provide a tangible measure
of the degree of stress to which an organism was exposed.

[1] Formerly:
Chief, Neuropsychiatry Section
U.S. Army Medical Research Team, Viet Nam
Walter Reed Army Institute of Research
Washington, D.C.

The emphasis on the adrenal glands proved most useful for stimulating research since it offered a specific structure for the center of attention. However, with further work in the field and the development of improved biochemical techniques, evidence has accumulated that other endocrine systems, in addition to those involving the adrenals, can respond to psychological stimuli. It now would appear that no endocrine system is free entirely from the influences of psychological stress (Mason, 1964).

Despite these recent advances, implicating virtually all endocrine systems, altered adrenal function in relationship to behaviour and to the handling of stress has remained the central focus for research in the field during the last fifteen years. Initially, the studies concentrated on observed elevations in adrenal cortical secretion produced by acute stimuli in the environment in both experimental and naturally occurring situations. Endocrinological reactions to movies (Wadeson et al., 1963), final exams (Bliss et al.; 1956), and hospital admission (Mason et al., 1965) were studied in human subjects as well as the responses to threatening and demanding stimuli in monkeys (Mason, Brady, & Sidman, 1957; Mason, Harwood, & Rosenthal, 1957). It also was shown that calming influences in the environment such as movies with a benign content and hypnosis produced an acute decrease in the level of secretion (Sachar, Cobb, & Shor, 1966; Wadeson et al., 1963). These studies, however, dealt only with the response of the organism to an acute and well-defined event. Subsequently, investigations of more chronic situations have shown that under circumstances of prolonged stress both elevations and depressions in the mean adrenal steroid secretion level can occur (Mason, 1959; Friedman, Mason, & Hamburg, 1963).

More recently, it has been appreciated that the degree of stress which an event is considered to provide, whether it be automobile racing or cardiac surgery, is based entirely on the subjective assessment of the event by the investigator. Thus the problem has become more complex, necessitating a re-examination of the earlier conceptualization of stress as a stimulus-response or threat-defense phenomenon. Instead, it is now appreciated that stress

can be defined only in terms of man's interaction with his
environment, and that an event is stressful for an individual only if he perceives it as such. By contrast with
the earlier viewpoint, it is clear that no component of
the stress reaction can be considered constant. Most
important in producing this shift in emphasis was the work
of several investigators (Fox et al., 1961; Wolff et al.,
1964; Sachar et al., 1963), all of whom demonstrated the
significance of individual difference in the psychological
and physiological handling of similar events in the environment. Specifically, they demonstrated that there was a relationship between the adrenal secretion of 17-hydroxy-
corticosteroid (17-OHCS) and an individual's characteristic
style of dealing with the day-to-day stresses of living.
The concept of ego defenses, and the manner in which they
were utilized to handle the perception of threatening
stimuli was used to explain the differences they observed.
As a result, it became experimentally feasible, on the basis
of observed behavior, to predict the chronic mean level of
17-OHCS secretion in a given individual over a period of
weeks or months (Wolff et al., 1964). It also was demonstrated in certain clinical situations that over more extended periods of time, with therapy or other factors which
alter the efficacy of the individual's defenses, changes
occur in this characteristic mean level.

There now is strong evidence that, in addition to individual differences, social factors may exert a significant
effect in altering an individual's perception of stress and,
hence, his level of adrenal cortical secretion (Mason &
Brady, 1964). In small groups, with free communication
among members of equal standing, there is a tendency for a
consensus to develop as to how a stress should be perceived,
which in turn minimizes individual differences in adrenal-
cortical response. The group support also serves to reinforce avoidance of prolonged feelings of arousal or uncer-
tainty. As a result, members of a group, when presented
with a threatening event, will tend to have more similar responses in the excretion levels of steroids than if they
were presented with the same event as isolated subjects.
It also is becoming increasingly apparent that aside from
mere group consensus in the perception of stress when all
members are equal, there also is an important potential

influence of assigned role when some members are designated
as leaders (Marchbanks, 1958). This has been shown to be
true particularly in primate societies, where animals high
in the social hierarchy of the troop present entirely
different endocrinological profiles in response to a given
stress than do animals who are low in the dominance order
(personal communication Rose, R. M. and Levine, M.). This
means that in the investigation of man's response to stress
attention must be paid to the threat itself, the psychological style of the individual in coping with his environment, and the social context in which he exists.

Following the first indications that levels of steroid
secretion from the adrenal gland could be a measurable parameter of an organism's response to stress, investigators
sought for naturally occurring events which appeared to pose
extreme threats to those involved. Race drivers, long dis-
tance runners, college oarsmen, and patients prior to open
heart surgery, as well as persons in a myriad of other
pursuits had their rates of steroid excretion measured to
assess their "level of stress." Workers in the field were
aware that combat, with its very real threat of death or
mutilation, might represent the ultimate in naturally
occurring events of stress, and that steroid levels could
be anticipated that would exceed those observed previously
in any civilian circumstance. Historically, the high incidence of psychiatric casualties in combat tended to support
this point of view, and it was assumed that even those who
functioned successfully would have significant biochemical
evidence of their ordeal. Combat also offered an opportunity
to study human aggressive behavior in its most overt and destructive form.

Even at the time of the Korean conflict, logistical
problems and the relatively unrefined biochemical techniques
then available for measuring endocrine excretion limited
research in this area. It also is true that the greatest
period of interest in the biochemical aspects of behavior
came after the Korean war was concluded. Fifteen years
later, improved methods of measuring steroid excretion and,
specifically, 17-OHCS levels as well as the greater mobil-
ity provided by the helicopter, the naturally occurring

stress laboratory of combat was ready to be taken advantage
of in Viet Nam.

METHODS

The study was carried out in two separate phases. In
each of these phases, a group of United States soldiers in
a distinct combat situation in Viet Nam were investigated.
The men in the first group were helicopter medics who were
exposed to periods of brief and acute stress interspersed
with relative security and relaxation. The second group
was comprised of the twelve members of a Special Forces
(Green Beret) "A" Team defending an isolated outpost in the
Central Highlands of Viet Nam. This latter group, as distinct from the former, were exposed to prolonged stress
without any significant periods of relief, and with the
state accentuated periodically by outbreaks of fighting.

Phase I

Subjects - The subjects in the initial phase of the
study consisted of seven medical aidmen serving on helicop-
ters evacuating combat casualties in South Viet Nam. All
were Caucasian, and five of the seven were married. Age
ranged from 19 to 39 years (median 28.5). Education ranged
from 11 to 13 years (median 12). Years of military service
ranges from 2 1/2 to 19 (median 8). The subjects came from
two different helicopter ambulance units stationed together
in South Viet Nam, and had been performing duties picking
up and evacuating by air combat casualties for three to nine
months at the time the measures began. This was carried out
frequently under heavy enemy fire, and several of their
colleagues had been killed. The situation, however, although clearly threatening, was not novel to the subjects.

One subject, #3, was taken off flight status for
disciplinary reasons the day after the study was initiated.
However, he had been flying regularly to that point, and he
was retained as a subject.

All the subjects were free of evidence of clinical
disease during the study, with the exception of #3. This
subject sustained a severe scalp laceration which became

infected and his steroid measurement for that day, to be
discussed later, was therefore excluded from general consideration.

Sample Collection - Fourteen separate 24-hour urine
collections were made on each man. These were made almost
continuously during the three week study period. Some of
the days during which urine collections were made were
days when the men engaged in intense combat, some were days
when they flew only in highly secure areas, and some were
days when they did not fly at all or had the days off. A
technician followed the subjects both on and off duty to
insure completeness of the samples. The collected urine
was frozen at six hour intervals and, at the end of twenty-
four hours, the collection for that day was thawed. It then
was pooled for each subject, the total volume was measured
and appropriate aliquots for various biochemical measurements were taken and refrozen. Analyses of these 24-hour
pools for 17-hydroxycorticosteroid concentration (17-OHCS)
were performed by a modification of the Glenn-Nelson method
(Rosenthal & Mason, 1959). A number of collections were
known to be incomplete and were discarded. Seventy-six
were considered complete and comprise the data presented.
Each man also was weighed at the start of the study.

Psychological and Behavioral Observations - Shortly
after selection, each subject was asked to fill out a 75-
item personal history questionnaire, as well as a copy of
the Minnesota Multiphasic Personality Inventory. The study
extended for a three week period, from January 10 through
January 31, 1966, except for the seventh subject for whom
it was continued an additional week. Each evening throughout the period of the study, the subjects were asked to
fill out a copy of the Daily Multiple Affect Adjective
Check List (D-MAACL). The results of this aspect of the
study are reported elsewhere (Bourne, Coli, & Datel, 1966).
During the course of investigation, each man was interviewed
individually and a psychiatric history was obtained. Particular emphasis was placed on the subject's general modes of
handling stress, as well as on his conceptualization of the
specific threat posed by his daily exposure to the danger
of death or mutilation. Every third day during the study,
the man was asked to fill out a self report form in which
he listed anything unusual that had happened to him in the

previous 72 hours, as well as any significant affective
experience.

During the three-week duration of the study, a careful
record was kept of each subject's activities, including
details of the missions he flew as well as events in his
private life. Close contact was maintained with each of
the men, and, utilizing informal interviews, additional
information was obtained regarding responses to various
combat events. Periodically, the author also accompanied
the subject on his missions to record his behavior and performance.

Phase II

Subjects - The subjects in the second phase of the
study consisted of the twelve members of a Special Forces
"A" team in an isolated camp near the Cambodian border in
South Viet Nam. Two of the subjects were officers and ten
were enlisted men. All of these subjects were Caucasian;
two were married and ten were single or divorced. Ages
ranged from 22 to 41 years (median 26). Education ranged
from 10 to 16 years (median 12). Years of military service
ranged from 1 1/2 to 20 years (median 5.5). Time in Viet
Nam ranged from 5 to 36 months (median 8.5), and time in
the camp ranged from 1 to 10 months (median 8).

Location and Mission - The camp was located in territory controlled by the Viet Cong. It was situated so as
to provide significant obstruction to the free flow of arms
and men from the Ho Chi Minh Trail into the Central Highlands of South Viet Nam. The mission of the twelve man
team was to train locally recruited villagers and tribesmen,
defend the camp against attack, and make frequent patrols
into the surrounding countryside. The constant threat of
attack by an overwhelmingly superior force was always present but was increased considerably at the start of the
monsoon season in early May. On May 10, 1966, the men in
the camp were notified that an attack was imminent. Intel-
ligence sources indicated that the attack would come between
May 18 and May 22, but most probably on the night of May 19.
Although this particular attack failed to occur, there was
mounting stress caused by this realistic external threat up
to May 19, which then tapered off gradually during the

following few days. A more colorful description of life in
this camp has appeared elsewhere (Mason, 1967).

    Sample Collection - Twenty-four hour urine collections
were made on each of the twelve subjects. The number of
collections ranged from one to seven. These were collected
over an eighteen-day period from May 9 through May 27, but
with the majority collected during the critical period of
May 18 through May 22. The urine was handled in the same
manner as in the first phase of the study with the helicopter ambulance crew members. It was stored in a field
refrigerator run on a portable generator and was kept
frozen until it could be removed from the camp by helicopter. Analyses were again made on the 24-hour pools for
17-hydroxycorticosteroid concentration. Collections known
to be incomplete were again discarded. Fifty-five collections were considered complete, and these comprise the data
presented. A record of each man's weight was obtained.

    Psychological and Behavioral Observations - Because of
the nature of the military operation in which these men were
engaged, it was not possible to conduct the same type of
formal psychological evaluations that were carried out with
the helicopter ambulance medics. The personal history
questionnaire and the Minnesota Multiphasic Personality
Inventory were not used in this instance. However, the
weekly form of the Multiple Affect Adjective Check List
(W-MAACL) was administered for a period of one month. The
results of this aspect of the study are reported elsewhere
(Bourne, Coli, & Datel, 1968). Informal interviews were
conducted with each of the subjects at intervals during the
study. In addition, the author and an assistant lived in
the camp as participant observers for the duration of the
study from May 1 to July 6, 1966. A daily log was maintained for all activities in the camp as well as the significant events in the lives of each of the subjects. Records
also were kept of all military activity in the area which
altered the level of perceived stress in the camp.

RESULTS

Phase I

    Daily twenty-four hour urinary 17-OHCS levels for each
of the seven helicopter ambulance medics are shown in

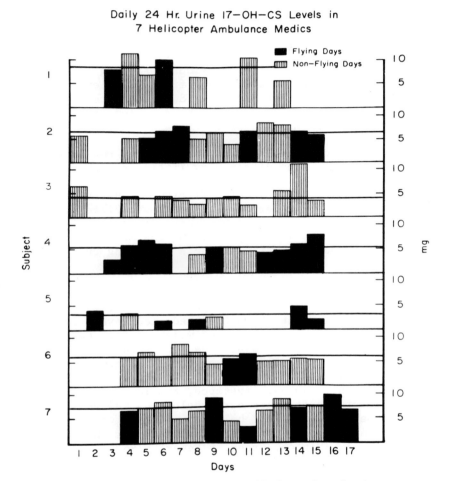

Figure 1.   Daily 24-hour urine 17-OHCS levels in seven
helicopter ambulance medics, showing the mean for each
subject.

Figure 1.   In all, 76 twenty-four hour collections were
analyzed.

It will be noted that, in all subjects, there is remarkably little difference in the observed level of 17-
hydroxycorticosteroid obtained on flying and non-flying
days.   In one-half of the instances, the highest levels of
excretion were found on days when the subjects did not fly
at all.   A graphic example of this is seen in subject #1,
who on January 14th flew five missions totalling four hours,
and encountering considerable enemy fire.   His level of
17-OHCS excretion on that day was 7.8 mg/24 hours.   The
same subject on January 17th, when he remained at his billet,
had a level of 11.2 mg/24 hours.

The levels obtained on each day, whether the subject
was flying or not, also differ very little from the overall
mean obtained for each individual during the time of study.
For the group as a whole, the coefficient of variance
(standard deviation as per cent of mean) was 27 per cent.
This is true, despite the highly episodic nature of the
danger to which they were exposed, and the markedly different behavior required of the subjects on flying and non-
flying days.

Figure 2 shows the mean 24-hour urinary 17-OHCS levels
obtained on each of the seven subjects during the period of
study.   In addition, it shows the predicted levels for each
subject calculated on the basis of weight alone, described
by Rose, Poe, and Mason (data to be published) in a group
of healthy young adult males in basic training.   The mean
of these two groups adjusted for sample size were significantly different.   In each instance, the level obtained
falls at least one standard error below the weight predicted
figure.   They also are well below the figures of Migeon and
Sachar which have been considered as means for the population as a whole (Migeon, Green, & Eckert, 1963; Sachar et al.,
1965).

Phase II

The chronic mean twenty-four hour levels of 17-hydroxy-
corticosteroid excretion for the members of the Special
Forces "A" team are shown in Figure 3.   Insufficient complete collections were obtained on one subject, #5, and he

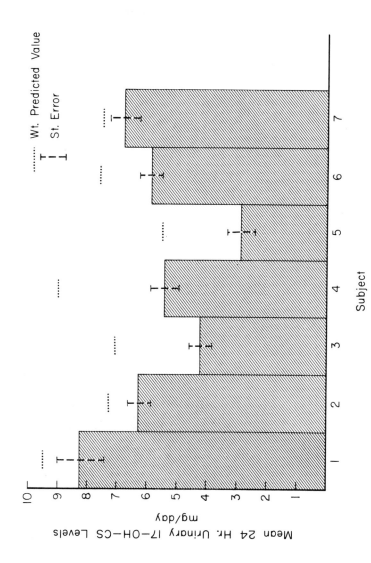

Figure 2.   Mean 24-hour urine 17-OHCS levels in seven helicopter ambulance medics.

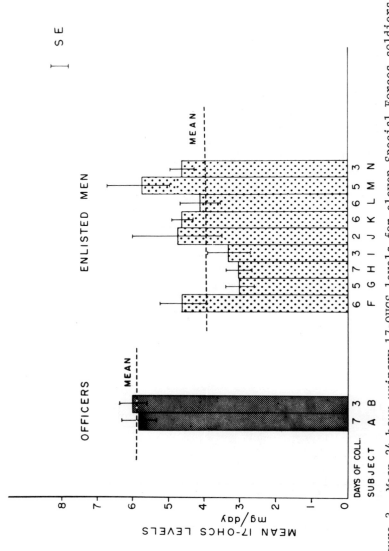

Figure 3.   Mean 24-hour urinary 17-OHCS levels for eleven Special Forces soldiers.

was, therefore, excluded from consideration.

It can be seen that there is a significant difference
between the group mean level for the two officers, subjects
number one and two, and the nine enlisted men, subjects
numbers six through fourteen. This amounts to 1.7 mg. or
40.5 per cent of the mean level of the enlisted group. It
also should be noted that the two officers have a chronic
twenty-four hour excretion level which varies only 0.07 mg.
from their group mean. The enlisted men have levels which
are also remarkably consistent, falling within 1.5 mg. of
the group mean. This is more significant when one takes
into account that the two subjects, number seven and
number thirteen, at the upper and lower extremes are also
the subjects with the most extreme body weights, weighing
120 and 230 pounts respectively. The group mean weight for
all the subjects,both officers and enlisted men, was 173
pounds.

Figure 4 shows the per cent change in twenty-four hour
17-OHCS excretion from a baseline level prior to the day
the attack was anticipated, to the day the attack was expected, and then for the days immediately following the
attack. Adequate collections on the day of anticipated
attack were obtained on one officer and six enlisted men.

It will be noted that, on the critical day, the officer
showed a 23.2 per cent rise in the level of his steroid excretion over the baseline, whereas five of the six enlisted
men showed a significant decrease in 17-hydroxycorticoste-
roid excretion. The single exception was the senior radio
operator, whose role in the camp, while it was under threat,
was quite different from that of the other enlisted men.
He worked very intimately with the officers and spent most
of that twenty-four hour period transmitting and receiving
the very large volume of communication which took place
between the officers and the higher command in Pleiku,
forty miles away. In terms of the type of demands placed
on him, his role was much closer to that of the officers
than to the other enlisted men, who were not at all involved
in the command interactions and decision making.

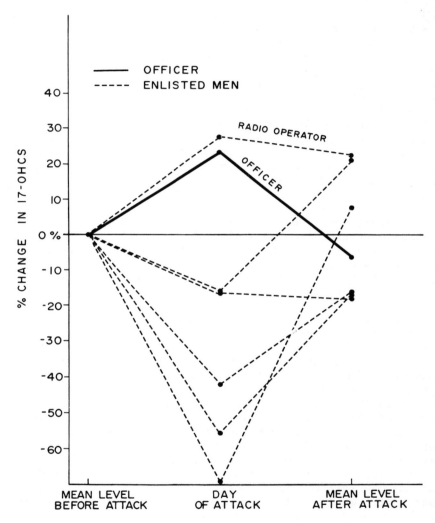

Figure 4.   Percentage change in 24-hour 17-OHCS levels.

DISCUSSION

It appears from the data, presented in the first phase of the study, that there are two major findings. First, that for these subjects the variation in the level of twenty-four hour urinary 17-hydroxycorticosteroid excretion deviates very little from the overall mean and bears no direct relationship to whether he was flying combat missions or not. Second, the chronic mean level of 17-hydroxycorticosteroid excretion for the entire period of study on each subject was lower considerably than that predicted by body weight alone, compared with a group of basic trainees at Fort Dix, New Jersey. These two features, stability over time and the chronic low level of 17-hydroxycorticosteroid excretion, suggest that flying versus non-flying cannot be interpreted alone as stress versus non-stress, nor can the objective threat of death and mutilation be interpreted as a stress without consideration of the manner in which each individual perceives the threat. It appears that each subject utilizes very extensive and effective psychological defenses to handle the events with which he is faced. These defenses enable the man to perceive reality in such a way that he minimizes the danger it represents, as well as creating for himself a feeling of invulnerability and omnipotence.

Interviews with the subjects revealed that they tended, in general, to stress the considerable gratification they achieved in their job that tended to balance the threat of the danger to which they were exposed. This was expressed particularly in terms of the prestige they obtained among other troops because they were helicopter ambulance medics, as well as frequent expressions of gratitude from the casualties they evacuated. With two exceptions, the threat of death or mutilation was minimized constantly. This threat was handled with a wide variety of defenses, but with equally effective results. Whether the defenses tended to deny the danger or bolster the individual's feeling of invincibility, they provided an altered perception of reality with which the man seemed to be able to function relatively comfortably.

One subject (#5) was a sincerely religious Catholic who believed that God would protect him no matter how great the danger. This feeling was reinforced considerably by his successful survival throughout the Korean War, where, at

times, he had been exposed to even more hazardous conditions than he was now being exposed to in Viet Nam. However, despite his rigid defense, this subject had a permanent tremor and described himself as nervous, dating his
problems from his experiences in the Korean conflict.

Another subject (#6) had calculated carefully from the
number of flights he flew, the number of casualties in the
unit during the previous year, and the length of his tour
in Viet Nam, a statistical estimate of the chance of his
being killed or injured on any given day. The result was
reassuringly small. This subject, following a near miss
in a mine explosion in Saigon, expressed far greater fear
of going into the city, a situation he could avoid, than
of flying, a situation he could not avoid.

In one subject, who was perhaps the least intellectu-
ally capable of the group (#1), there was evidence of considerably ritualistic compulsive behavior. This subject
had experienced great difficulty in learning the skills
the Army had taught him, and performed all of his tasks in
a painstaking systematic manner. While flying out to a
combat area for a pick up, he would review mentally in
minute detail every single action he would perform from
the moment the helicopter touched the ground. It seemed
that he had taken literally the old Army adage that if you
do your job right you will stay out of trouble, and had
expanded it to cover even the intransigencies of combat.

Another clearly definable manner in which the combat
situation was handled was demonstrated in subjects #2 and
#7. Both of these men were describing constantly how near
the bullets had come, how close they were to the Viet Cong,
and how miraculously they had been saved. In the group,
this was a socially acceptable way to behave, including the
admission of having been afraid. These stories were accepted without question, even when everyone present knew them
to be exaggerated considerably. When asked to explain what
they gained from the job when it was apparently so dangerous, they both stated openly that they were motivated considerably by the medals they received, the increased pay for
flying, and the prestige. It also was evident that these
men utilized their exaggeration of the danger to reinforce
their own sense of omnipotence, and the belief that they
could survive and handle any eventuality in combat. Inter-
estingly, these two subjects were rated as the best per-

formers in the group when evaluated by the pilots with whom they flew.

In most instances, the defensive maneuvers were considerably more complex than would appear from the present description, and no subject used just one type of defense to the exclusion of all others. However, it is apparent that the type of defense used is of minimal consequence in terms of the effect in lowering the level of steroid secretion. What seems of significance is the extent to which it is successful in providing the individual protection against having to face the danger in the environment as well as enhancing his own feelings of invincibility.

The concept of varying defences, used to exclude overwhelmingly threatening events from conscious appreciation, is not new. As long as twenty-five years ago, Rado made the following statement in discussing the psychodynamics of combat stress (Rado, 1943).

"By far the most efficient technique at the soldier's disposal in resolving this conflict is completely to ignore the dangers surrounding him as though disregarding his own life, and thus stop the entire working of emergency control. Transformed from a sensitive man into an insensitive technician of war, he then interprets combat not as a continued threat of injuries but as a sequence of operational demands to be responded to by precise military performances. He is able to take this remarkable attitude because the situation touches off in the depths of his mind the eternal human illusion of one's invulnerability and immortality. With his self-love thus powerfully protected he can afford to lose his identity in the military unit, can give himself entirely to the job in hand and may even perform deeds of heroism."

What is new is the demonstration that such well established behavioral concepts can be substantiated at a physiological level. That such a specific measure of stress as 17-OHCS excretion should remain relatively impervious to the clear-cut threat of death or mutilation suggests that when the threat in the environment achieves sufficient magnitude, altered perception of the situation becomes a necessary and indispensable method of adaptation. This is required when social pressures are so great that physical avoidance is totally unacceptable to the individual.

Both in his handling of the danger and the consequences of his own aggressive behavior, the individual is able to repress the usual component of affective arousal and induce in himself a state of psychological anaesthesia. In his book, Air War : Vietnam, Harvey (1967) describes the phased initiation that pilots undergo permitting them to become acclimated to the dropping of bombs and straffing of those on the ground without incurring any emotional reaction. It seems that the process of affective denial once aroused spills over to other areas of the man's life leading to a generalized emotional withdrawal, and hence a lowering of steroid secretion.

In the second phase of the study, the data obtained on the twelve members of the Special Forces (Green Beret) "A" team demonstrate several important findings. With these subjects, as with the helicopter ambulance medics, the mean levels of 17-OHCS excretion are lower considerably than might be anticipated on the basis of body weight and studies of non-life threatening experimental stress situations. At the same time, the levels for the officers and enlisted men deviate little from their respective group means.

It appeared that, as in the first phase of the study, these findings can be attributed largely to the similar manner in which the external threat posed by the dangers of combat was handled. For instance, one Special Forces soldier was a very religious individual who would drive many miles in a jeep over treacherous jungle roads so that a Vietnamese Catholic Priest, who spoke little or no English, could hear his confession. By making this hazardous journey with sufficient frequency, the man was able to maintain his strong belief in divine protection, and felt he had little to fear in combat.

Although a wide variety of defenses were observed in these subjects, all of which would be interpreted as effective ways of protecting each man from a sense of overwhelming threat, an additional factor appears to be operative among these men. More so than the helicopter ambulance medics, the members of this Special Forces team demonstrated an overwhelming emphasis on self-reliance, often to the point of omnipotence. This was true, both for the individual and for the team as a whole. The members expressed the belief that the team was invincible, gaining for themselves considerable support by virtue of their membership. Most of the members had an inordinate faith in their own capabilities, the result of pre-existing personality traits, their very comprehensive training, and their past successful survival through the most hazardous combat experiences. In some of the men, especially those who had spent years in counter insurgency operations in Laos and Viet Nam, their faith in their own invulnerability bordered on a feeling of immortality.

In addition, it was apparent that these subjects were action-oriented individuals who spent characteristically little time in introspection. Their response to any environmental threat was to engage in a furor of activity which rapidly dissipated the developing tension. Externally directed aggressive behavior, which enjoyed a maximum of group condonence, tended to relieve the individual of any feelings of vulnerability, and, particularly, protected him from the fear of being challenged beyond what he believed to be the limit of his capacity.

The second point of interest, which the data raise, is that there is a significant difference in the adrenal cortical response demonstrated by the enlisted men and that exhibited by the two officers in the camp. Although, generally, all members of the group are exposed equally to the realistic dangers surrounding them, this suggests either an inherent difference in the psychological adaptive capacity of the two officers or that their assigned role in the group provides additional stresses which cannot be as easily dealt with as those confronting the enlisted men. The data supports the latter hypothesis. The enlisted men are required generally to perform tasks in which they are highly trained and which tend to be of a mechanistic nature, such as building defenses and maintaining equipment. Their concern in combat, or in the event of an attack on the camp, revolves around their satisfactory performance of these tasks and the preservation of their own lives. Their competence in the former leaves little room for ruminative apprehension, and the fear for their own survival is handled conveniently by their feelings of invulnerability and by a heightened industriousness with their tasks.

Unlike the enlisted men, the officers are influenced primarily in their behavior by radio messages coming from the
higher command outside the camp. This involves rapid
decision-making on their part and the tactful handling of
commands made with the weight of superior rank, but
hampered by the ignorance of a 40-mile physical separation.
The demands created by this situation, as well as the
responsibilities inherent in their own command situation,
cannot be as easily dealt with or defended against as can
the more vaguely defined and distant threats of death or
injury. These demands require immediate solutions and tend
to keep the officer in a state of, at least, mild interpersonal conflict with either his superiors or his subordinates. In addition, the very nature of his job limits
the possible avenues available to him for the dissipation
of tension. He rarely can engage in the more physical and
less emotionally demanding chores around the camp, but must
remain constantly on the alert for new instructions which
may call for new and unique patterns of behavior that he
can never be sure how he will accomplish.

The sense of responsibility felt by the officers for
the lives and safety of the ten enlisted men under their
command, and the additional stress which this provides is
hard to gauge. Although this was easily kept from immediate awareness by such rationalizations as the often
heard statement, "If they overrun us it is every man for
himself," there is no doubt that the traditional responsibility of rank creates a real social stress. Of greater
significance is the constant demands on the generally
young officers to reinforce their role as leaders. Despite
their official position, they are in constant competition
with older, often highly battle scarred, senior enlisted
men for informal control of the group and the respect of
the other members. This leads them to take extreme
personal risks in order to gain acceptance as the rightful
leaders. The temptation to prove themselves in this way
is not always yielded to, but the social pressure to do so
is always there.

The separation of roles between the officers and enlisted men in the camp, which appears to explain the difference in levels of chronic 17-OHCS excretion, were further
accentuated when the expectation of an enemy attack on the
camp arose. This was reflected also by an increase in the
separation of 17-OHCS levels. The drop in the level of

excretion shown by five out of six of the enlisted men co-
incided with heightened activity in the form of laying
additional mines, reinforcing barbed wire defenses, check-
ing ammunition stores, and preparing the medical bunker for
casualties. All of these are well-practiced activities
which they had been taught to carry out in response to this
type of emergency. They remained so busy, coping with the
immediacy of the threat by practical measures, that they
had little time to ruminate about the impending danger.
Group cohesion was emphasized and accentuated and a feeling
of euphoric expectancy pervaded their preparations for the
attack.

The officers at the time of the expected attack also
experienced an intensification of their previous role
behavior. They were in almost constant radio communication
with their superiors, both relaying information from the
camp and coordinating their plans with those of other units
in the general area. They were very much aware that the
ability of the camp to withstand an attack was in their
hands and that they were facing a crucial opportunity to
prove their capabilities. The rise in level of 17-OHCS
excretion exhibited by the one officer from whom urine
could be collected, at this time, is consistent with these
findings.

The observations in this second phase of the study
reconfirm the initial findings with the helicopter ambulance
crew men that individual psychological defenses, and behavior patterns, enable man to perceive his environment in
such a way that he denies the very real threat of death or
mutilation in combat. They also suggest the importance of
group influences and assigned role in modifying the individual's adrenal cortical response to a stressful environment. In group situations, where the possible alternative
methods for handling stress are limited, the group factors
tend to minimize the effect of individual differences. The
observations, made in the present study, are highly consistent with the findings of Marchbanks (1958) in his study
of B-52 crews. He found that, on a long and stressful
flight, the instructor pilot showed significantly higher
levels of 17-OHCS excretion than the other members of the
group, all of whom demonstrated lower but remarkably
similar levels of excretion. It appears that in both
instances the higher levels of 1y-OHCS excretion shown by
those in the leadership position is related more to their

assigned role than specific personality factors, and that
they are responding to the demands imposed by the group
rather than to the major threat in the external environment.
The similarity of response seen in the other group members
suggests that there is considerable conformity in the way
any threat is perceived and in the manner in which it is
handled.

A number of other possible explanations for the biochemical findings in this study must be considered. All
United States military personnel in Viet Nam are required
to take weekly a tablet containing 300 mg. of Chloroquine
base and 45 mg. of Primaquine base as prophylaxis against
malaria. There are two ways in which ingestion of these
anti-malarial drugs might produce falsely low levels of
17-OHCS in the urine. Firstly, the drugs might interfere
at higher wavelengths with the spectrophotometric readings
upon which determination of the concentration of 17-OHCS
in the urine is based. Secondly, there might be a direct
pharmacological effect upon adrenal function. Careful
examination of the absorption spectra on a number of the
samples showed no evidence of a contaminating substance,
thus ruling out the former consideration. To the present
time, there has been no definitive study which would
preclude absolutely the latter possibility, although we
believe, on the basis of a great deal of empirical evidence, that there is no significant effect of these two
drugs on the activity of the pituitary adrenal axis.

An alternative explanation for the low level of 17-
OHCS excretion might be that, in a condition of chronic
stress to which these subjects are exposed with constant
stimulation of the pituitary adrenal axis, a state of
"adrenal exhaustion" develops. However, a naturally
occurring event involving one of the subjects in the first
phase of the study tends to refute this. During the period
of the investigation, subject #3 was involved in a fight
and sustained a scalp laceration which became infected
severely. At that time, his level of excretion rose to
more than three times what it had been prior to the in-
fection, returning to the previous levels twenty-four hours
after antibiotic therapy was instituted. This suggested
certainly that a considerable adrenal reserve existed.
Similar evidence which supports this belief was obtained by
Freidman (1963) when studying a group under chronic stress.

In that instance, considerable adrenal reserve was shown to be present in response both to naturally occurring events and to challenge with ACTH.

An additional variable might be the necessary adaptation to heat which occurs in Viet Nam. However, although the helicopter crews were operating in a tropical environment, the Special Forces camp located in the highlands enjoyed cool and equitable weather conditions.

It might be suggested that the groups under study are highly selected and their responses are not representative of combat troops in general. They are highly trained and have learned to handle stress with a high level of military arousal while at the same time preserving broad emotional tranquility. However, we believe that the wide range of personality types, the variety of past histories, and the varying degrees of investment in the job, tend to refute this hypothesis.

At first glance, it might appear that these findings in humans contradict the extensive data on the physiological aspects of aggressive behavior in animals. However, closer examination indicates that, for many reasons, warfare among nations cannot be equated either psychologically or physiologically with aggressive behavior in animals. First, it is highly institutionalized with the individual soldier having virtually no control over and little emotional investiment in the decisions made by his leaders. He finds himself compelled to follow their wishes, and his concern becomes one of surviving in a socially acceptable way rather than being in a state of personal aggressive arousal. Second, warfare, particularly for the pilot dropping bombs or even the foot soldier using a gun, has become a mechanistic act which in most instances is quite depersonalized. Much of the time the soldier feels he is merely doing a job and experiences little sense of animosity or aggressivity. Third, human psychic processes enable man to divorce himself emotionally from events that are threatening or aggressive in a way which presumably animals are incapable of doing.

The data presented on the Special Forces "A" team which demonstrated steroid elevations for the two officers is more comparable with the observations on animals. These two men were engaged in interpersonal conflict with the

other members of the team, and, although not expressed
violently, is still more comparable to aggressive behavior
in animals than actual combat with those labelled as
"enemy." By virtue of their psychological defence of
omnipotence, they felt capable of dealing with any eventuality in battle, whereas a challenge from among their own
men represented a far greater threat to their sense of
survival. It seems, therefore, that meaningful study of
aggressive behavior in humans must focus upon the reactions
of the individual in highly personal conflicts with others
rather than on events where his identity is submerged in
group acts in which he has little real investment.

ACKNOWLEDGMENTS

The author wishes to express his appreciation to
William M. Coli, B.A., for his assistance in the collection
of data in Viet Nam and to John W. Mason, M.D., and Robert
M. Rose, M.D., of the Department of Neuroendocrinology,
Walter Reed Army Institute of Research, for making possible
the biochemical determinations on the specimens collected.

REFERENCES

BLISS, E. D., MIGEON, C. J., HARDIN-BRANCH, C. H., &
    SAMUELS, L. T. Reaction of the adrenal cortex to
    emotional stress. Psychosom. Med., 1956, 18, 56-76.

BOURNE, P. G., COLI, W. M., & DATEL, W. E. Anxiety levels
    of six helicopter ambulance medics in a combat zone.
    Psychol. Rep., 1966, 19, 821-822.

BOURNE, P. G., COLI, W. M., & DATEL, J. W. Affect levels
    of special forces soldiers under threat of attack.
    Psychol. Rep., 1968, 22, 363-366.

CANNON, W. B., & de la PAZ, D. Emotional stimulation of
    adrenal secretion. Am. J. Physiol., 1911, 27, 64-70.

ELMADJIAN, R. Adrenocortical function of combat infantry
    men in Korea. Ciba Colloquium on Endocrinology, 1955,
    8, 627-655.

FOX, H. M., MURAWSKI, J. G., BARTHOLOMAY, A. F., &
    GIFFORD, S. Adrenal steroid excretion patterns in 18
    healthy subjects and tentative correlations with per-
    sonality structure. Psychosom. Med., 1961, 23,
    364-376.

FRIEDMAN, S. B., MASON, J. W., & HAMBURG, D. A. Urinary
    17-hydroxycorticosteroid levels in parents of
    children with neoplastic disease. Psychosom. Med.,
    1963, 25, 364-376.

HARVEY, F. Airwar : Viet Nam. New York: Bantam, 1967.

MARCHBANKS, V. H. Effects of flying stress on 17-hydroxy-
    corticosteroid levels. J. Aviation Med., 1958,
    29, 676-682.

MASON, J. Psychoendocrine approaches in stress research.
    Symp. on Med. Asp. of Stress in the Milit. Clim.
    Washington, D. C.: Walter Reed Army Institute of
    Research, 1964, pp. 375-417.

MASON, J. F. Whom the gods love. Reporter, 1967, 37,
    37, 21-25.

MASON, J. W. Psychological influences on the pituitary-
    adrenal cortical system. In G. Pincus (Ed.) Recent
    Progress in Hormone Research. New York: Academic
    Press, 1959, pp. 345-389.

MASON, J. W., & BRADY, J. V. The sensitivity of psycho-
    endocrine systems to social and physical environment.
    In P. H. Leiderman and D. Shapiro (Eds.) Psychobio-
    logical Approaches to Social Behavior. Stanford,
    California: Stanford University Press, 1964.

MASON, J. W., BRADY, J. V., & SIDMAN, M. Plasma 17-hydroxy-
    corticosteroid levels and conditioned behavior in the
    rhesus monkey. Endocrinology, 1957, 60, 741-752.

MASON, J. W., HARWOOD, C. T., & ROSENTHAL, N. R. Influence
    of some environmental factors on plasma and urinary
    17-hydroxycorticosteroid levels in the rhesus monkey.
    Amer. J. Physiol., 1957, 80, 429-433.

MASON, J. W., SACHAR, E. J., FISHMAN, J. H., HAMBURG, D. A., & HANDLON, J. H. Corticosteroid response to hospital admission. Arch. Gen. Psychiat., 1965, 13, 1-8.

MIGEON, C. J., GREEN, O. C., & ECKERT, J. P. Study of adrenocortical function in obesity. Metabolism, 1963, 12, 218- 239.

RADO, S. Pathodynamics and treatment of traumatic war neurosis (Traumatophobia). Psychosom. Med., 1943, 43, 362-368.

ROSENTHAL, N. R., & MASON, J. W. Urinary excretion in normal rhesus monkey. J. Lab. Clin. Med., 1959, 53, 720-728.

SACHAR, E. J., COBB, J. C., & SHOR, R. E. Plasma cortical levels during hypnotic trance. Arch. Gen. Psychiat., 1966, 14, 482-490.

SACHAR, E. J., MASON, J. W., FISHMAN, J. R., HAMBURG, D. A., & HANDLAN, J. H. Corticosteroid excretion in normal young adults living under 'Basal conditions.' Psychosom. Med., 1965, 27, 435-455.

SACHAR, E. J., MASON, J. W., KOLMER, H. S., & ARTISS, K. L. Psycho-endocrine aspects of acute schizophrenic reactions. Psychosom. Med., 1963, 25, 510-520.

SELYE, H. Thymus and adrenals in the response of the organism to injuries and intoxications. Brit. J. Exp. Pathol., 1936, 234-248.

WADESON, R. W., MASON, J. W., HAMBURG, D. A., & HANDLON, J. H. Plasma and urinary 17-OHCS responses to motion pictures. Arch. Gen. Psychiat., 1963, 9, 146-156.

WOLFF, C. T., FRIEDMAN, S. B., HAFER, M. A., & MASON, J. W. Relationship between psychological defenses and mean urinary 17-OHCS excretion rates. I. A. Predictive study of parents of fatally ill children. Psychosom. Med., 1964, 26, 576-591.

AGGRESSION: SUMMARY AND OVERVIEW

Bryan W. Robinson

Department of Psychology
Florida State University

Tallahassee, Florida

This symposium on fighting and defeat produced a rich variety of new data and new ideas. It rapidly became apparent that the general purpose of the symposium of bringing together current work in the biochemical and neurophysiological correlates of agonistic behavior in mammals was much too ambitious. Such a goal could not have been reached in a single day or probably in a single week. There are too many species of mammals and too many varieties of agonistic behavior to review. However, the symposium was immensely stimulating, and was very valuable for its participants. Everyone was brought into confrontation with our exciting but completely inadequate knowledge of aggression not just in our laboratory animals but, more importantly, in man. The roles of species uniqueness, of seemingly insignificant environmental factors, and of neural circuitry produced many questions, but few final answers. These issues and others were debated energetically during the symposium and in a special discussion group the following morning.

The purpose of this final chapter is to present a brief summary of the various papers, and to discuss the major themes and problem areas which were identified. The discussion necessarily is, in part, subjective and I hope no injustice will be done. However, by attempting to place the primary issues in context, there is the possibility of touching some of the deeper issues not obviously highlighted by the details covered in the preceding chapters.

The symposium had the general purpose of bringing together present work in biochemical and neurophysiological
correlates of agonistic behaviors in mammals. Recent work
indicates that both fighting and defeat produce striking
changes in both brain biochemistry and levels of blood
hormones. Such agonistic behaviors also have effects upon
the testes and accessory sex glands, although it is not yet
clear how much this affects sexual behavior and reproduction.

Using a realistic situation in which two monkeys living
together have their brains stimulated by remote radio control,
R. Plotnik, D. Mir, and J. M. R. Delgado found that fighting
between monkeys can be elicited by noxious brain stimulation
or by external foot shock. When there was a dominance-subordination relationship between the two animals, only the
dominant animal could be stimulated to be aggressive. These
results indicate the importance of the effect of training
and experience upon aggressive behavior and raise the
question of whether all aggressive behavior elicited by
brain stimulation may simply be the result of pain and
similar noxious stimulation. The authors interpret their
experiment as evidence against the existence of an aggression "center." Evidence was presented at the symposium
that non-noxious aggression could be evoked from the monkey
hypothalamus and that, under the influence of stimulation
of such areas, subordinate monkeys would readily attack
dominant animals. Furthermore, continued evocation of such
non-noxious aggression could effect a permanent social
change in the group so that the dominant-subordinate pairs
would reverse roles (Robinson, Alexander, & Bowne, 1969).
Such evidence would appear to contravert the notion that all
fighting elicited by brain stimulation depends on the noxious
properties of such stimulation and greatly modifies the concept of the non-existence of an aggression "center."

J. P. Flynn found that several areas in the brain of
the cat will induce aggressive behavior, the midbrain and
hypothalamus being the most important. In his theoretical
discussion K. E. Moyer proposed the hypothesis that each
kind of aggressive behavior (identified by the kind of
stimulus which evokes it) has a separate neurological basis.
Thus predation, which is essentially food-gatting behavior,
is physiologically distinct from agonistic behavior or
social fighting.

New discoveries concerning the way in which hereditary factors produce sex differences in fighting were reported by Bronson and Desjardins. Early in the postnatal life of the mouse, there is a critical period during which treatment with the male sex hormone will increase the incidence of fighting in later life in either sex. At least in mice the nervous systems of the two sexes become definitely different in this way.

New techniques for the chemical assay of hormones, and other substances concerned in brain metabolism during fighting and defeat, are making it possible to analyze the changes that take place under these conditions. Annemarie Welch reported that male mice in isolation become progressively more irritable and likely to start fights, and that these changes are accompanied by changes in brain chemistry. Such substances as norepinephrine, dopamine, and serotonin are metabolized more slowly. This and similar facts may lead to an understanding of the chemical basis or irritability and its control.

While physiological changes preceding fighting are difficult to find, major changes are produced as a result of fighting and defeat. C. Desjardins reviewed work showing that defeat produces long-lasting changes in plasma hormones of mice, one of which corticosterone, exhibits high levels over periods of many hours and days. B. E. Eleftheriou reported that these endocrine changes are accompanied by decreases in RNA in certain areas of the brain, the latter caused by increased ribonuclease activity. In successful fighters, these changes are transitory, but in defeated animals the changes persist over long periods, resulting in distrubances of protein synthesis and general neural activity.

Corresponding data in man are difficult to obtain for obvious reasons. P. G. Bourne reported the fact that urinary corticosteroid levels, which would be expected to rise as a result of either fighting or defeat, were unexpectedly low in men involved in conbat situations in Viet Nam, but that the level was higher in officers than in enlisted men. The military situation thus appears to be different from that involved in individual combat.

PROBLEMS

Several problem areas of major importance were highlighted by the symposium. Some of these do not seem to be
of truly fundamental importance since they probably reflect
an area of science still in its early stages. Others, however, appear more formidable and it is not clear that they
will ever cease to trouble us. Let us discuss an example
of each type.

2. The irrelevant detail problem. It is by no means
uncommon in aggression research for similar experiments by
different investigators to result in differing or even
opposite conclusions. Indeed, the situation is worse.
Even the data generated by different workers may be different or opposite. This is true in widely separated species
such as mice and monkeys. Examples are easily given. With
mice, the strain of mouse used and the age and sex of the
mice obviously are important. But, the exact conditions
of feeding and watering, of caging, and of isolation are
shown by studies reported here to be important. The
results of biochemical analyses of mouse brains may vary
greatly with the details of the experimental protocol used
- how soon after fighting the animal was killed, how often
and how long it fought, and so on. One gains the very
definite impression that not all of these "irrelevant"
details have been uncovered. The problem, incidentally,
is vastly complicated by the reluctance of journal editors
to publish full technical details of such experiments.
Thus, workers have no opportunity to become aware of these
details except by personal contact, a most inefficient way
of clarification.

Another example, in more detail, is provided in the
fine study of Plotnik, Mir, and Delgado. They investigated
whether the aggressive responses evoked by brain stimulation
were "natural"; that is, could the social effects of natu-
rally-occurring aggression be duplicated by electrically
evoked aggression? The technique of brain tele-stimulation
made such an experiment feasible, for the animals could be
put in social groupings. They found that socially effective
aggressive threats and fights could be evoked only from a
dominant animal in the presence of a subordinant, then only
from sites in the mesencephalon, and finally only as an
after-effect of stimulation. They obtained no social
aggression from sites in the hypothalamus, traditionally

the place from which both lesions and stimulation modify agonistic behavior. Their conclusion was that the aggression they observed was most likely due to the noxious effects of mesencephalic stimulation, since noxious foot stimulation also produced attacks only from dominant to submissive monkey. This strict one-way relationship also suggested to them that there was no aggression center.

In work described at the symposium and published elsewhere (Robinson, Alexander, & Bowne, 1969), Dr. Murray and I reported opposite results! The question as to the "naturalness" of evoked aggression had also intrigued us and we also had access to the technique of brain tele-stimulation. Using the same primate species, $\underline{M}$. $\underline{mulatta}$, we were able to elicit aggressive responses from the hypothalamus. One strange fact was that the response of the animal when it was unrestrained and with other monkeys could not be entirely predicted from the response obtained when that same animal was confined to a restraining chair. And, the best aggressive responses came from loci which did not produce particularly convincing aggressive behavior in the chair. Investigation of these aggressive responses showed them to be fundamentally different from those being studied by Plotnik, Mir, and Delgado in that stimulation of these loci was effective in evoking aggression from subordinant to dominant animal as well as vice versa. Further, the effects occurred during stimulation and was stimulus-bound, permitting the duration and intensity of the response to be freely manipulated. Finally, some of the loci were shown to be non-noxious.

Now, the immediate question arises as to why two similar studies yielded vastly different results and, inevitably, different implications for the nature of the agonistic response. The answer may reside in the slightly different technical features of the tele-stimulators or in the somewhat different placement of the electrodes. However, and this is the important point to be made here, the chances are eeually likely that factors of which the two groups are unaware are responsible. For example, some unconscious bias by the investigators may have led to subtle selection or molding of the group behavior so as to produce the results which were desired all along. Alternatively, the past history of the individual animals may be critical. Since rhesus monkeys are usually captured in adolescence or young adulthood in the feral state, it is certain that they

have already had individually and collectively many forma-
tive experiences by the time they reach the laboratory.
Thus, sampling error may be present - there is no way at
this time to be sure that New Haven and Atlanta rhesus
monkeys are equivalent subjects in aggression experiments.

     2. The species problem. The preceding section
illustrated some of the difficulties arising from irrelevant but theoretically conquerable technical details. Let
us now consider a different type of problem, namely, the
difficulties arising from a theoretically insoluable
problem, namely, the species problem. The dilemma is
simply stated: How valid are the conclusions of experiments performed on lower species for man? In some biological areas, the concern is slight and the dangers of
extrapolation seem minimal. But, in the areas of group
behavior, of aggression, and of brain-behavior relationship the situation is entirely different. It is very
difficult to make meaningful comparisons between the nature
of aggression shown by, for example, mice and rabbits. The
cat and the monkey are very dissimilar in social organization, and the basic reasons for aggression are equally
dissimilar. For example, cats have very little group
hierarchecal organization and there is correspondingly
little social fighting. They are carnivores and usually
must kill to eat, so that predatory fighting is frequent.
In monkeys, the emphases are placed oppositely. Social
organization is highly developed and social fighting is
very common. Usually, such fighting is non-injurious to
the combatants, but on occasion injuries are deliverately
inflicted and death can result. On the other hand,
predatory fighting is poorly developed and rarely occurs.

     Where does man fit into this spectrum? Man demon-
strates both social and predatory fighting. His social
patterns and stimuli for aggression is not too dissimilar
from those of the rhesus monkey or the baboon, but civiliza-
tion has put powerful yet changing constraints on how such
social aggression is expressed. No animal has felt a
corresponding set of constraints. Is man's central nervous
system changed, and possibly still changing, to help man
adapt to these different ground rules? My personal feeling
is in the affirmative. Man is also a hunter and predator,
although less so than in centuries past. But, he does have
a strong biological heritage of predation. So, from the

standpoint of aggression, he is both monkey and cat. He is more. There is increasing evidence that he may be part fish, bird, and rodent. Urbanization and crowding produce aggressive and at times self-destructive behavior which is most easily mimicked at the present time by experiments on these lower forms. So, which species can serve as a model for human behavior - the monkey, the cat, the fish, the bird, the rodent?

Or can any? Man demonstrates yet another form of aggressive behavior for which there so far is no animal analogue. War and institutionalized fighting are prominent human traditions. Do they arise from the other kinds of aggression? If so, can we understand and control war by studying only the other types of aggression in their related species? Or, is man's tendency a reflection of some aspect of neural organization - a hormone, another nucleus, a network in the limbic system or some more subtle brain modification - unique to Homo sapiens. If this be true, then no studies of non-human species will tell us much about man's formalized fighting. Bourne's work, reported above, is truly a pioneer study. For the first time scientific physiological studies were carried out under battlefield conditions. That the results were not predictable from animal experiments is not surprising. This dis-. crepancy may be interpreted as evidence that warfare is uniquely human behavior with its own physiology. If so, what then can animal experiments tell us about this particular kind of aggression? I think we must recognize the uniqueness of man.

FUTURE TRENDS

It is always risky to try, in science, to see very far into the future. Events change the basic orientation of investigators, - in simpler language, there are fads in science as in every area of human activity. Nonetheless, there are some basic, fundamental currents which can be recognized.

1. Technical sophistication and inter-disciplinary orientation. Aggression is a uniquely social activity. Solitary aggression is not defined in lower forms and, in higher, is usually considered pathological. It must, therefore, be studied in animals who are living in relatively unrestrained groups. At the same time, there is a growing

interest, as the speakers of this symposium have convincingly shown, in the electrophysiological, hormonal, and
biochemical details occurring <u>during</u> fighting and defeat
rather than <u>afterwards</u>. There will be an increasing
emphasis on the development and use of remotely controlled
devices. Brain tele-stimulation and telemetry of neural
or cardiac activity are already in use. Other procedures,
such as micro-electrode driving and recording, chemical
stimulation of the brain, biopsy of the brain, and with-
drawing blood samples could be performed remotely as well.
No fundamental technical research is needed. Micro-elec-
tronic and micro-mechanical methods used in industry and
space have provided the hardware. It is up to the working
scientist to recognize the unique value of such experiments
and to commit himself to them - and to persuade fund-grant-
ing agencies that in the study of aggression such techniques are necessary.

Although aggression research is still quite primitive
and is producing a bewildering complexity of new findings
which often seem distantly related and perhaps somewhat
divergent, there are areas of overlapping interests which
require the joint efforts of investigators from different
disciplines to be fully exploited. As an example, the
relationships between the activity of the amygdala and
other portions of the limbic system and the function of
the pituitary-adrenal axis during fighting and defeat are
almost certainly close. We know that electrical stimulation and lesions of the limbic system cause modifications
in agonistic behavior and also cause major changes in
corticosteroid production and metabolism. It is also clear
that spontaneous agonistic behavior is accompanied by large
changes in corticosteroid levels. The exact relationship
between these three areas is not known and is not likely to
be known except by an interdisciplinary approach.

2. <u>More human studies</u>. The newer electronic tele-
techniques together with a renewed and much belated interest in man will result in more studies on fighting and
defeat in man. The range and variety of man's aggression
is unique among animal species and, as Bourne has shown,
man can be studied even during warfare. Studies are also
possible during those often three popular modes of human
aggression: business life, sports, and hunting. There is
no compelling reason at present to believe that all these
forms of aggression have a common physiology and that the

study of one will lead to an understanding of the others.
The personal belief of the writer is that major differences
in neural organization underlie institutional aggression
(war), predation (hunting), and social aggression (business,
sports). Of course, there may be areas of overlaps, particularly as one nears the final common pathway in the limbic
system.

3. Human pathology. We are apparently just beginning
to recognize that a significant part of human aggression,
perhaps a large part, can be caused by brain pathology.
This is particularly true in social violence. Poverty, un-
employment, crowding, and substandard housing play a major
role in producing urban unrest and riots. However, the
brain is unique in that it incorporates the environment
into itself by storing past experiences as memory. Activation of certain neural structures is necessary for aggressive behavior to ensue. If the activation follows certain
sets of stimuli, it is then by definition appropriate, or
normal. But, what if some of the cells which make up the
circuits are damaged and posses very low thresholds? They
then may be activated by seemingly insifnificant or even by
inappropriate stimuli. Aggression may ensue for no apparent
reason at all, particularly if "spontaneous" electrical
activity occurs in these circuits.

The relationship between behavioral abnormality and
neural dysfunction has been studied by a number of authors
(Ellington, 1955; Fischgold & Gastaut, 1957; Hill, 1950,
1952; Jasper, Solomon, & Bradley, 1938; Kennard,
Robinovitch, & Fister, 1955; Knott & Gottlieb, 1944).
Sweet and co-workers (1969) cite a number of interesting
cases in which violent behavior occurred "spontaneously."
Medical examination, however, showed the presence of central
nervous system pathology. Perhaps the most fascinating was
the case of Charles Whitman, responsible for the University
of Texas mass murders. His postmortem examination revealed
the presence of a gliobastoma multiforme, an infiltrating
and malignant tumor located "probably in the medial part of
one temporal lobe." Exact localization was impossible due
to gunshot wounds of the brain.

Perhpas the commonest neural dysfunctions related with
aggressive behavior are ictal or post-ictal states, particularly of the temporal lobe. Gastaut et al. (1955) noted
rage behavior. Others have likewise investigated the re-

lationship of epilepsy to the behavior disorders.

It is difficult, however, to produce anger by artificial brain stimulation in humans who are undergoing brain surgery. Why this paradox which suggests that the effect of focal lesions and attendant seizure activity is only indirect? There are at least two reasons why brain stimulation in humans has not yet produced violent behavior. First, the electrodes may not be properly placed. Second, especially suggested by our studies and those of Delgado et al. (see Plotnik, Mir, & Delgado, this symposium), the response elicited by brain stimulation is not predictable solely from the location of the electrode and the stimulus parameters. The environment must be suitable for the full expression of electrically evoked behavior. The operating theater is the epitome of control and depersonalization and thus may inhibit the appearance of aggressive feelings and responses in the patient. Perhaps when human brain stimulation is carried out in the proper environment, one in which the stimulation is controlled remotely and the patient is in his usual surroundings, there will be no difficulty in evoking anti-social behavior.

All of which suggests, in contradistinction to the strict environmentalism in vogue today, that there may be certain brain dysfunctions, acquired or inherited, which are responsible for much of the violent behavior seen in humans. And, if that is granted (and it would seem nearly impossible to deny it), then by extrapolation there may be a spectrum of limbic organizations in normal brains which effectively determines whether an individual is passive, active, aggressive, violent, or uncontrolled.

4. Control of aggression. In light of the preceding paragraphs, it follows that many types of aggression potentially are controllable, i.e. treatable. Let us admit quickly that aggressive behavior due to obvious brain pathology such as seizure disorders, mass lesions, and temporal lobe scars should be treated.

A more subtle and difficult issue is barely beyond this one. If we grant that the neural circuits underlying aggression vary in effectiveness, then the question arises as to whether physical techniques should be used to temporarily enhance or suppress aggressiveness?

The answers to this question are by no means easy to reach - and no answers will be given here. The symposium has raised the issue and suggested how it may be possible in a few decades to manipulate aggression in individuals virtually at will.

To put the issue in perspective, let us consider whether society now has the means for controlling aggression and, secondly, whether aggression is all bad.

Western thought has emphasized the importance and dignity of the individual. Individual self-determination and freedom have high priorities in the value systems of most of us. Yet, controlling influences abound in everyday life, most of them with our knowledge - and approval. The list is long indeed and includes the manipulation of stimuli, use of reinforcement, use of aversive stimulation, punishment, pointing up the contingencies of reinforcement, deprivation and satiation, emotion, and the use of drugs such as alcohol and tranquillizers. Controlling agencies are also numerous and operate with marked success. We are all familiar with the effectiveness of government, law, religion, psychotherapy, economics, and education as controlling agencies. There can be little doubt that while we prize self-determination, we are all our lives under the influence of forces that shape our behavior.

So, a certain amount of control now exists and the average man accepts that control, agrees with its necessity, and uses it in his own family - all within limits.

Man has yet to come to full grips with his aggressivity. Most of us think, upon hearing the phrase "control of aggression," of measures which <u>reduce</u> aggression or its expression. Yet, any technique or agent which can reduce aggression can also, theoretically, enhance it. Is there a place for enhanced aggression?

Most social thinkers have felt that a certain amount of aggression is necessary for an individual to function productively in his particular society. This level of aggression may be greater or less depending on the society, but cannot be dispensed with completely. An individual may have a little more or a little less aggressivity than his group members, but he mustn't differ very much or he becomes nonproductive. Those oriented towards mental health will note

that the above statement is another way of defining normal-
ity. Although definitions of such differ widely and gener-
ate considerable heat, the concept of productive functioning is central.

Excessive aggressivity may lead to crimes of violence,
personal tragedies, and protracted and non-productive
strivings for dominance. However, a large amount of mental
illness, failure, and sorrow is caused by lack of effective
competing and inability to achieve any dominance. Just as
a completely subordinate monkey leads a constricted and
basically neurotic life, so does a completely subordinate
human. And, just as enhanced aggressivity may derive in
many cases from discrete brain lesions or from physiological quirks in structurally normal limbic tissue, so
may reduced aggressivity.

So, while the overly aggressive person is more noticeable because his behavior is more visible, there may be an
equally important counterpart in the overly subordinate
person. The author, for one, does not believe all aggression is bad but that a certain amount of aggression is
healthy - and perhaps few would disagree if aggression is
properly and broadly defined. For example, every contri-
butor to this symposium must have displayed or sublimated
enough aggression to not only formulate and write a paper,
but to achieve all that is implied in science: getting a
laboratory and competing for space and funds, fighting off
the distractions (at least for science) of teaching, of
family, etc.

Aggression, then, is not inherently bad - what is bad
is too much of it, or too little, or misdirected aggressivity. As we learn more about the biological bases of
aggression, the ability to control aggression will follow.
It is conceivable that experiments such as we have heard
about in this symposium will lead to techniques or drugs
that will selectively modify, or perhaps manipulate is a
more honest word, human aggression. A very real problem
then arises of who will do that manipulating and of exactly
what will be modified. Will the basic decisions be medical
or political? And can certain individuals, classes of
peoples, or nations be made more or less aggressive? The
questions, sobering as they are, can only be mentioned here.
It would be presumptuous for a personal discourse to be

given in a chapter such as this. But, the problem is a
real problem, and before too many more years have passed
will be an immediate real problem.

REFERENCES

ROBINSON, B. W., ALEXANDER, M., & BOWNE, G. Dominance
    reversal resulting from aggressive responses evoked
    by brain tele-stimulation. Physiol. Behav., 1969,
    4, 749-752.

ELLINGTON, R. J. The incidence of EEG abnormality among
    patients with mental disorders of apparently non-
    organic origin: a critical review. Amer. J.
    Psychiat., 1955, 111, 263-268.

FISCHGOLD, H., & GASTAUT, H. Conditionenment et Réactivité
    en Électroencéphalographie. Paris: Masson et Cie,
    1957.

HILL, D. Psychiatry. In D. Hill and G. Parr (Eds.)
    Electroencephalography. London: Macdonald & Co.,
    1950, Chap. XI.

HILL, D. EEG in episodic psychiatric and psychopathic
    behavior. Electroenceph. Clin. Neurophysiol., 1952,
    4, 419-442.

JASPER, H. H., SOLOMON, P., & BRADLEY, C. Electroencephlo-
    graphic analyses of behavior problem children. Amer.
    J. Psychiat., 1938, 95, 641-652.

KENNARD, M. A., ROBINOVITCH, M. S., & FISTER, W. P. The
    use of frequency analysis in the interpretation of
    the EEGs of patients with psychological disorders.
    Electroenceph. Clin. Neurophysiol., 1955, 7, 29-38.

KNOTT, J. R., & GOTTLIEB, J. S. Electroencephalographic
    evaluation of psychopathic personality--correlations
    with age, sex, family history and antecedent illness
    or injury. Arch. Neurol. Psychiat., Chicago, 1944,
    52, 515-522.

SWEET, W. H., ERVIN, F., & MARK, V. H. The relationship
     of violent behavior to focal cerebral disease. In
     S. Garattini and E. B. Sigg (Eds.) Aggressive Behav-
     ior. Amsterdam: Excerpta Medica, 1969.

GASTAUT, H., MORIN, G., & LESÈVRE, N. Étude du comporte-
     ment des épileptiques psychometeurs dans l'internalle
     de leur crises: les troubles de l'áctivité globale
     et de la sociabilité. Ann. Med. Psychol., 1955,
     113, 1-15.

ROGER, A., & DONGIER, M. Corrélations électrocliniques
     chez 50 épileptiques internés. Rev. Neurol., 1960,
     83, 593-602.

                      GENERAL REFERENCES

     Listed to enable the general reader to more easily
become familiar with selected works of value in the area
of agonistic behavior.

ALTMANN, S. A. A field study of the sociobiology of
     rhesus monkeys, Macaca mulatta. Ann. N. Y. Acad. Sci.,
     1962, 102, 338.

ANDREW, R. J. The origin and evolution of the calls and
     facial expressions of the primates. Behavior, 1963,
     20, 1.

CARPENTER, C. R. A field study of the behavior and social
     relations of howling monkeys. Comp. Psychol. Monogr.,
     1934, 10, 1.

CLEMENTE, C. D., & LINDSLEY, D. B. (Eds.). Aggression and
     Defense. Berkeley: University of California Press,
     1967.

DARWIN, C. The Expression of the Emotions in Man and
     Animals. London: John Murray, 1872.

GARATTINI, S., & SIGG, E. B. (Eds.). Aggressive Behavior.
     Amsterdam: Excerpta Medica, 1969.

GLASER, G. (Ed.) EEG and Behavior. New York: Basic Books,
     1963.

LORENZ, K. On Aggression. New York: Harcourt, Brace,
    and World, Inc., 1963.

SKINNER, B. F. Science and Human Behavior. New York:
    The Free Press, 1965.

TINBERGEN, N. Social Behavior in Animals. New York:
    John Wiley, 1953.

WASHBURN, S. L., & DEVORE, I. The social life of baboons.
    Sci. Am., 1961, 204/6, 62.

SUBJECT INDEX

Acetylcholinesterase, 89

Actinomycin, 47

Adenine monophosphate, 66, 74, 76, 77-80

Adrenalectomy, 50

Adrenal glands, 95, 108, 126, 127, 128, 262, 263

Aggression
  affective, 221
  brain stimulation, 201
  control, 244
  instrumental, 241
  isolation, 103, 104
  measurement, 102
  noxiousness, 161, 185
  primary, 7, 141, 143, 191
  secondary, 7, 141, 143, 192
  types, 220

Aggressive behavior, 153
  brain stimulation, 7
  emotionality, 5, 15
  irritability, 8, 33, 35
  hormones, 4
  inhibition, 242, 244
  learning, 243
  neural organization, 8
  types, 8

Aggressor, 5, 6, 35

Agonistic behavior, 1, 2, 19
  adaptation, 3, 12, 16
  catharsis, 22
  dominance, 29, 42
  evolution, 12, 13, 17
  hunger, 29
  learning, 3
  occurrence, 11, 14
  origin, 12, 20
  reinforcement, 21, 25
  sex, 29, 30, 31, 36, 38, 39
  sexual jealousy, 17
  sublimation, 22, 31

Amphetamine, 33, 34, 37, 94, 95, 99, 101, 106, 117, 118

Amphibia, 11, 12

Amygdala, 22, 24, 47, 63, 68, 117, 188, 224, 229, 232, 235, 236

Androstenedione, 49

Androsterone, 50

Aspartic acid, 89

Assaultive behavior, 210, 245

Avoidance learning, 69, 71, 74

Brainstem, 91

Biogenic amines, 63, 65

Blood pressure, 126, 128

307